COMMUNICATING IN THE WORKPLACE

A GUIDE TO BUSINESS AND PROFESSIONAL SPEAKING

Lynne Kelly
University of Hartford

Linda C. Lederman
Rutgers University

Gerald M. Phillips
The Pennsylvania State University

1817

HARPER & ROW, PUBLISHERS, New York
Cambridge, Philadelphia, San Francisco,
London, Mexico City, São Paulo, Singapore, Sydney

Sponsoring Editor: Barbara Cinquegrani
Project Editor: Susan Goldfarb
Text Design Adaptation: Lucy Krikorian
Cover Design: Maura Fadden
Cover Photo: © Carol Lee/Boston, The Picture Cube
Text Art: ComCom Division of Haddon Craftsmen, Inc.
Photo Research: Alice Lundoff
Production Manager: Jeanie Berke
Production Assistant: Paula Roppolo
Compositor: ComCom Division of Haddon Craftsmen
Printer and Binder: R. R. Donnelley & Sons Company
Cover Printer: Phoenix Color Corp.

Photo Credits (page numbers appear in italics):
6: © Ann Chwatsky/Leo de Wys, Inc.; *46:* © Frank Siteman/Taurus Photos; *50* © Marilyn L. Schrut/Taurus Photos; *69:* © Michael Kagan/Monkmeyer; *70:* © John Coletti/Stock, Boston; *99:* © Ann Chwatsky/Leo de Wys, Inc.; *103:* © Michael Kagan/Monkmeyer; *110:* Courtesy AT&T Archives; *124:* © Fujihira/Monkmeyer; *126:* © Fredrik D. Bodin/Stock, Boston; *154:* (*above*) © Arthur Grace/Stock, Boston, (*below*) © Joseph Schuyler/Stock, Boston; *203* © Michal Heron/Woodfin Camp & Associates; *226* (*above*) © Joseph Nettis/Photo Researchers, (*below*) © Rhoda Sidney/Monkmeyer; *240* © Bryce Flynn/Stock, Boston; *242* © Arlene S. Collins/Monkmeyer

COMMUNICATING IN THE WORKPLACE: A Guide to Business and Professional Speaking

Library of Congress Cataloging-in-Publication Data

Kelly, Lynne.
Communicating in the workplace : a guide to business and professional speaking / Lynne Kelly, Linda C. Lederman, Gerald M. Phillips.
p. cm.
Includes bibliographies and index.
ISBN 0-06-043628-X
1. Communication in management. 2. Public speaking.
I. Lederman, Linda Costigan. II. Phillips, Gerald M. III. Title.
HD30.3.K45 1989 88-22831
658.4'5—dc19 CIP

88 89 90 91 9 8 7 6 5 4 3 2 1

To my parents, for encouraging me to pursue my education

—L.K.

To my son, Joshua B. Lederman

—L.C.L.

Contents

To the Student

At long last the telephone rings. You got the job! Your extensive research into companies and your hours of preparation have helped you in the employment interview process. You have demonstrated strong communication skills and have persuaded the interviewer that you are right for the position.

Today is your first day on the new job. You have been anticipating this day for weeks, imagining what it would be like. You smile at other employees as you find your way to your supervisor's office to report in. Your supervisor is friendlier and more enthusiastic than you expected, and you feel relieved. As your supervisor shows you around, explaining your duties and responsibilities and the company policies, you try to commit the information to memory. You also ask about co-workers and key people in the organization, trying to get a feel for what the people you'll be working with are like.

As you settle in your tiny new office, the telephone rings. The department manager's secretary reminds you of the afternoon staff meeting. You then check your computer to see if there is any electronic mail, and you smile as you read a message welcoming you as a new member of the family.

Later in the day, at the meeting, you are asked to stand and introduce yourself and say a few words about your background. Then the meeting gets under way. You are assigned to a project team that will meet the next day. At the end of the staff meeting, other employees introduce themselves to you and either give you advice or fill you in on the "ropes" in the organization.

* * *

From this scenario, you can get an idea of the importance and pervasiveness of communication in the workplace. Communication takes many forms in the organization, and it takes up a major portion of the time spent at work. Your success as an organization member is determined in part by your ability to communicate effectively in a variety of situations.

This text is designed to help you develop communication skills in key situations you are likely to encounter, including interviews, public presentations, and group meetings. It also discusses the use of communication technology in the performance of day-to-day tasks.

LYNNE KELLY
LINDA C. LEDERMAN
GERALD M. PHILLIPS

To the Instructor

This text offers three unique features. First, we have included a chapter on the use of technology in the performance of daily tasks. Computers and other forms of technology have dramatically changed how work is done in the organization, and new equipment and procedures for communication are continually being introduced. Skill at using new communication technologies is becoming increasingly necessary for all employees.

A second unique feature is the chapter on communication and the socialization of employees. In recent years, scholars have focused on what they call "organizational culture"—an organization's predominant values, norms for behavior, customs, and rituals. Each organization develops a unique culture that guides the actions of its members. Some actions are valued and rewarded within the organization's culture, and other actions are discouraged or even punished. In order to make effective behavioral choices, employees need to be aware of the company's culture and must learn how to "fit in." It is through the process of socialization that newcomers become a part of the organization and adapt to its culture. Unsuccessful socialization can leave an employee feeling isolated and "different." Therefore, we offer suggestions for taking an active role in the socialization process.

The third unique feature of this text is the inclusion of "L&L Associates" as a model of an organization. The material on "L&L Associates" can be used in two ways. One option is that it can be viewed as an extended example of the concepts presented in the text. "L&L Associates" is described fully in Chapter 3 and is used to provide examples in all subsequent chapters. You can simply teach about "L&L Associates" as you discuss each chapter.

The other way the material on "L&L Associates" can be used is as a full simulation in which students in the course become the "employees" and operate the "business." Students fill all of the positions in the company, from president to project group member. Participation in the simulation provides the opportunity for students to experience a variety of communication activities in an organizational context. Participants conduct interviews, lead meetings, participate in groups, deliver presentations, become socialized into the company, and perform everyday tasks.

The instructor's manual provides all of the information and materials necessary to run the simulation. The manual follows two tracks: one for instructors who wish to employ the "L&L Associates" simulation, and a second for instructors whose preference is to use "L&L Associates" as an extended example of course concepts. Additional student activities are provided at the end of each chapter in the text and in the instructor's manual. These activities provide more opportunities for students to develop their communication skills.

The text is divided into two parts. Part I, "The Organizational Context of Communication," contains three chapters. Chapter 1 examines the process of communication and its components. Chapter 2, "Organizational Influences on the Communication Process," provides a definition of the term *organization* and highlights three key features of organizations—formal structure, informal communication networks, and organizational culture—that influence the communication process. Chapter 3 presents a complete description of "L&L Associates" as a sample organizational context.

The remaining chapters constitute Part II, "Communication Activities in the Organization." Chapters 4 and 5 focus on fundamentals of interviewing and on five types of interviews: employment interviews, performance appraisal interviews, information-gathering interviews, disciplinary interviews, and exit interviews. The emphasis of these chapters is on the role of the interviewee in the interview process.

Chapter 6, "Working in Groups," examines types of groups common to the organization, the purposes of group meetings, and the nature of small groups. It also includes an extensive section on effective participation in work groups. Chapter 7 covers the subject of leading groups and managing meetings and includes discussion of how to plan meetings and lead them effectively.

Chapters 8 and 9 explore public presentations in great detail. In Chapter 8, five stages of preparation for presentations are outlined, and in Chapter 9, the delivery of presentations is discussed. Guidelines for choosing a method of delivery, preparing notes, using visual aids, rehearsing, and managing speech apprehension are presented.

Chapter 10 covers communication and the socialization process, examining the phases of socialization and the roles of upper management, co-workers, and immediate supervisors in the socialization process. The chapter provides suggestions for taking an active role.

Chapter 11, "Technology and the Performance of Everyday Tasks in the Organization," concludes the text. Types of information and communication technologies are discussed, along with effective telephone techniques. Business letters and memos and the role of the computer in communication technology are examined.

Many people have contributed to the development of this book. We would like to acknowledge the help of Patrick Collins, John Jay College of Criminal Justice; Susan Brown Flechtner, Texas A&M University; John A. Daly, University of Texas at Austin; Pam Edwards, University of Northern Iowa; Christy Greene, Louisiana State University; Judy Jones, University of California, Santa Barbara; and Elaine Klein, Westchester Community College. Finally, we would like to thank Barbara Cinquegrani, sponsoring editor, and Susan Goldfarb, project editor, for their help with this book.

LYNNE KELLY
LINDA C. LEDERMAN
GERALD M. PHILLIPS

PART I

THE ORGANIZATIONAL CONTEXT OF COMMUNICATION

CHAPTER

1

The Process of Communication

It is tempting to begin this book on business and professional communication by emphasizing the importance of communication in the organization. Other authors have used this approach, and we feel a certain urgency to do the same. But we suspect that you will express little surprise when we assert that people in organizations, particularly managers and executives, spend a minimum of about 50 percent of their time involved in communication.[1] And we doubt that you would find it startling to know that a number of studies have reported that communication skills rank among the top qualifications required for organizational success and advancement.[2] So we will take a slightly different tack. Let's look at what can happen to employees who have a tendency to avoid communicating at work.

These employees experience communication apprehension, which is fear or anxiety associated with the act of communicating.[3] Although they are not necessarily incompetent communicators, their lack of initiative in and avoidance of communication may result in others perceiving them as deficient in communication.[4] You may not always be troubled by communication apprehension, but most people experience some degree of apprehension in some situations. If those situations occur in the work context, your success in the organization may be compromised. Researchers have found that communication apprehension is detrimental to employees in several ways. As compared to those with low communication apprehension, high apprehensives received more negative ratings on the basis of selection interviews and were less likely to be offered employment.[5] In addition, they reported less job satisfaction,[6] preferred occupations with low communication requirements (occupations which tend to be of lower status and offer lower economic rewards),[7] and were more likely to perceive that they would not be promoted within their organizations.[8]

Difficulty communicating is clearly detrimental to the individual employee. You may not be among the approximately 20 percent of the population who experience high levels of communication apprehension in most contexts,[9] but like most of us, you could improve your ability to communicate. Deficiencies in communication can interfere with your employment opportunities, your job satisfaction, and your promotability.

This book is designed to provide you with information about communicating in organizations and with opportunities to develop communication skills needed for daily life in organizations. We start with a discussion of the process of communication. In Chapter 2 we will show how that process is influenced by features of contemporary organizations, and we argue that an understanding of those features is useful for making effective communication choices at work.

COMMUNICATION AS PROCESS

Communication is a term for which we all have a commonsense understanding, but we may not be able to define it. In this section we will explain what we mean when we say that communication is a process. Later we will examine the components of that process. Keep in mind that there are many different ways to define communication. We will offer you one perspective out of the many alternative approaches to defining communication.

Communication Has No Beginning or End

In 1960 David Berlo articulated a process view of communication,[10] a view which has greatly influenced the field of speech communication. To say that communication is a process means that it is dynamic, not static. Something that is in process is not completed; it is changing continually. Communication as a process has no clearly discernible beginning or end. Suppose, for example, that you decide to ask your supervisor for a raise. You make an appointment to talk to her, and on the appointed day at the appointed hour, you meet with her and ask for the raise. Although we often arbitrarily designate a particular moment or event as the beginning of communication, further examination reveals multiple points which could be labeled as the beginning. We might be inclined to say that communication with the supervisor began when you walked into her office and uttered your first words. But what about when you asked for the appointment? When you first got the idea to ask for the raise? Or when your supervisor mentioned one day that your work is excellent? Couldn't all of these also be considered the start of communication?

At some point, of course, you must decide to initiate communication, to ask for the raise. At that point you can begin to think through what you want to say and how you will say it. We believe careful preparation of this kind is important. However, by recognizing that communication is a process, you will realize that the interaction for which you are planning is part of an ongoing stream of interaction between you and your supervisor. Your past encounters will shape future encounters. So will many other factors, as we will now discuss.

Mutual Influence

As a process, communication is a continual cycle of mutual influence. Everything about the participants—their attitudes, values, experiences, beliefs, and needs—influences the communicative choices they make. Their choices regarding with whom to talk and the topics about which they talk are constrained by this complex set of factors. Once a decision to talk has been made, past experience, present attitudes, interests, values, and goals combine with features of the specific communication situation to affect choices of what to say and how to say it. As people communicate, they are each changed by the interaction, which further affects what is said and how it is said. Thus the cycle continues. Although we all depend on our experience for guidance in our communication behavior, no two communication situations or events are the same. They are only similar.

We can illustrate this continuous cycle of influence by examining the process of asking for a raise. If your past experiences with asking for raises have been successful, you may enter this situation believing that you deserve a raise and confident in your ability to persuade your supervisor that you do. Suppose that when you arrive for your meeting, your supervisor is tense and preoccupied. You may recognize that you have never encountered a situation similar to this before. All the other times you asked for a raise, the supervisor was receptive and friendly. Suddenly you lose confidence and you wonder if you should even ask. You may decide that this is not the time to ask for a raise, but here you are, in the presence of your supervisor, and you must say something. She will not put up with foolishness and you do not want her to remember your wasting her time the next time you try for a raise. You may decide to ask a question. But that means you have to think of it on the spot. It cannot be a trivial question and cannot look like a cover-up. The right kind of question could please your supervisor, who then could become more friendly toward you. At that point, you might decide to throw caution to the winds and risk asking for a raise. Note that we have introduced only one additional factor—the

Before asking his supervisor for a raise, this employee needs to consider many factors that will influence his message and how it is received.

present state of mind of the supervisor. This obviously is an oversimplification, because in actuality, multiple factors interact to create a unique and complex situation.

We could write a variety of scenarios with different beginnings and endings. Each scenario would illustrate the proposition that each person in a communication situation influences each other person and is influenced by past experiences, present attitudes, values, beliefs, goals, needs, and so on. Of more immediate importance, each person is influenced by events in the situation itself.

Symbols

Communication is a process in which participants are influenced by assigning meaning to symbols intentionally and unintentionally exchanged. Let's examine this statement to clarify its meaning.

We have explained the idea of mutual influence; each individual influences and is influenced by each other individual. Assigning meaning to symbols is the process by which that influence is exerted. A *symbol* is a representation of a thing, idea, place, event, or person. A company's logo, for instance, is a symbol because when people see it, they associate it with that particular company.

Symbols can take many forms. We will focus primarily on two major forms: verbal and nonverbal symbols.

Verbal Symbols Verbal symbols (words) are arbitrarily accepted within a given culture to stand for the things they represent. The things they represent are called *referents.* For example, the word *desk* stands for an object (the referent) with which we are familiar. The French use the word *pupitre* for the same object. Words are social conventions which allow for shared meaning.

Because words have meaning due to social convention, they are imperfect representations of the things they stand for. They can have multiple meanings, particularly words with nontangible referents. Words with physical referents—*desk,* for example—can be made very specific by pointing to the particular object for which they stand. On the other hand, words like *fairness, job enrichment, creativity, prestige, initiative,* and *dependability* can have many different meanings. For example, for one person creativity may mean doing something that has never been done before, while for another person, it may mean doing something you have never done before. If we are evaluating an employee, the difference in meaning could be crucial. A supervisor who accepts the first interpretation will give employees high ratings on creativity only when they perform a task or generate an idea that is completely new to that supervisor. Accepting the second meaning would lead a supervisor to evaluate employees very differently. That supervisor would rate employees high on creativity if they performed tasks or suggested ideas that they had never done or thought of before. As we will explain in more detail in the chapters on interviewing, performance appraisals form the basis of many promotion and salary adjustment decisions. Therefore, the meaning of words that serve as criteria for evaluation of employees has important consequences for the individual in the organization.

When we use a word, we cannot assume that another individual understands it the way we do. Words have both denotative and connotative meanings. *Denotation* refers to the generally accepted meaning or meanings associated with a given word. Definitions provided in dictionaries represent denotative meanings. But we know that words suggest or imply other meanings, called *connotations.* A single word can have many connotations, and what a particular word connotes depends on the individual. Individuals will assign meaning to words on the basis of their own experiences, attitudes, values, goals, states of mind, and a variety of other factors. As a result, disagreements and misunderstandings frequently are sparked by divergent interpretations of words. So if a superior tells you, for instance, that you do not demonstrate sufficient initiative on the job, your disagreement with that superior is likely to revolve around different connotations of the word *initiative.*

Given the problems associated with language use, organization members need to be conscious of the verbal symbols they choose and of how they interpret words used by others. We offer the following guidelines for using and interpreting language:

1. *Be precise in choosing words.* When we are not careful about selecting our words, we may use language that is sloppy and imprecise. Even though we know what we intended to say, it is unlikely that the other person will know. Precision in language use will help reduce the possibility of misunderstanding.
2. *Ask for clarification.* When you are unsure about how to interpret a word or phrase, you should usually ask. This is difficult to do in organizations because people fear (and rightly so sometimes) that they will be perceived as inept or uninformed. However, there are many instances in which it is perfectly appropriate and sensible to seek clarification. For example, if you are currently working on several reports and a supervisor says, "I want to see that report on Friday," you should ask which report he means unless you are absolutely certain which one he wants to see. That may seem commonsensical, but it is exactly in the day-to-day routine interactions that people fail to get the clarification they need. We usually know enough to ask for clarification of particular words when our supervisor is presenting a new procedure. But in our daily interactions, we take more for granted. We have seen papers in which students have written "We take more for granite"—a perfect example of needing clarification of a commonplace expression. In a case like this, and in other situations in which you feel you ought to know the meaning of a word, a more sensible approach might be to use a dictionary. That way you won't risk your reputation.
3. *Avoid unnecessary jargon.* All organizations and all professions develop jargon, specialized language with precise meaning. Jargon allows for efficient communication among the people within a profession, an organization, or a subdivision of an organization. It is appropriate and useful to use jargon when interacting with people who use and understand it. It does not make sense to use it with people who do not understand it, yet this happens regularly. When an employee in sales talks to an employee in advertising, they each need to avoid the specialized language of their fields unless they are certain the other understands it. As we stated earlier, people are hesitant to ask because they do not want to appear uneducated or incompetent. If you use jargon, others may not ask what it means. Of course, using jargon to impress others or exert power over them is a common occurrence in organizations. However, we believe that being a good communicator is a better way to impress people and become powerful.

Nonverbal Symbols Nonverbal symbols take a variety of different forms (summarized in Exhibit 1.1). These include kinesics (posture, body movements, gestures, and facial expressions); haptics (touch); oculesics (eye behavior); proxemics (space and distance); and paralanguage (vocal characteristics). We will briefly examine each of these.

1. ***Kinesics*** *Kinesics* refers to the use of movement to communicate. Movements of the face, the hands, or the whole body convey messages about the speaker, how the speaker perceives the situation, and how the speaker sees the listener. Facial expressions, for example, often tell us a great deal about the emotional state of another. We can recognize happiness, sadness, fear, and anger when they are reflected in people's faces. (There are some people who seem to be able to keep their faces from revealing their emotions. This can be useful in an organization because sometimes employees prefer not to display their feelings.) Other movements of the body and hands are more difficult to interpret. However, in interpreting the meaning of movements, we focus on the total package; we don't typically zero in on a single feature.
2. ***Haptics*** Touch is another type of nonverbal symbol. We use touch for a variety of purposes—to convey warmth, support, sexual attraction, or ridicule, or to exert power. These last two purposes require explanation. If one person pats another on the head as if that person was a child, the first person is using touch to ridicule the other. Patting or slapping a person on the buttocks can also convey disdain or a lack of respect. In both of these examples, touch is used to ridicule and also to exert power. In the American culture it is generally the high-status person, the one in the superior position, who initiates touch.[11] It is considered generally inappropriate for the subordinate to touch the superior. In superior-subordinate interactions, then, touch has the potential to be used to display power.
3. ***Oculesics*** Eye gaze and eye movement provide another means of communicating nonverbally. In some respects, eye behavior is one of the most easily controlled nonverbal codes. For instance, we have all deliberately stared at another to convey our displeasure or have avoided eye contact to communicate that we do not want to talk.

Exhibit 1.1 TYPES OF NONVERBAL COMMUNICATION

1. Kinesics (use of movement of the face, hands, and entire body)
2. Haptics (use of touch)
3. Oculesics (eye gaze and movement)
4. Proxemics (use of space and distance)
5. Paralanguage (vocal characteristics)

In our culture, eye contact is valued and expected. When people are unable or unwilling to make eye contact, we make attributions of insecurity, lack of confidence, untrustworthiness, and other negative characteristics. Eye contact, but not staring, is expected in the organizational setting.

4. ***Proxemics*** People use space and distance to communicate. For example, how close or far we stand from another may convey something about the relationship we have with that person. We tend to stand or sit nearer to people with whom we have a close or intimate relationship than to people who are acquaintances. Space functions as an important symbol in organizations. In an article on symbols of power, Michael Korda suggests that the location and size of the space given to managers and executives (specifically, their offices) communicates how much power they wield.[12] Korda also offers advice regarding how to use office furnishings to symbolize power. How chairs and desks are arranged and the distances between them can either minimize or maximize perceptions of power.[13]
5. ***Paralanguage*** *Paralanguage* refers to vocal characteristics, such as tone of voice, vocal inflection, loudness, pitch, quality of voice, and pauses. How we say something provides others with information about the meaning of what we said. Sarcasm, for example, depends on a contradiction between the verbal and the nonverbal, particularly paralanguage. If a co-worker said "Nice job" in a tone that contradicted those words, you would recognize it as a sarcastic remark meaning "Poor job." By refusing to acknowledge paralanguage, we could even deny that a message was sent. For instance, if you confronted your co-worker to express your displeasure about his remark "Nice job," he of course could reply, "I said you did a nice job, didn't I?" You might continue to think he had been sarcastic, because when the verbal and nonverbal messages contradict one another, we tend to believe the nonverbal message.[14] However, your co-worker's insistence that he had been sincere might cast some doubt in your mind about what he really meant.

When communication occurs, people assign meaning to the total package of verbal and nonverbal messages. That is why we are unable to give you a list of specific nonverbal behaviors and how they should be interpreted. All we can do is advocate increased awareness of your own and others' nonverbal communication. As you attempt to assign meaning to messages, consider the nonverbal communication and its relation to the verbal. In trying to sort out how others have reacted to your communication, think about what messages your nonverbal behavior might have conveyed.

Just as verbal symbols have multiple meanings, so do nonverbal symbols.

When we think of communication as a process in which people assign meaning to symbols, we must understand that people can assign meanings that differ from those we have in mind. We are often surprised to find out that someone interpreted as sarcastic a remark we had made sincerely. All symbols are ambiguous, and as such, they allow for a variety of interpretations.

Intentionality

A common saying about communication is "One cannot not communicate" when in an interactional situation.[15] This simply means that everything a person does can be interpreted. When you sit still and say nothing, people can interpret you as thoughtful, apathetic, confused, or even asleep. As long as you are in contact with other people, what you say and do and what you do not say and do not do will be interpreted. You will have meaning to other people. Recall that we characterized communication as a process in which people assign meaning to verbal and nonverbal symbols. An implication of that statement is that people can and often will assign meanings to behaviors that were not intended to be communicative. For example, suppose someone with whom you work greets you each morning with a happy "Hello." One day when you come in, the person does not say a word. You may assume that something is wrong because you assign meaning to the other's silence. But that person may not have intended anything by being silent. She may have been lost in thought, may not have seen you, or may have been about to sneeze. Clearly the possibility exists that she did intend to use silence to communicate, but you do not know that. You could ask her directly; you could "test the waters" by saying "Hello" and watching her response; or you could overlook the incident and see what happens.

In essence, then, communication is a process in which symbols are exchanged, either intentionally or unintentionally. Regardless of intentionality, however, people assign meaning to those symbols and, as a result, are influenced by one another. Exhibit 1.2 highlights these important aspects of the communication process. In the next section of this chapter, we will discuss four components of the communication process to further elaborate our perspective.

Exhibit 1.2 THE COMMUNICATION PROCESS

As a process, communication

1. Has no beginning or end
2. Is a cycle of mutual influence
3. Involves assignment of meaning to verbal and nonverbal symbols
4. May be intentional or unintentional

COMPONENTS OF THE COMMUNICATION PROCESS

Four elements of the communication process must always be present in order for communication to occur. These components are the communicators, the relationships, the context, and the exchange of symbols.

The Communicators

For communication to occur, there must be at least two people. As we suggested earlier, communicators observe one another and are influenced by each other's talk and behavior. But each person also brings to the interaction the total of his or her past experiences and present feelings, goals, needs, attitudes, knowledge, and sense of the shared situation. People cannot set these things aside when they interact. Instead, these aspects of the communicators influence what they say; how they say it; how they assign meaning to symbols used by each other; and how they perceive one another, themselves, and the situation in which communication occurs. Although it might sound like a cliché, each person is unique because no two people have identical experiences or perceptions of those experiences. Communicators carry their unique histories with them, histories that affect their current selves.

However, an individual is not a static entity. The process of communication changes each individual, no matter how minute and unobservable the change. Our feelings, attitudes, values, beliefs, goals, needs, and relationships are subtly shaped in the process. That is why we described communication as a cycle of mutual influence. Each individual influences the communication process and is influenced by it.

What does this mean for you? How does this information assist you as you attempt to improve your communication skills? The essence of our answer is this: *Knowing that communicators are influenced by their histories can help you in planning communicative choices, in interpreting the actions of others, and in recognizing the complexity of the communication process.*

As you plan for communication encounters, think about your past experiences both with the particular person and in similar contexts. What have you learned from those encounters? What do you know about the other person's goals, values, interests, needs, communication style, perceptions of you, and perceptions of the situation? Answering these questions can provide you with a great deal of valuable information about how to adapt your communication to that particular individual. The more you can tailor your message to another, so that it is appropriate for that person, the greater your chances of a successful interaction. If you know, for instance, that the other has been persuaded by statistics in the past, using statistics to support your point of view may be an appropriate choice. Examining past experiences you have had in similar contexts can also help you plan. You can consider communicative choices that you made which were effective and appropriate and those which did not accomplish what you had intended. Of course, as we have emphasized, each communication situation is complex and no two situations are identical, so you cannot simply transplant communication choices from one situation to the next, assuming they will always work. But you can use past strategies to inform your thinking about present situations.

You may be thinking that it is not always possible to plan for communication situations. That certainly is true, and as a result, you may not have the opportunity to utilize past experiences consciously. That doesn't mean that past experiences and choices are not influencing your present behavior. It simply means that you may not be consciously thinking about how you have approached this type of situation or this particular person in previous encounters. However, we believe that for many communicative situations you will experience as a member of an organization, it is possible and desirable to prepare and plan. It is certainly possible to prepare for interviews, presentations, meetings, appointments, and even conversations you intend to have. Planning should be more extensive for some situations than others, but it is necessary for many situations.

Furthermore, when you recognize that communicators are influenced by their histories, you have some insight into their behavior. The more you know about a person's history, the better able you are to interpret his or her behavior in the context of that history. For example, perhaps you know that the manager of your department had only a high school education and had to work very hard to get to the position as manager. In approaching that manager to apply for reimbursement for a night course you took, that knowledge could help you understand the response you receive. Your manager's experience may have taught him that education is an unnecessary luxury, and he may be less than enthusiastic about supporting your academic endeavors. Another possibility (and there are many) is that he may feel that employees should have the education he was unable to obtain, and he might be very supportive. Regardless of the specific reaction, recognition that communicators are affected by their experiences can help you assign meaning to your manager's response.

Finally, when you understand that communicators are influenced by their histories but that they also are constantly changing, you will recognize the tremendous complexity of the communication process. People are often surprised when others misunderstand their messages. It is probably more surprising that we ever understand each other, because there are a multiplicity of factors influencing our communication. The importance of viewing communication as complex is that it encourages us to think before we speak, to be more precise and careful about what we say and how we say it. It also illuminates the fact that listening is an active process; we need to exert effort to listen and attempt to understand what others are trying to communicate.

The Relationships

The second element of the communication process is the relationships among the communicators. The minute communication begins, a relationship is formed. The nature of the relationship we have with another strongly influences our communication behavior. There are many ways to describe relationships; one way we find useful was presented by Gerald Miller.[16] Miller suggests that relationships can be placed along a continuum from noninterpersonal to interpersonal.[17] A *noninterpersonal* relationship is one in which we deal with the other as a stereotype or as a representative of a social role rather than as a unique individual.[18] We make predictions about the other's behavior on the basis of sociological information such as race, socioeconomic status, occupation, and religious affiliation.[19] We do not know anything about this person at the psychological level; all of our understanding is at the descriptive level.[20] In other words, we cannot predict what the other person will do on the basis of what we know about his or her individual likes and dislikes or attitudes and values. Any predictions we make are based on what we expect from people from that group or in that social role.

At the other end of the continuum are relationships that can be called interpersonal. In an *interpersonal* relationship we respond to the other as a unique individual, not as a representative of some social role. We have psychological knowledge of the other and can predict his or her behavior on that basis.[21] For example, we know that a co-worker who values hard work will get annoyed when she sees people slacking off. We therefore can predict how she will respond when she learns of an employee taking it easy on the job.

Both within the organization and in general, we have relationships at various points along the continuum. Our relationships with people with whom we work closely may develop into more interpersonal relationships. That doesn't necessarily mean that our interaction with those people is primarily social and rarely task oriented (although it could be). On the other hand, many of our relationships at work fall at the noninterpersonal end of the continuum, particularly with members of the organization with whom we have limited contact. Without interaction either at work or outside, relationships don't have the opportunity to become more interpersonal.

How people communicate with one another in an organization, then, depends on the nature of their relationships. The topics about which they choose to speak, their language choices, and to whom they choose to speak and in what way are all affected by their relationships.

The Context

In addition to being influenced by their histories and their relationships, communicators are influenced by the surroundings in which communication takes place. This third element of the communication process is the situation, or context, of communication. When communicators interact, they do so at a particular time, in a particular place, and for a particular reason. All features of the context have the potential to influence the communicators. There are a number of these we should consider. In this section we will examine the general features of purpose, place, and time, which have an impact on any type of communicative encounter. In Chapter 2 we will discuss specific aspects of the organizational context that influence the communication process.

First, the *purpose of the encounter* can influence the communicators. People behave differently, depending on the purpose for communication. For instance, communication at the company picnic is likely to be less formal and less task oriented than at a staff meeting—unless, of course, there is a very important social contact to be made. If a person with whom you are romantically involved is there, the situation may be very tense indeed, or you may find his or her presence comforting. A staff meeting may be unthreatening and even boring if none of it involves you or anything you do. On the other hand, it could be an opportunity to sell your idea to your supervisor and co-workers.

Skilled communicators adapt to the situation so that what they choose to talk about and how they talk about it are appropriate. If an employee meets with a supervisor for a performance appraisal interview, the employee will discuss topics relevant to the purpose of the meeting and will choose language appropriate for the relationship that exists. On the other hand, a not-so-skillful communicator may not adapt. He may come to the performance appraisal interview as if he were at the picnic. The impropriety may not escape notice and the interview could be a catastrophe—unless, of course, the interviewer was bored and was looking for some levity.

The second general feature of the context is the *place or setting* in which communication occurs. Our behavior varies from place to place because norms and rules are different for each setting. For instance, places can differ in degree of formality or informality. A meeting of the board of trustees that occurs in the boardroom is likely to be a more formal occasion than their meeting in the lobby prior to or after the meeting in the boardroom. Note that the purpose and place, two features of the context, interact to affect behavior. The formality that exists in the boardroom setting is there in part because of the purpose of the meeting, not just because of the setting itself. All of the features of a communication context are interdependent; we are discussing them separately to highlight the individual aspects of a situation, but it is important to recognize that they interact to affect communication behavior.

The third general feature is the *time of day* at which communication occurs. Although this aspect of the context is not as influential as either the purpose or the place, it can affect the communication process. The supervisor who tries to motivate an employee to work harder is likely to have greater success early on a Monday than late on a Friday afternoon. At the end of a long week, an employee is concerned more with getting home and having a few days off than with improving job performance. The employee who tries to talk to a co-worker about a problem right before lunch may not receive the kind of response he or she would receive at a better time. As a member of an organization, you need to take time of day into account as you plan for communication, in order to try to maximize the likelihood of success.

These three features of the situation or context can have a tremendous impact on communication. The point we want to stress is that communicators do not interact in a vacuum. They interact in a specific context, to which they must adapt in order to enhance the possibility of effective communication. What this means for you is that you need to analyze each communication situation for which you prepare. If it is within your control to select the time of day and the place for a specific encounter, consider the impact of various times and places and select those that seem to be most suited for your purpose. If it is not within your purview to choose these features of a situation, you can still consider how they will affect the communication process and can be prepared to adapt. For example, if the other communicator seems to be in a rush when you meet to discuss a proposal, consider whether this may be a function of the time of day. Perhaps it is late in the day or just before lunch. To adapt to this situation, you might keep your remarks brief and suggest another meeting to develop the details. Of course, the other person may be rushed for a variety of reasons—she may not like your proposal, she may have many appointments scheduled, she may not like you, or any combination of these; poor timing is only one possibility. In your analysis of the situation, you may decide it is probably not the time of day that is affecting the other's response. If that is the case, you need to consider other possibilities, taking into account your relationship and what you know about the other person. Note that your analysis of the communication process should focus on all of the components, not just the specific context. We will elaborate on this idea at the end of this section.

The Exchange of Symbols

The fourth and final component of the communication process is the exchange of symbols, which may be intentional or unintentional, as we have noted. In order for communication to take place, we must assign meaning to the verbal and/or nonverbal behaviors of the other communicators. If two individuals are seated in a room reading, neither one assigning meaning to the other's behavior,

Exhibit 1.3 COMPONENTS OF THE COMMUNICATION PROCESS

1. The communicators
2. The relationships among communicators
3. The context
4. The exchange of symbols

communication has not taken place. Of course, one or both people could interpret the other's behavior as indicative of disinterest. Before we can say that communication has occurred, someone must assign meaning to another's actions.

In assigning meaning, communicators are influenced by all of the factors we discussed earlier—their personal experiences, knowledge, goals, feelings, attitudes, and beliefs. As these aspects of themselves are changed in the communication process, the meanings the people assign to symbols may be changed. If, for instance, an employee who doesn't appear to listen well does an impeccable job of following instructions, his supervisor may assign new meaning to the employee's behaviors that had been interpreted as a sign of poor listening. This will influence the supervisor's behavior, which undoubtedly will affect how the employee acts. Note that each individual is simultaneously sender and receiver of messages. As the supervisor receives a message from the employee and interprets his behavior, her response sends a message at the same time.

The communicators, the relationships among communicators, the context, and the exchange of symbols are the four components of the communication process (see Exhibit 1.3). These four components are interdependent; each influences the others. As you prepare for communication situations, you need to analyze these four components of the process. Consider your own goals, needs, interests, values, and past experiences that relate to the situation you are about to encounter. What might be the needs, goals, and interests of the other? What kind of relationship do you have with the other, and what information does that provide you about his or her goals, interests, needs, and likely behavior? How might the purpose, place, and time of day influence your communication and that of the other person? Finally, what messages do you intend to convey, and how can you adapt those messages so that they are appropriate for the other person, the context, and your relationship with the other? By answering these kinds of questions, you will be well prepared to plan your communication so it is suited to you and the context as well as adapted to the other individual.

THE USE OF THIS BOOK

This book is designed to help you develop oral communication skills you will need as an organization member. We will examine a variety of types of skills, including interviewing, group problem solving, public presentations, meeting management, employee socialization, and the use of new communication technologies.

In Chapter 2 we examine features of the organization that influence the communication process. The process of communication is shaped by and helps shape several important aspects of organizations, such as the organizational structure, the development of informal networks, and the organizational culture.

In Chapter 3 we present an organizational context to help illustrate many of the ideas developed in Part I of this text. We describe a sample organization called "L&L Associates," which can function as an organizational simulation if your instructor chooses to utilize it that way. We have provided the details necessary to use L&L Associates as a simulation, in order to give you the opportunity to develop your skills in a context that simulates some of the conditions of the work environment. Even if you do not participate in the simulation, the discussion of L&L Associates will highlight important aspects of organizations that affect the communication process.

Activities are provided at the end of each chapter to assist the development of your skills. Through these and classroom activities, you will have the opportunity to develop oral communication skills that are vital for success in the organization.

SUMMARY

In this chapter we have focused on the process of communication and its importance in the organization. Communication is a process in which each individual influences, and is influenced by, other individuals through the assignment of meaning to symbols intentionally and unintentionally exchanged. Because it is a process, communication has no discernible beginning or end. It is a continual cycle of mutual influence, in that communicators affect each other's communicative choices. Both verbal and nonverbal symbols are exchanged in the process, and all symbols have the potential to be interpreted, whether the communication was intended or not.

The communication process consists of four major elements: the communicators, the relationships, the context, and the exchange of symbols. Everything about the communicators—their unique histories—influences the choices they make as they communicate. The relationships they have with one another and the context in which the interaction occurs also affect their communication. As they exchange verbal and nonverbal symbols, the communicators are simultaneously senders and receivers of messages. To increase the possibility of effective communication, people need to analyze these components of the process as they prepare for communication situations.

CHAPTER 1 ACTIVITIES

1. Write your own definition of communication, and be prepared to discuss how you arrived at it.

2. For a few days, keep a journal of your communication interactions, either at school or at your place of employment. Note each of the following:
   a. With whom you interacted
   b. The nature of your relationship
   c. The purpose of the interaction
   d. The place where it occurred
   e. The time of day it took place

   After completing your journal entries, write down your impressions. How did the situational features of time, place, and purpose affect these interactions? How did the nature of your relationship with the other communicator(s) influence your communication?

3. Choose a communication situation for which you can prepare. The situation could be a conference with your advisor, a discussion with a professor, a conversation with a classmate, an interview with a potential employer, or any situation of your choice. Prepare for the situation by writing answers to the following questions:
   a. What do I know about the person with whom I'll be communicating?
   b. What does he or she know about me?
   c. What is the nature of our relationship? How will that affect our communication?
   d. Where will our interaction occur? How might that influence our communication?
   e. At what time of day will this situation take place? How might that affect our interaction?
   f. What is the purpose for our interaction? How will that affect our communication?
   g. Given what I know about the other person, our relationship, and the purpose and the context of the encounter, what should I do and what shouldn't I do when we communicate?

   After you have completed the interaction, write your impressions of it. In what ways was the situation different from what you had anticipated? How did you adapt? How helpful was your preparation? In what ways did it help you?

CHAPTER 1 NOTES

1. E. T. Klemmer and F. W. Snyder, "Measurement of Time Spent Communicating," *Journal of Communication,* vol. 22, 1972, pp. 142–158.
2. James Belohlov, Paul Popp, and Michael Porte, "Communication: A View from the Inside of Business," *Journal of Business Communication,* vol. 11, 1974, pp. 53–59.
3. James C. McCroskey and Virginia P. Richmond, "The Impact of Communication Apprehension on Individuals in Organizations," *Communication Quarterly,* vol. 27, 1979, pp. 55–60.

4. Ibid., p. 57.
5. Virginia P. Richmond, "Communication Apprehension and Success in the Job Applicant Screening Process," paper presented at the International Communication Association Convention, Berlin, West Germany, 1977.
6. Raymond L. Falcione, James C. McCroskey, and John A. Daly, "Job Satisfaction as a Function of Employees' Communication Apprehension, Self-Esteem, and Perceptions of their Immediate Supervisor." In *Communication Yearbook I,* B. D. Ruben (Ed.), New Brunswick, NJ: Transaction, 1977, pp. 263–276.
7. John A. Daly and James C. McCroskey, "Occupational Choice and Desirability as a Function of Communication Apprehension," *Journal of Counseling Psychology,* vol. 22, 1975, pp. 309–313.
8. Michael D. Scott, James C. McCroskey, and Michael E. Sheahan, "Measuring Communication Apprehension," *Journal of Communication,* vol. 28, 1978, pp. 104–111.
9. McCroskey and Richmond, p. 56.
10. David K. Berlo, *The Process of Communication: An Introduction to Theory and Practice,* New York: Holt, Rinehart and Winston, 1960.
11. Nancy M. Henley, *Body Politics,* Englewood Cliffs, NJ: Prentice-Hall, 1977, p. 181.
12. Michael Korda, "Symbols of Power." In *Organizational Reality: Reports from the Firing Line,* 3rd ed., Peter J. Frost, Vance F. Mitchell, and Walter R. Nord (Eds.), Glenview, IL: Scott, Foresman, 1986, pp. 145–157.
13. Ibid., p. 146.
14. Mark L. Knapp, *Nonverbal Communication in Human Interaction,* New York: Holt, Rinehart and Winston, 1972, p. 9.
15. Paul Watzlawick, Janet H. Beavin, and Don D. Jackson, *Pragmatics of Human Communication: A Study of Interactional Patterns, Pathologies, and Paradoxes,* New York: Norton, 1967, pp. 48–49.
16. Gerald R. Miller, "The Current Status of Theory and Research in Interpersonal Communication," *Human Communication Research,* vol. 4, 1978, pp. 164–178.
17. Ibid., p. 167.
18. Ibid.
19. Ibid.
20. Ibid., p. 168.
21. Ibid., p. 167.

CHAPTER 2

Organizational Influences on the Communication Process

Human beings are organizing creatures. We organize daily schedules and annual objectives. Our tendency to organize is also manifested in our continual attempts to coordinate our lives with other human beings, forming relationships, families, companies, communities, governments, and societies. Because individuals in our complex society cannot take care of all of their own needs, our organizations are a vital part of our lives.

As you begin your study of business and professional speaking, it is important that you have some understanding of the context in which the communication skills you are developing will be used. That context is the organization—more precisely, the business organization. As a member of a business organization, you will participate in communication activities that help shape that organization and which, at the same time, are shaped by it. In this chapter we will examine ways in which the organizational context influences the process of communication. Much about the process of communication is the same regardless of context, but there are features of organizations that make communication in the organization unique. We will begin by describing the fundamental elements of an organization. We will then look at three important features of organizations: formal structure, informal networks, and culture. As we discuss these three features, we will focus on their relationships to the communication process. Finally, we will provide a discussion of communication media that are commonly used in the organization.

WHAT IS AN ORGANIZATION?

Although we can all recognize one when we see it, we many not be able to explain what an organization is. What is it that churches, schools, hospitals, manufacturing plants, and so forth have in common that makes them organizations? In explaining what an organization is, we are relying heavily upon the very influential writing of Chester I. Barnard.[1] Although Barnard offered his definition in the late 1930s, it is sufficiently general and comprehensive so as to be timeless. One renowned scholar in the field of organizational communication, Philip K. Tompkins, has helped revive interest in Barnard's work. In a recent work, Tompkins used Barnard's view as the basis for his own definition of organizational communication.[2]

Barnard was one of few organizational theorists who wrote a fairly complete theory of organization and who recognized the vital role of communication in organizations. It is important to note that Barnard was interested in explaining the nature of organizations in general, not just business organizations. Extensive experience in a wide variety of organizations[3] gave Barnard a special vantage point from which to gather observations about organizations in general.

Barnard defined an organization as "a system of consciously coordinated activities or forces of two or more persons."[4] Let's look at the components of that definition so that you can gain a fuller understanding of the nature of an organization.

Systems Perspective

First of all, Barnard's definition tells us that an organization should be seen as a system. This is the perspective adopted by many organizational theorists.[5] From this point of view, an organization is seen as consisting of interrelated parts such that any change in one part of the organization reverberates change throughout it. And, as a system, an organization is part of larger systems, such as a community, a state, a country, an industry, and so forth. Changes in the larger systems of which the organization is a part can produce change within the organization.

Perhaps it will help you understand this concept of organizations as systems if you think of your family as a system. It is composed of parts—your parents, your siblings, and yourself, for example. When you talk about an individual in your family, you are not talking about your family. The individuals are part of the family because of the roles they play in it and the relationships they have with other members.

Note also that family members are interdependent; something that happens to one member has repercussions for everyone. When a child leaves home to go to college, for instance, there will be more changes throughout the household. Perhaps rooms will be rearranged because of the additional space. Perhaps your parents will treat you and your siblings differently. You might treat your parents differently. There are many changes that could occur, but the point is that a change in one part of a system produces change, regardless of how subtle, throughout the system.

In addition, change outside the system (in the larger systems of which it is a part) has an impact on the system. A series of burglaries in your neighborhood may alter some family policies and habits. The closing of businesses in your community may bring about financial hardship for your family.

Like your family, organizations are systems that cannot be understood completely by looking at individual parts. Rather, they are best understood by examining interrelationships between the parts and between the parts and the larger systems to which they belong. Charles Perrow, a noted sociologist, believes it is very informative to examine an organization as a part of a larger system, such as an industry or a network of organizations.[6] Such a perspective reveals information that could not be uncovered by looking at an organization or its parts in isolation.

Coordinated Activity

The second component of Barnard's definition concerns his notion of "consciously coordinated activities . . . of two or more persons." Barnard viewed an organization not as a collection or group of people, but as an aggregate of actions performed by people.[7] It is the coordination of actions performed by various people that results in the achievement of a purpose. One could gather a group of people for the purpose of trying to reach some objective, but that objective can be reached only through the *coordination* of actions or activities performed by those people.

For example, in your family, members take on roles which must be coordinated. Money must be earned, bills paid, meals cooked, supplies purchased, the sick provided for, and so on. Each family member takes on one or more of these roles and performs it on behalf of the others. When the role is not played well, other family members suffer the consequences. Thus, there is usually a person whose role it is to coordinate activity, to supervise, direct, and evaluate the activities of others.

In formal organizations like businesses, employees are assigned tasks to perform on behalf of the company. Supervisors oversee the work to make sure it is accomplished properly. On a higher level, administrators and executives plan what must be accomplished and calculate what personnel are needed to accomplish it. Employees (members) are added to or deleted from the organization in order to accomplish the goals. Thus, activity is coordinated.

In addition to offering a definition of an organization, Barnard discussed three major elements of an organization: (1) willingness to cooperate, (2) common purpose, and (3) communication.[8] These three elements are necessary for an organization to exist.

Willingness to Cooperate

An organization depends upon the willingness of individuals to cooperate and contribute their efforts and energy to the system.[9] This element is so central to an organization that we can easily overlook it. People must be willing to cooperate with one another if the organization is to exist and survive. Without cooperation there can be no coordination of activities and consequently no achievement of purpose. Barnard argues quite persuasively that individuals' willingness to cooperate depends upon their satisfaction with the organization.[10] If the rewards received by an organization member outweigh the sacrifices he or she must make, that individual is likely to be satisfied and thus willing to cooperate.

Think of your own experiences with organizations, whether with places of employment or campus clubs. You have probably felt less satisfied in some organizations than in others because you felt that what you were putting in exceeded what you were getting out of the organization. This probably had a detrimental effect on your willingness to serve that organization and to cooperate with the system.

A major activity of most organizations is to induce people to cooperate. This is accomplished in part by the offering of incentives—both material (such as money, life insurance, or bonuses) and nonmaterial (including responsibility, prestige, power, and a sense of being worthwhile). For a variety of reasons, not all people are willing to cooperate. In business organizations, members may be replaced if they are not willing and able to cooperate with organizational goals by performing required tasks satisfactorily.

Common Purpose

The second essential element of an organization is a common purpose. Most organizations actually have multiple purposes that guide activity. Without a common purpose or objective, there would be no reason for people to cooperate.[11] Moreover, they would not know what specific actions they need to perform. The purpose gives the organization members a focus for their efforts. For example, knowing that an organization's objective is to manufacture and sell computers, the members can identify and perform the activities that are necessary to achieve that objective. Note that we are talking here about the organization's purpose, not the personal objectives of the individuals in that organization. An individual's purpose (or motive, as Barnard refers to it)[12] may be to earn a substantial salary, but what we are talking about here is the organization's purpose.

Organizations' purposes can vary widely. The purpose of a family could be to sustain and support the growth of the members. The purpose of a government unit is to raise funds and provide necessary service. The purpose of a company is usually to distribute goods and services. Each member of an organization tries to achieve personal goals within the framework of the organization. Barnard believed that to the extent the organization facilitates personal accomplishment without sacrificing its own goals, members are willing to cooperate.[13] This view may overstate the individual's power to decide whether or not to comply with the organization's requirements, however. People often continue to cooperate in organizations in which their personal goals remain unfulfilled.

Communication

The third essential element of the organization, in Barnard's view, is communication. Barnard's perspective is that without communication, cooperation cannot be achieved; thus, neither personal nor organizational purposes can be accomplished.

Communication is essential to the organization for two reasons. First, the common purpose of the organization must be communicated to members.[14] Second, members must communicate in order to coordinate their activities to achieve that purpose.[15] Imagine an organization without communication, particularly without verbal communication. It is almost impossible to conceive of such a situation because it is hard to imagine how the organization could accomplish anything.

Drawing upon Barnard's work, we define an organization as *a system of consciously coordinated activities of two or more persons.* For an organization to exist, members must be willing to cooperate, there must be a common purpose, and there must be a system of communication (see Exhibit 2.1). In the next section, we will look at three features of the organization that both influence and are influenced by the communication process.

Exhibit 2.1 BARNARD'S THREE ELEMENTS OF AN ORGANIZATION

1. Willingness to cooperate
2. Common purpose
3. Communication

FEATURES OF ORGANIZATIONS

In Chapter 1 we briefly discussed the importance of adapting communication to the specific situation in which it occurs. We suggested that you analyze the general features of purpose, place, and time and then make communicative choices appropriate for the context. In this section we will elaborate that discussion by focusing on several features of the organizational context. It is important that you understand these features because they have implications for the communicative choices you will make as an organization member. As Charles Conrad, organizational communication scholar, notes: "Being able to communicate effectively at work requires two kinds of knowledge. First, it requires an understanding of the relationships that exist between communication and the operation of organizations. . . . Second, effective communication depends on employees' understanding how to choose appropriate communication strategies in different situations."[16] Your analysis of communication situations will need to be expanded to include the features discussed in this section. Although there are many aspects of organizations, the three we consider to be most significant are formal structure, informal communication networks, and organizational culture.

Formal Structure

One of the key features of organizations is their formal structure. Formal structure refers to the design of an organization, that is, the arrangement of all of its divisions, departments, or units. Formal structure is illustrated by an organization chart such as the one depicted in Exhibit 2.2. The formal organizational structure is what appears on paper as a hierarchy of positions, and it depicts who has authority over whom. Each individual has a specific role within the organizational structure, a role that involves specified job duties and specified relationships with other members. By looking at the organization chart, you can identify who reports to whom, and you can gain an understanding of all of the component parts of that organization.

Communication in organizations is greatly influenced by formal organizational structure. For example, much of the communication that occurs follows the chain of command delineated by the organization chart. A salesperson who has a question about a sales procedure is not likely to direct that question to the vice president of finance. Rather, she will ask her immediate supervisor or a department co-worker in this instance. Not all communication follows the prescribed lines of communication represented by the organization chart, as we will discuss when we examine informal networks. However, much communication is directly influenced by the presence of formal structure, so much so that organizational communication theorists have described communication in

Exhibit 2.2 SAMPLE ORGANIZATION CHART

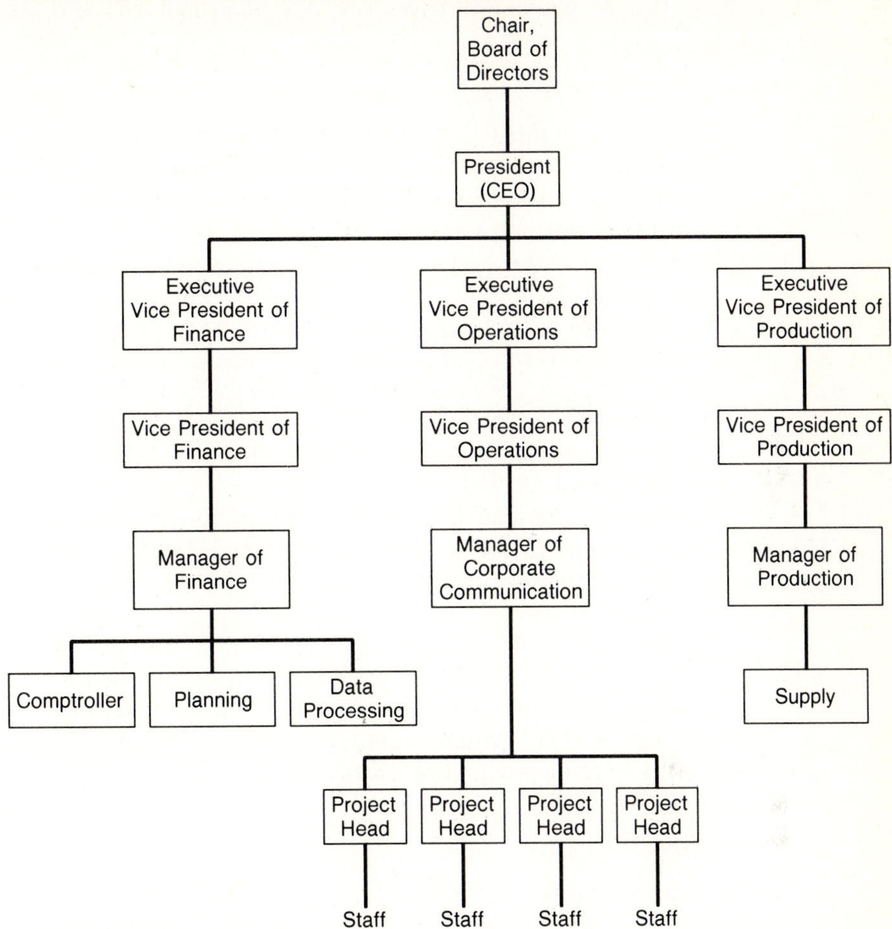

terms of the direction it follows on the organization chart. Organizational communication can be categorized as downward, upward, and horizontal.

Downward Communication Communication is often initiated by those in superordinate positions and sent to subordinates; this is *downward communication.* When we think of communication within an organization, we are likely to think of downward communication, with a superior giving job instructions, information, or feedback to a worker. Although this is an important type of communication, communication also flows in other directions, as we will examine shortly.

Downward communication is used for a variety of reasons. Superiors communicate with their subordinates to provide them instructions, to share information, to criticize and commend, to seek information, and to motivate. In fact, Daniel Katz and Robert Kahn identified five types of downward communication:[17]

1. ***Job instructions*** Job instructions are messages about what an employee is to do or is not to do in carrying out job responsibilities. Messages about the way to adjust a machine or the format for writing a report are job instructions.
2. ***Job rationale*** Sometimes employees are also given explanations of why they should do a job in a particular way. "If you follow this format when you write your reports, we will have consistency throughout the department, making it easier to compare reports" is a job rationale.
3. ***Information*** Some downward messages concern more general information about the organization, such as rules, policies, company benefits, and procedures. Explaining a safety regulation is one way of providing information.
4. ***Feedback*** When an employee is given information about his or her job performance, the superior is providing *feedback.* Feedback may be given casually, through the formal performance appraisal process, or in both ways.
5. ***Ideology*** *Ideology* refers to downward messages intended to create loyalty to the organization and a sense of identification with its objectives. The university president who, in a speech to faculty, reminds them of their primary mission to educate young people is presenting this type of downward message.

Unfortunately, however, employees often are not satisfied with the downward communication they receive.[18] They sometimes believe that the amount of information they receive is inadequate[19] or that it is not the kind of information they want or need.[20]

Upward Communication Communication can also be initiated by subordinates and sent to those in superior positions; this is *upward communication.* Perhaps most organizational communication is directed downward; however, that does not undermine the importance of upward-directed communication.

Subordinates communicate upward to make suggestions, to air dissatisfactions, to seek information, to impress superiors, to provide feedback about job problems, and perhaps to reduce the psychological distance between themselves and their superiors.[21] One problem that seems to occur frequently is that subordinates distort their upward communication.[22] They may delete information that could be perceived as reflecting negatively on their job performance.[23] They may withhold criticism of their superiors for fear of punishment, and they may neglect to send information that they deem irrelevant when in fact it is not. Sometimes subordinates claim that their superiors are not receptive to upward communication, and the subordinates withhold information for that reason.[24]

Horizontal Communication Communication between persons on the same level in an organization is referred to as *horizontal communication.* Employees on the same level communicate in order to coordinate work activities, to solve problems, to share information among departments, to resolve interdepartmental conflicts, and to establish emotional and social support systems.[25] Horizontal communication is essential for cooperation and coordination in the organization.

There are a few problems that may occur in horizontal communication. First, there is often competition among employees at the same level of an organization, competition for promotions and recognition.[26] This can result in employees withholding information from one another or a lack of cooperation. Second, increased interaction among workers may lead to increased conflict and more misunderstandings.[27] Just because people have the opportunity to communicate does not mean that their communication will be beneficial. Third, with increasing specialization, employees in different departments often have difficulty making themselves understood. Specialized fields have specialized language—jargon that is understood only by those within that field, as we explained in Chapter 1. When people from different fields communicate, they can have trouble interpreting each other's language, and this can cause misunderstandings and frustration.

All three directions of communication—downward, upward, and horizontal—are necessary for the coordination and cooperation that must exist if organizational objectives are to be met. But each is not without potential problems, which may or may not be addressed by management. How successfully or unsuccessfully these problems are managed can affect the extent to which communication fulfills its functions in the organization.

Functions of Organizational Communication Together, downward, upward, and horizontal communication fulfill many functions in organizations. Taking our cue from Charles Conrad's discussion, we will examine three major functions of organizational communication: the command, relational, and ambiguity management functions.[28]

1. ***The command function*** Communication is essential to the coordination of activities designed to achieve an organization's objectives. The reason for an organization's existence is to achieve some specified objectives. Members' work must be coordinated in order to achieve

those goals. For example, if the salespeople do not coordinate with the advertising people, advertising may be created that does not emphasize those aspects of the product that enhance the ability of salespeople to sell the product. Communication is the essential element of this kind of coordination: a manager must direct employees' actions and must provide feedback about the adequacy of those actions.[29] As Conrad explains, direction and feedback are the two aspects of this *command function* of communication.[30]

2. ***The relational function*** Members of an organization form relationships with one another. In fact, the formation of some relationships is dictated by the formal organizational structure.[31] Because many of these relationships are imposed, they remain at the noninterpersonal end of the continuum described in Chapter 1. However, regardless of the specific nature of these relationships, communication is the process through which they are formed and maintained. Successful maintenance of employee relationships is important to the coordination necessary for organizational effectiveness because the quality of those relationships can affect job satisfaction and willingness to perform tasks.[32]
3. ***The ambiguity management function*** We have described organizations as having common purposes, systems of communication, and formal structures. Our discussion may have suggested that organizations run smoothly and everything is clear to everyone. That is not the case, however. There is a great deal of uncertainty in organizations. Goals are ambiguous, lines of communication may be unknown or not utilized, and people may be uncertain of many aspects of their tasks. Even if the organization's management attempts to provide clarification, some degree of ambiguity will continue to exist, in part because the environment in which the organization operates will fluctuate. Communication fulfills an *ambiguity management function* in that organization members interact with one another in order to make sense out of ambiguous situations and to create agreed-upon ways of interpreting those situations.[33] For example, when a rumor about possible layoffs circulates, employees talk with one another to find out if there is any truth to the rumor, how many people are expected to be out of work, the reason for the layoffs, and any other details that are of interest to them. Moreover, they may come to share a common view of the situation as a result of their communication. Through interaction, for instance, they may believe that the rumor is untrue and no layoffs are imminent.

These three functions of communication—command, relational, and ambiguity management—operate in all organizations and are fulfilled by horizontal, upward, and downward communication. Now that we have examined formal structure as an influence on communication, let's turn to some suggestions designed to help you adapt your communication to the organizational context.

Suggestions for Communicating in Formal Structures Knowing that organizations have formal structures that influence the communication process can assist you as you develop your organizational communication skills. As a member of an organization, you should try to heed the following advice:

1. *Learn the formal structure.* Most organizations have a prepared organization chart that is available to interested parties. A copy of the chart may be included in materials distributed to new employees. If it is not, you should ask for a copy and familiarize yourself with the structure. It is a way to learn more about the organization as a whole and, more specifically, to become aware of the formal chain of command and lines of communication.
2. *Follow the formal lines of communication.* In most cases, you should use the proper channels of communication, although when we discuss informal networks you will see that it is not always necessary to do so. (However, people who use informal lines privately may still present a public display of utilizing formal channels of communication.) Until you develop sophistication as an organization member, it is best to follow the formal lines of communication. If you have a request to make or a question you need answered, the person to whom you report is the most appropriate person to ask in most instances. There may be times when you can approach an experienced person in your department, but you need to determine first if that person can grant your request. When people do not follow the chain of command, they risk alienating or angering the person or persons they have bypassed. In fact, if you bypass your immediate supervisor and speak to the manager of the unit, that manager may advise you to talk to your supervisor or may reprimand you for not having done so. As difficult as it is to do, in most instances you need to begin with your immediate supervisor, even if he or she is the problem. In this case, however, you would be wise to investigate the procedure for dealing with such matters that is followed by the company or union (if you belong to one).
3. *Utilize all directions of communication.* Information can be obtained, problems solved, and coordination achieved by communicating with superiors, subordinates, and co-workers. Learn to use all three directions of communication rather than relying exclusively on one. You need to make judgments about when it is appropriate to communicate in each direction, on the basis of your analysis of the situation and your experience in the organization. For example, sharing your ideas with co-workers may be enjoyable, but if you are truly interested in seeing

a change in the organization, you will need to communicate upward with those who have the authority to approve and implement the change.

It is clear that the formal structure of an organization influences the communication process. The structure establishes lines of authority and communication and dictates the formation of some relationships. We do not get to choose our immediate supervisor or the manager of our department, except perhaps in rare cases. It is important to understand the formal structure in order to avoid unintentionally bypassing appropriate lines of communication. Not all communication within the organization follows designated channels, however, as we will discuss in the next section.

Informal Communication Networks

The second feature of organizations that influences and is influenced by communication is the existence of informal networks of relationships, referred to by Barnard as the *informal organization.* Barnard defines the informal organization as "the aggregate of the personal contacts and interactions and associated groupings of people" within an organization.[34] As Barnard explains, people in an organization come in contact with one another, interact, and form informal groups even though such contacts and groupings are not specified or governed by the formal structure. Sometimes these relationships are formed because of proximity—two or more people who work near one another are likely to form an informal group. Sometimes these associations are more intentional, in that people seek out other organization members for various reasons. Regardless of how they come about, relationships form between organization members even though those relationships are not mandated by the organizational structure. "Learning the ropes" in an organization, says Barnard, "is chiefly learning [the] who's who, what's what, and why's why, of its informal society."[35]

Informal organizations develop inside all formal organizations. People make friends, form cliques and political alliances, and sometimes even fall in love. Mentor relationships develop. It is through the relational function of communication that these relationships are established and maintained. At the same time, the presence of these networks of relationships influences communication in the organization. Unwritten rules evolve regarding with whom information should be shared, from whom it should be withheld, or to whom to talk about particular issues. This communication that occurs outside of the formal lines dictated by the organization chart is often referred to as informal communication. It is communication between individuals who have no mandated relationship. Informal communication often occurs outside of working time, such as at lunch and breaks and after hours. It often involves bypassing the official chain of command, such as when an employee in one division seeks information from a supervisor in another division, even though the two people have no formal relationship.

Both formal and informal communication seem to be necessary to the continued existence of an organization. On the whole, informal communication augments communication throughout the organization. If formal communication alone existed in organizations, there would be less interaction and, as a result, less coordination than would be desirable. Informal communication augments and supports the formal structure and the people who take part in it. In addition to increasing the amount of communication overall, informal communication serves a variety of important functions.

Functions of Informal Communication Networks There are many functions of informal networks of communication. The three functions of organizational communication in general—the command, relational, and ambiguity management functions—are fulfilled by informal networks, especially the relational and ambiguity management functions. In this section we will examine three additional functions of informal communication networks:

1. ***Emotional and social support*** Through informal interactions, organization members develop support systems—networks of people to whom they can turn for emotional and social support. Even people who are highly satisfied with an organization have complaints about it at one time or another. They often do not want to register those complaints formally, but they want to air their feelings with people who understand the situation. It is with employees in the informal network that they share their dissatisfactions. Enlightened management now attempts to build opportunities for development of friendships, mentor relationships, and casual contact because it is imperative to maintenance of morale as well as organizational effectiveness. Isolated and alienated members or employees can destroy an organization.
2. ***Increase in willingness to cooperate*** Because of the development of social and emotional support systems through informal communication, employees may experience an increase in their willingness to cooperate toward the achievement of organizational objectives. Very often, it is not possible to use the formal structure to appeal emotionally to employees. Sometimes arrangements made informally can be used to bypass the formal structure in order to accomplish tasks that could not otherwise be done. It is very important to an organization that members develop personal loyalties to their leaders and supervisors as well as to each other. Conversely, interpersonal hostilities can materially interfere with formal communication in an organization.

3. *Increase in member satisfaction* As Barnard points out, the informal organization allows employees to maintain a feeling of self-respect and independent choice.[36] This is due to the fact that informal interactions are not dictated by the formal organization and, consequently, give members a sense of choice. This is likely to produce increased member satisfaction with the organization.

Suggestions for Communicating in Informal Networks Earlier we offered suggestions for communicating effectively within the formal structure of the organization. It is also important to be conscious of the communicative choices you make as you become part of informal networks. Although there is no formal penalty for making a mistake, there can be serious consequences. For example, "spilling the beans" with the wrong person could get you labeled as a blabbermouth from whom others should withhold important information. We offer several suggestions for using the informal communication networks in an organization:

1. *Cultivate informal relationships.* Because of the functions fulfilled by informal networks, it is important that you attempt to develop informal relationships within the organization. It usually takes some effort to form these relationships, even if others initiate them with you. Show some interest in others by asking them about themselves. Be responsive to them, and offer minor assistance if possible. Informal relationships with people at upper levels of the organization can be rewarding, so they shouldn't automatically be overlooked. A superior can become your mentor, which can potentially help you advance in the organization. There are no specific prescriptions for successfully cultivating informal relationships. All we can suggest is that you be conscious of the choices you make and exert the effort it takes to become part of an informal network.
2. *Exercise restraint.* As a new employee eager to develop informal relationships, be careful not to try to force them. Relationships take time to develop; people need to learn about each other and whether or not they can trust the other person. Take your time and get to know others before attempting to initiate a more interpersonal relationship. Sometimes the people who seem to be most eager to get to know the newcomer have a "hidden agenda"—they are looking for an ally because they are outcasts from the informal network. Be respectful but cautious when employees show a lot of interest in you as the new employee.
3. *Be discreet.* There are two parts to this suggestion. First, when you are given information in confidence, don't betray it. People may be testing you to see if you can be trusted, or they may genuinely trust you with

their secrets. Sharing confidential information can earn you the label of untrustworthy or perhaps ruin a potentially satisfying relationship. Second, as author Ronald Adler advises, "Don't flaunt informal shortcuts."[37] One of the advantages of being part of an informal network is that it provides shortcuts for getting tasks done. A friendly relationship with someone in purchasing can speed the process of obtaining a purchase order. Be discreet about your ability to use these shortcuts. Bragging to others may alienate them or cause them to register a complaint against the department personnel who are "playing favorites." You could make enemies as well as lose your connection.

The development of informal relationships can make life in an organization very pleasant and can increase your ability to get your job done efficiently. Working to cultivate these relationships is well worth your time, but you need good judgment in making communicative choices.

Organizational Culture

We will consider one more feature of an organization: its culture. Like the other features of organizations, culture affects and is affected by communication. In this section we will examine the concept of organizational culture, discuss its relationship to communication, and suggest ways to adapt communication to that culture.

What Is Organizational Culture? In recent years, the application of the concept of culture to organizations has received a great deal of attention.[38] When we travel to another country, we sometimes experience "culture shock"; that is, we recognize that the country's culture differs from our own, and we have to adapt our ways to "fit in." An organization can also be thought of as having its own culture. Culture is a shared view of life in an organization, including its predominant values, norms for behavior, customs, and rituals. As Conrad notes, "the members of a culture develop distinctive ways of perceiving, interpreting, and explaining the events and actions that they observe around them."[39]

Each organization develops its own unique culture, and that culture evolves over time. Thomas Peters and Peter Waterman, in their popular book *In Search of Excellence,* suggest that some cultures foster greater organizational effectiveness than others.[40] This has resulted in executives attempting to change the culture of their organization, but this has not always been successful.[41]

Because organizational cultures differ, people feel "more at home" in some organizations than in others. Popular magazine articles provide advice about sizing up an organization's culture in order to determine whether you will "fit in." This is difficult to do, however, prior to accepting employment with a particular company. The company's literature and your interactions with recruiters can give you only a limited sense of the organization's culture. To thoroughly understand an organization's culture, you probably need to be immersed in it over a period of time. Two communication scholars, Michael Pacanowsky and Nick O'Donnell-Trujillo, suggest that studying an organization's rites and rituals, metaphors, stories, vocabulary, and several other indicators is a way to come to understand its culture.[42]

It is not important for you to conduct a thorough analysis of your organization's culture. What is important is that you understand the relationship between culture and communication because of the implications of that relationship for your behavior as an organization member.

Communication and Culture Organizational cultures are created through communication. The values, customs, norms, and rituals that characterize a culture are shared and altered through communication.

The other aspect of the situation, more important to our purpose, is that culture influences communicative behavior. As Conrad states, "It is through communication that members of cultures (and thus of organizations) learn who they are, what their roles are, and what kinds of actions are expected of them."[43] Moreover, the culture provides the backdrop for interpreting situations; consequently, it suggests guidelines and imposes limitations on behavior.[44] If a predominant cultural value is self-sacrifice for the good of the organization, some situations in which a choice must be made are likely to be interpreted with that value in mind. Organization members may go to extremes to demonstrate their willingness to sacrifice for the organization. Behavior that appears to be self-interested is discouraged in such a culture, and unselfish behavior is encouraged. Thus, culture affects the behavioral and communicative choices people make.

Culture also influences people's perceptions and interpretations of events and situations, which can affect their behavior. In an organization that has favored speed over quality, employees are likely to perceive many situations as requiring fast, not necessarily accurate, results. This affects their daily work habits and their communication with others. It probably would not be unusual to hear employees emphasize the speed with which a task was completed. Those who did not accept this value would undoubtedly be influenced by it, even as they grumbled to others that all that counts is speed, not quality.

Adapting to Organizational Cultures As we have discussed features of organizations that influence communication, we have provided suggestions for your own communication behavior. We would like to end this discussion of culture by again offering suggestions to help you communicate more effectively in the organizational context:

1. *Listen carefully.* Although in this text we emphasize the speaking part of the communication process, good listening habits are crucial. In order to adapt to an organizational culture, you need a sense of what that culture is like—what is valued, what is expected, and what is forbidden. By listening carefully, you can begin to understand that culture. As Pacanowsky and O'Donnell-Trujillo suggest, you can learn about the culture by listening to the stories told about people and events in the organization, the metaphors used to describe the organization, and the specialized vocabulary shared by employees.[45] You will learn about the culture and what is expected of you by listening intently.
2. *Observe others.* You can also learn about the culture of an organization by observing the behavior of others, both those who are successful and those who are less so. An important way to improve communication is by modeling the behavior of people who are effective. As you observe others, you can attempt to model those who are effective communicators and successful in the organization. Observe those who have been labeled as not fitting in. Try to determine in what ways their behavior is inappropriate for, or not valued in, the organization's culture. Sometimes it is just as useful to know what behaviors to avoid as it is to know what behaviors to model.
3. *Fulfill your role.* Through careful listening and observation, you can learn what is expected of you. Then you must choose behaviors that fulfill your role in the organization if you want to signal a willingness to participate in the culture.[46] Performing the behaviors expected of you does not mean blind conformity or total subordination to the organization. Remember, the culture provides guidelines for behavior, not strict rules that allow only one behavioral option.

Formal structure, informal communication networks, and culture are three features of organizations that affect communication (see Exhibit 2.3). It is important that you be aware of these features so that you can adapt your communication to the organizational context in which it occurs. In the next section we will examine various media of communication that you will use as an organization member.

Exhibit 2.3 FEATURES OF ORGANIZATIONS

1. Formal structure
2. Informal communication networks
3. Organizational culture

MEDIA OF COMMUNICATION

There are many ways in which information is communicated in an organization. These media of communication, sometimes called channels of communication, traditionally took two forms: oral and written. With widespread use of the computer, we can now talk about three forms: oral, written, and machine-mediated. However, it is clear that these forms overlap. For example, with electronic mail, an employee may write a memo and send it directly to other employees through the use of computers. The memo never needs to be written on paper. Thus, the written form overlaps with the machine-mediated form of communication. In addition, oral communication overlaps with machine-mediated communication in such forms as videotaped presentations and telephone conferences. In the past, research was conducted to determine which medium—oral or written—was more effective in communicating a message.[47] With so many new media available for communication, future studies will need to focus on their effectiveness.

In this section we will look at three major communication media. Keep in mind, however, that these categories overlap. Our purpose is to acquaint you with the wide variety of media used for communication within an organization.

Oral Communication

Oral communication takes a variety of forms, as summarized in Exhibit 2.4. First, and perhaps most frequent, is face-to-face interaction between two individuals. An employee approaches a superior to ask a question or make a suggestion; a supervisor gives instructions to a worker; or two workers talk to coordinate their efforts.

Second, oral communication takes place in committee meetings. We will discuss meetings in Chapters 6 and 7, but for now we want to point out that communication frequently takes this form in the organization. Department heads may meet on a regular basis to coordinate the activities of the various departments. Employees may be assigned to task forces to help solve problems in their departments. And executives meet to make decisions of wider scope for the company.

A third form of oral communication is the interview. There are a variety

Exhibit 2.4 ORAL COMMUNICATION MEDIA

1. Face-to-face interaction
2. Committee meetings
3. Interviews
4. Presentations
5. Training sessions

of types of interviews taking place within the organization. There are selection interviews for hiring purposes, performance appraisal interviews for annual or semiannual evaluations, and counseling interviews for employees with problems. In Chapters 4 and 5 we will discuss interviews in great detail.

Presentations are also a form of oral communication. An employee may make a presentation proposing a new idea or may give a speech to people in the community. Presentations serve many purposes; we will examine them fully in Chapters 8 and 9.

The training session is a special form of oral communication. Employees at all levels in an organization require training programs to teach them a variety of skills or concepts. In fact, many large organizations have a corporate training department with a full-time staff. Smaller organizations often hire teachers from outside the organization to run training sessions on a periodic basis.

All employees should be skillful in oral communication in its various forms, because oral skills are important on a daily basis. In addition, some research has indicated that oral communication skills are rated at the top of the list of skills important to job success.[48] Typically only low-level jobs involve little interaction.[49] As people move up in an organization, their oral skills become more and more important. Our major objective in this text is to help you improve the oral communication skills necessary for life in a business organization.

Written Communication

Written communication can also take many forms. One very common form is the letter or memo. *Letters* are generally longer and more formal than memos. *Memos* are a common form of communication, and they serve a variety of functions within the organization. They may serve to remind employees of meetings, summarize a previous discussion, or share a bit of information.

Bulletin boards are another medium for written communication. They are often used for making general announcements, such as meeting dates or information about the company picnic. They are also used to provide information about achievements made by organization members.

Many organizations have a *house organ,* such as a magazine or newsletter. These often include information about organization members; events of interest to employees; and information about the company itself, such as latest developments, new plans and policies, and accomplishments.

Another type of written communication is the *annual report* or other reports. These are detailed descriptions of proposals or outcomes of projects. If a new health insurance plan was adopted by an organization, for example, undoubtedly someone would prepare a written report on the progress of the new plan.

Exhibit 2.5 WRITTEN COMMUNICATION MEDIA

1. Letters
2. Memos
3. Bulletin boards
4. House organ
5. Annual report or other reports

There are many more types of written communication used in the organization. Since our focus in this book is on oral communication, we will not go over all of the written forms. However, those that we have discussed should give you a sense of the importance of written communication within the organization. For some types of jobs, effective writing skills may be even more important than oral skills. If you are unsure of your career direction, you probably should work to develop both oral and written communications skills while you are in college. See Exhibit 2.5 for a summary of these written communication media.

Machine-Mediated Communication

Many interactions between organization members are mediated by machines of various types, principally the computer. In this section we will give you an overview of some of types of machine-mediated communication. Technology is developing so rapidly that even as we write this, new forms of machine-mediated communication are being developed.

One of the most common forms of machine-mediated communication is the use of the telephone. All kinds of business is accomplished via the telephone, and the number of ways the telephone can be used has been increasing in recent years. Computers have expanded the capabilities of telephones tremendously. An employee at a phone outside the organization can dial a code number that allows her to find out what messages have been left on her answering machine. Note how this frees employees to work on other tasks. Employees do not have to wait for important calls. They can go on with the day, calling the code number to find out if the call has come through. New technology has also made it possible for greater numbers of people to have phones in their cars. People can be working as they are on the road. Imagine what a benefit this is to salespeople who do a great deal of traveling.

Computers mediate communication in another important way through on-line communication. Organization members have computer terminals that allow them to contact other people, both inside and outside the organization. Messages, manuscripts, reports, charts and graphs, and so on can be transmitted directly to other individuals through the use of these computer links. Think of the tremendous amount of time saved by avoiding the use of the typewriter, the copier, and the mail.

Not all that long ago, all meetings were face-to-face. This meant that employees had to travel a great deal to coordinate with others in different parts of the country and the world, at great expense to the company. With developments in technology, that is no longer true. *Teleconferencing* has made it possible for people to meet without traveling to the same location. Teleconferencing can take a variety of forms. First, there is the *audioconference,* in which a group of employees can interact through the use of the telephone. Second, *videoteleconferencing* makes it possible for groups of employees to both see and hear one another, even though they are hundreds of miles apart.

Videotape mediates a great deal of organizational communication. Instead of sending a trainer to another location, the organization can use videotaped presentations for training. Videotape is used for a variety of other organizational functions as well.

There are many, many more types of machine-mediated communication in the organization. Those that we have mentioned are among the most commonly used, especially in larger organizations. New technologies producing new forms of machine-mediated communication will require individuals to develop new skills for communication. Making a videotaped presentation, for example, is different from speaking to a live audience, and the speaker must use techniques appropriate for each situation. In this book we will try to help you develop oral communication skills for some of the new forms of machine-mediated communication.

SUMMARY

In this chapter we have defined an organization as a system of consciously coordinated activities of two or more persons, a definition that was originally proposed by Chester I. Barnard. An organization is composed of three essential elements: willingness to cooperate, common purpose, and communication.

We looked at three features of organizations that influence and are influenced by communication. First, we examined formal structure, which is represented by the organization chart. Each individual has a specified role in the formal structure, and relationships among individuals are dictated. Communication in the organization has been categorized on the basis of the direction it follows on the organization chart: downward, upward, and horizontal. These three types of communication are characterized by several unique problems. Organizational communication fulfills three major functions: command, relational, and ambiguity management functions.

Second, we discussed informal communication networks. All organizations develop an informal organization, which is the aggregate of contacts and interactions among people in the organization. These contacts occur because people work closely with one another and because people seek out interaction for a variety of reasons. Relationships that develop through informal contacts are not specified by the organization chart or organizational policies. The communication that establishes and maintains these relationships is referred to as informal communication. Informal communication serves the functions of providing emotional and social support, increasing cooperation, and increasing member satisfaction.

Third, we considered the ways an organization's culture affects communication. Culture is a shared view of life in the organization—its predominant values, norms for behavior, rituals, and customs. Culture is created through communication and influences communicative behavior.

Three primary media are used in organizational communication. Oral communication is perhaps the most common medium. It takes a variety of forms, including face-to-face interaction between two people, committee meetings, interviews, lectures and speeches, and training sessions. Written communication is a second medium, also taking many forms. Finally, much communication is machine-mediated, such as the use of the telephone, on-line communication, and teleconferencing. This last category overlaps the first two, because machines may be used in either oral or written communication.

CHAPTER 2 ACTIVITIES

1. Write your own definition of an organization. How does it differ from Barnard's definition? In what ways is it similar?
2. Obtain a copy of the organization chart for an organization with which you are familiar (preferably for your college or university or a company for which you've worked). But before you look at the chart, try to draw your own version. In your drawing, try to include the major divisions of the organization and the lines of communication. Now compare your version with the actual chart. How accurate is the chart that you drew? How familiar are you with the formal lines of communication?
3. Keep a journal of your interactions with others, either at work or in school, for one week. Note with whom you talked, for how long, the purpose of your interaction, and whether the interaction represents an informal relationship you have established or is dictated by the formal structure of the organization. Then analyze your journal to see what percentage of your interactions are mandated by the formal organization and what percentage could be considered informal contacts.
4. Conduct an informal study of an organization's culture (perhaps your school or place of employment would be an appropriate subject). In a notebook, record your observations in the following categories: specialized vocabulary (jargon) of organization members, stories told about people or events in the organization, metaphors used to describe the organization or the way it is run, rituals that are performed, and values that seem to be rewarded.

CHAPTER 2 NOTES

1. Chester I. Barnard, *The Functions of the Executive,* Cambridge, MA: Harvard University Press, 1938.
2. Philip K. Tompkins, "The Functions of Communication in Organizations." In *Handbook of Rhetorical and Communication Theory,* C. C. Arnold and J. W. Bowers (Eds.), Boston: Allyn & Bacon, 1984, pp. 659–719.
3. For a biography of Barnard, see William B. Wolf, *The Basic Barnard: An Introduction to Chester I. Barnard and His Theories of Organization and Management,* Ithaca, NY: Cornell University Press, 1974.
4. Barnard, p. 73.
5. See, for example, Daniel Katz and Robert Kahn, *The Social Psychology of Organizations,* New York: Wiley, 1966.
6. Charles Perrow, *Complex Organizations: A Critical Essay,* 3rd ed., New York: Random House, 1986.
7. Barnard, p. 76.
8. Ibid., p. 82.
9. Ibid., p. 83.
10. Ibid., p. 85.
11. Ibid., p. 86.
12. Ibid., p. 88.
13. Ibid., pp. 93–94.
14. Ibid., p. 89.
15. Ibid., pp. 106–107.
16. Charles Conrad, *Strategic Organizational Communication: Cultures, Situations, and Adaptation,* New York: Holt, Rinehart and Winston, 1985, p. 5.
17. Katz and Kahn, pp. 239–243.
18. Jerry W. Koehler, Karl W. E. Anatol, and Ronald L. Applbaum, *Organizational Communication: Behavioral Perspectives,* 2nd ed., New York: Holt, Rinehart and Winston, 1981, p. 88.
19. Barry K. Spiker and Tom D. Daniels, "Information Adequacy and Communication Relationships: An Empirical Examination of 18 Organizations," *Western Journal of Speech Communication,* vol. 45, 1981, pp. 342–354.
20. Ibid.
21. Koehler, Anatol, and Applbaum, p. 91.
22. John C. Athanassiades, "Distortion of Upward Communication in Hierarchical Organizations," *Academy of Management Journal,* vol. 16, 1973, pp. 207–225.
23. Koehler, Anatol, and Applbaum, p. 97.
24. Gerald M. Goldhaber, *Organizational Communication,* 4th ed., Dubuque, IA: Wm. C. Brown, 1986, p. 234.
25. Koehler, Anatol, and Applbaum, pp. 101–102.
26. Tom D. Daniels and Barry K. Spiker, *Perspectives on Organizational Communication,* Dubuque, IA: Brown, 1987, p. 90.
27. Koehler, Anatol, and Applbaum, p. 104.

28. Conrad, pp. 8–14.
29. Ibid., p. 8.
30. Ibid.
31. Ibid., p. 10.
32. Ibid., p. 11.
33. Ibid., p. 13.
34. Barnard, p. 115.
35. Ibid., p. 121.
36. Ibid., p. 122.
37. Ronald B. Adler, *Communicating at Work: Principles and Practices for Business and the Professions,* 2nd ed., New York: Random House, 1986, p. 39.
38. See, for example, Terrence E. Deal and Allen A. Kennedy, *Corporate Cultures: The Rites and Rituals of Corporate Life,* Reading, MA: Addison-Wesley, 1982; Michael E. Pacanowsky and Nick O'Donnell-Trujillo, "Communication and Organizational Cultures," *The Western Journal of Speech Communication,* vol. 46, 1982, pp. 115–130, and "Organizational Communication as Cultural Performance," *Communication Monographs,* vol. 50, 1983, pp. 126–147.
39. Conrad, p. 200.
40. Thomas J. Peters and Robert H. Waterman, *In Search of Excellence: Lessons from America's Best-Run Companies,* New York: Harper & Row, 1982.
41. Peter C. Reynolds, "Imposing a Corporate Culture," *Psychology Today,* vol. 21, March 1987, pp. 33–38.
42. Pacanowsky and O'Donnell-Trujillo, 1982, pp. 124–126.
43. Conrad, p. 200.
44. Ibid., p. 201.
45. Pacanowsky and O'Donnell-Trujillo, 1982, pp. 124–126.
46. Conrad, p. 201.
47. See, for example, Dale A. Level's study as discussed in R. Wayne Pace, *Organizational Communication: Foundations for Human Resource Development,* Englewood Cliffs, NJ: Prentice-Hall, 1983, p. 43.
48. Adler, p. 5.
49. Ibid., p. 4.

CHAPTER

3

L&L Associates: An Organizational Context

As we explained in Chapter 2, an organization can best be viewed as a system of consciously coordinated activities of two or more people. We like that definition because we think it really applies to the ways in which organizations work in the everyday world. As Kurt Lewin has pointed out, "There's nothing as practical as a good theory." And our definition of an organization is based on a theory about the nature of the phenomenon being defined. To illustrate the way you can apply this definition in analyzing the communication you will encounter in your working life, we have created for you a working model of an organization that we call *L&L Associates.* L&L Associates is designed as an extended sample context in which communication occurs.[1]

To be true to its purpose, L&L has been designed to model organizational communication as it exists in the real world. Thus, as discussed in Chapter 2, it has structure, including channels for formal communication; it has networks for informal communication; and it has its own unique culture—the third feature of any organization, according to the definition we are using.

Because L&L's design models the aspects of communication that exist in a real-world counterpart, it is a sample context that can be called an *organizational simulation*—that is, a working model of a real organization. You can use L&L Associates as an ongoing case in point to which to refer when applying the principles developed throughout the text, and/or as a participatory simulation in which to experience these phenomena firsthand. Each way is a means for increasing your practical understanding of the materials discussed in this text. In Chapter 2 we discussed the structural properties that are associated with organizations in general. Let's introduce you to L&L Associates as a sample context by describing its organizational structure.

WELCOME TO L&L ASSOCIATES

Like many real-world organizations, L&L Associates is a hierarchically structured organization which has been created for a specific purpose, and which therefore needs employees who perform the various jobs necessary if the organization is to achieve its purpose. In order to familiarize you with L&L Associates, we'll discuss (1) the system, or organization; (2) coordinated activities, or the business; (3) the jobs in L&L Associates; and finally, (4) the scenario, or the current events taking place at L&L. In other words, we'll give you the detail that goes along with the organizational structure when you look at any specific organization.

The Organization

L&L Associates is a complex organizational structure consisting of three divisions: the production division (which produces information packages and/or services for clients); the finance division (which handles all corporate financial management); and operations (which deals with all internal workings of the

L&L Associates headquarters houses all three divisions of the organization.

corporation, including its internal and external communication functions). *The division of the organization that we use for the purpose of discussion and/or participation in the simulation is the operations division.* One specific department of the operations division, the corporate communications department, is the location of most of the activity we will take part in at L&L.

We focus on this part of the organization, both for discussion purposes and for the simulation, in order to examine communication as a central function in this part of an organization. Naturally, communication takes place throughout the organization; but in the operations division, which includes the communication functions of the organization, communication activity is one of the central tasks in which people are involved.

As mentioned in Chapter 2, an organization displays the ways in which its parts are divided and organized by creating what is called an *organization chart.* Most organizations have organization charts. Knowledge of the chart in any organization provides information about the hierarchy within that organization and about the departmentalization of the organization's enterprise. Exhibit 3.1 presents a part of the organization chart for L&L Associates. You may recognize it from Chapter 2. Here, it will take on more meaning for you, because you need to make sense of it in order to understand what we are going to be saying about communication in L&L. And that's the way an organization chart works: it means the most to those people who need to understand the specific workings of a specific company, though it may be simply a chart with lines and boxes to anyone else.

This segment of the organization chart of L&L Associates indicates the top personnel in all three divisions of the corporation, even though we will focus on communication activities in the operations division. The only department presented in detail in the organization chart is the corporate communications department. This is because corporate communications is the department used as our sample context. Communication at L&L illustrates the principles discussed in Chapter 2 in terms of upward, downward, horizontal, formal, and informal communication.

For our purposes, the organization chart in Exhibit 3.1 shows you the slice of the organization in which activity takes place in the examples we will be using in the text. (Naturally, the chart could be more complete, as it is in Exhibit 2.2, in which all the divisions are shown.)

Chain of Command As we discussed in Chapter 2, one of the significant aspects of organizational communication is how much it is affected by structure and hierarchy. Organization charts, like the one in Exhibit 3.1, indicate the hierarchy of an organization and therefore lay out the formal channels of communication. These channels form the *chain of command:* who reports to whom about what (as well as who can talk directly to whom, and who has to

Exhibit 3.1 ORGANIZATION CHART, L&L ASSOCIATES

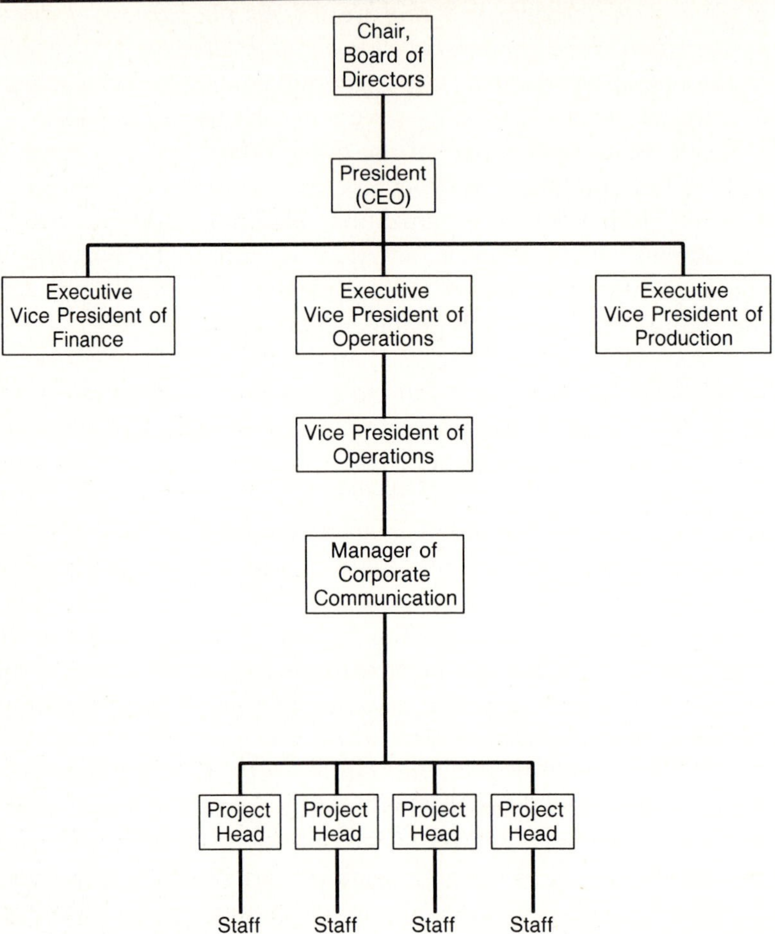

go through whom to talk to someone else). Exhibit 3.2 presents the chain of command in L&L Associates.

As you can see in Exhibit 3.2, upward and downward communication exist hierarchically within the organization: both types of communication follow the chain of command. What that means is that staff members cannot go directly to the president; they need to report through their project heads, who then report through managers, who report through vice presidents, and so on. As we discussed in Chapter 2, communication also travels horizontally: staff–staff, project head–project head, manager–manager, vice president–vice president.

This, then, is how L&L Associates is organized. It is a system consisting of interrelated parts: any change in one part of L&L reverberates throughout the entire organization. The system has three divisions, or subsystems, and each

Exhibit 3.2 CHAIN OF COMMAND IN L&L ASSOCIATES

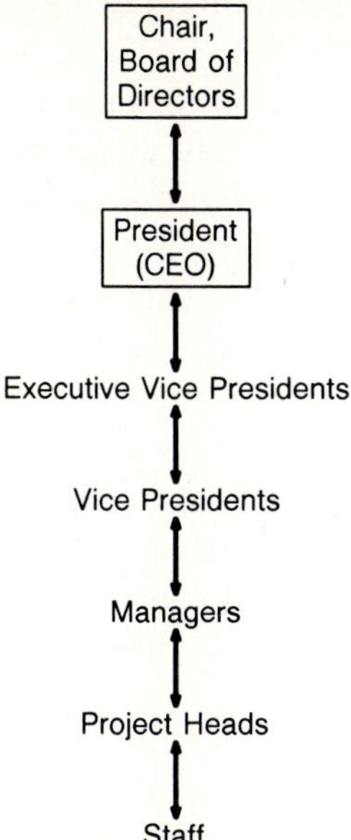

is compartmentalized. The organization chart shows how the divisions are related to one another, and it shows the titles of the people who head up the divisions and departments. The chain of command indicates the reporting (communication) functions—who reports to whom. The coordination of activities at L&L depends on this communication. In L&L, just as in any organization, knowing the divisions and the hierarchy of job responsibilities also tells you something about power in that context.

Having presented a picture of the structure, or skeleton, of the organization at L&L, let's look now at the second part of what makes up an organization: consciously coordinated activities. In the case of L&L, that means what the corporation has been created to do: its business.

Coordinated Activity: The Business

L&L Associates is a company in the business of producing health-related information or services for clients who hire the company for some specific project. Some of these projects are ongoing and are renewed on a yearly basis. Most, however, are onetime projects that take anywhere from a month to a year and a half to complete.

L&L works with a wide variety of clients. Some of them are profit-making corporations; some are not-for-profit organizations; some are private; some are public; some are very large, Fortune 500–type companies; some are small, family-held organizations. As a consequence, employees of L&L who deal directly with clients must have good skills for communicating with a variety of people.

Employees of L&L also need to have a range of skills for creating the kinds of products or services that are required by clients. While all are health information products or services, no two projects are exactly alike. Some of the kinds of information products or services produced by L&L in the last year include materials on how to quit smoking, produced for the National Association of Smokestoppers; videotapes on substance abuse, produced for one school district, which then became the prototype for a home videotape project on substance abuse that was adopted in towns and cities across the nation; and, most recently, the design for AIDS Help lines, hot lines for people concerned about AIDS. As is clear from these examples, L&L deals with a vast range of services and products. The company is therefore structured in such a way that project teams can work together, much as they do in marketing firms, research institutions, and advertising agencies.

Because L&L believes that it contributes to the quality of life by providing its health-related products and services, it has dedicated itself to treating its employees, as well as its clients and potential clients, with care and respect. One of the ways it tries to achieve this goal is by providing employees with opportunities to participate in quality circles (work groups formed to address special organizational problems—see Chapter 6); employee assistance groups (support groups formed to address problems of substance abuse and other personal

At L&L Associates, employees have the opportunity to participate in a variety of work groups.

Exhibit 3.3 L&L CREDO

L&L Associates is dedicated to creating a healthy work environment, in which we strive to

1. Produce high-quality information and services for our clients, which profits ourselves as well.
2. Maintain a working environment in which employees are assured of a healthy atmosphere in which to pursue their work.
3. Dedicate ourselves to contributing to the health and information needs of ourselves and others.
4. Create a working atmosphere in which race, religion, creed, and gender are never considerations in the respect and dignity with which L&L employees treat one another.

problems—see Chapter 6); and other employee groups designed to make working at L&L Associates better. Another way the company tries to contribute to employees is by conforming to the L&L credo, which was created in 1971 by S. A. Savitt, company founder and first president. Exhibit 3.3 presents the L&L credo, which has remained the philosophy of L&L Associates since its inception.

In terms of both the kinds of employee groups mentioned above and the L&L credo, L&L has an organizational culture that distinguishes it from other organizations. People are treated in a way to put this culture into action; the ways in which they behave, their expectations of the organization and other employees in it, and the general climate at L&L reflect its culture (see Chapter 2 for further discussion of organizational culture).

This, then, briefly describes the business in which L&L Associates engages and the commitment it has to working toward its common purposes. L&L is a profitable company that has complex profit-sharing plans for its employees in order to motivate them to high performance. It considers itself up-to-date, and many employees are trained in the latest technological innovations.

L&L Associates also has a commitment never to employ more than 600 employees, in order to maintain a small-company atmosphere in which people know their fellow workers. There are a variety of jobs at L&L, depending upon the division and the level in that division. In the next section, we will go over the job titles and job descriptions of the positions in the operations division.

Jobs at L&L and the Organizational Hierarchy

All employees in organizations need to have descriptions of the jobs they are to be performing. Jobs have purposes, and people work together in order to coordinate their work and to accomplish the specific goals of the organization as a whole. As pointed out by Daniel Katz and Robert Kahn, job descriptions are one of the forms of downward communication in the organization.[2] Superiors communicate the information that each member of the organization needs in order to fulfill his or her job responsibilities.

In order to provide you with a sense of what these jobs at L&L actually are and what they entail, we will briefly describe these jobs. Each job description (a good term to know in any organization) lists the employee's title, the major activities and responsibilities of the position, and the interfaces in the organization—that is, to whom that employee reports (if anyone) and whom that person supervises (if anyone). Job descriptions tell a lot about an organization in terms of (1) who is responsible for what job and (2) who reports to whom and who talks to whom (and by implication, who does *not*). Following are the brief descriptions of the jobs at L&L:

1. ***Chair, board of directors*** Has authority to approve all decisions and to empower the president to act as decision maker.
2. ***President (CEO)*** Coordinates all activities; serves as liaison to the chair of the board of directors; assumes final responsibility for all division activities; makes final oral presentation to the chair. Directly supervises the executive vice president of operations. Is responsible for all decisions and all outcomes.
3. ***Executive vice president of operations*** Coordinates all operations of the division. Attends meetings with the president and vice president. Reports to the president and directly supervises the vice president. Is responsible for passing down all information regarding the president's requests and for ensuring that what is supplied to the president is appropriate.
4. ***Vice president of operations*** Coordinates all internal communication within the division; is responsible for all communication. Reports to the executive vice president of operations. Directly supervises the manager of the corporate communications department. Is responsible for making sure that the material supplied by corporate communications for the president's presentation is appropriate.
5. ***Manager of corporate communications*** Manages the production of all communication projects in the department. Reports to the vice president of operations. Directly supervises all project heads in the department. Is responsible for giving out specific assignments in order to fulfill the requests as passed along by the vice president of operations.
6. ***Project head*** Responsible for organizing and leading project groups in the development of the communication activities. Reports to the manager of corporate communications. Directly supervises and works with a project group.
7. ***Group member*** Responsible for tasks assigned by the group project head. Staff position: reports directly to group project head and does not supervise anyone.

Each of these jobs involves a number of communication activities. In the next section we will discuss what is currently happening at L&L Associates.

Scenario: What Is Currently Happening at L&L Associates?

The scenario about to be described is one of the central events happening at present as L&L Associates conducts its everyday business. The president of L&L Associates has to prepare the annual report (an oral presentation) for the chair of the board. It is the president's first year at L&L Associates. The president needs to meet with the executive vice president of operations, the vice president of operations, and the manager of corporate communications in order to brief them on what he or she needs for the presentation of the annual report. After that briefing session, the manager meets with the project group heads, who afterwards meet with department staff to brief them and to pass along the specifics of the assignments and tasks.

Once the information has been communicated downward to the departmental level, the tasks are divided up and assigned to project groups by the department manager. Group members complete their assignments and turn them in to an immediate supervisor, as requested. These products are passed upward until they reach the highest levels appropriate in the organization. The process ends after the president presents the annual report to the chair.

The ultimate organizational goal of this activity is the successful completion and presentation of an oral report by the president to the chair of the board. Departmental and individual goals are determined by their various specific functions. Thus, for example, the goal of the executive vice president of operations is to provide the report for the president to deliver. The executive vice president supervises the person beneath him or her in the organization in order to get that done. The goal of the staff members in the corporate communications department is to complete the projects assigned by the project head—assignments that might involve research, creation, typing, or other activities.

Events end with the presentation of the oral report and the reaction to it. This series of events is the basis for our discussion of what is happening at L&L Associates and for the participatory simulation of L&L. See the last sections of this chapter for more information on participation in L&L.

COMMUNICATION ACTIVITIES AT L&L ASSOCIATES

Communication follows both formal and informal channels at L&L Associates, just as it does in other organizations. Workers at L&L take part in formal communication when they participate in briefing sessions, meetings, conferences, interviews, preparation of written reports, writing of interoffice memos, debriefing sessions, one-to-one meetings, telephone interactions, and oral presentations. They participate in informal communication when they talk with one another about work-related and personal matters.

These activities take place just as they do in any organization: in relation to the specific jobs that specific people have. But since communication is a process, as we discussed in Chapter 1, it is an ongoing part of everything that is happening at L&L Associates, just as at any other organization.

At L&L Associates, just as at any other organization, some people will do more of some kinds of activities than others. Exhibit 3.4 lists the jobs at L&L that we described above, along with the formal communication activities in which these employees often participate and the chapters of this text that deal with these activities. Naturally, employees also communicate informally as they do their jobs in the organization.

We have designed L&L Associates and explained it to you as a sample context in which to apply your understanding of the complexity and diversity of communication in the various forms it takes in the business and professional world. In order to provide you with opportunities to take part in that organizational process, L&L Associates is designed as more than a case study—it is an interactive simulation. Participation in it will allow you to put into practice the communication activities you are learning about in this text.

Exhibit 3.4 JOBS AT L&L ASSOCIATES

Job Title	Formal Communication Activities	Chapter
Chair, board of directors	Meetings	6, 7
President (CEO)	Speeches	8, 9
	Interviews	4, 5
	Meetings	6, 7
Executive vice president of operations	Interviews	4, 5
	Meetings	6, 7
Vice president of operations	Interviews	4, 5
	Meetings	6, 7
Manager of corporate communication	Interviews	4, 5
	Meetings	6, 7
Project heads	Interviews	4, 5
	Meetings	6, 7
	Everyday tasks	11
Staff members	Interviews	4, 5
	Meetings	6, 7
	Speechwriting	8, 9
	Everyday tasks	11

ACTUAL PARTICIPATION IN L&L ASSOCIATES

L&L Associates is designed to present you with an operating model of an organization. Its purpose is to provide a working structure within which you, cast in the role of a member of an organization, can have a firsthand experience of what it is like to work in an organization.

In this chapter we have presented you with a detailed explanation of L&L Associates (the organization, the business, job descriptions, and the scenario of current events). Now let's give you a brief overview of what *you* will be doing in L&L Associates.

You participate in the simulation as an employee at L&L Associates, cast in a role as an organization member with a specified title, job description, and work objectives. You and the other students, who play the parts of other organization members, interact in job-related activities, and you follow appropriate channels within the organization in order to contact them (see Exhibit 3.1 on page 48). Participants are provided with specified tasks to perform, with responsibility for designing tasks, and with responsibility for implementing solutions. The simulation ends when the organization's objectives have been reached. Let's talk next about what you will do if you participate in the simulation—how you will work at L&L.

Working at L&L Associates

You enter the simulation as an employee at L&L Associates who has a position with a job title and job description and a set of responsibilities and goals. Let's go step by step through what takes place:

1. To get started, the instructor will assign you a role to play in the simulation during the weeks you participate in it. The instructor will decide whether to assign roles randomly, to ask for volunteers, or to have you submit résumés and applications.
2. After assigning roles, the instructor will review L&L Associates with the class, going over the organization chart, chain of command, job descriptions, and scenario. When the simulation has been clarified enough for participation to begin, the instructor and students will then take on the roles they will play as L&L employees in the simulation.
3. The simulation is ready to begin. You will be given an L&L employee identification badge to wear whenever you are working at L&L Associates, and you will be assigned a place to go to do your work in the simulation.
4. At the same time as you are beginning to play your role, the student

who is cast in the role of chair of the board meets with the student playing the role of president to brief him or her on the time, date, and topic of a formal presentation the president has to make to the chair.

5. The president then meets with the members of the organization to brief them and identify what he or she needs from them for the presentation. The next time you come to class, you will enter the simulated organization, L&L Associates, and you will work on your specific job in the project of developing various aspects of the presentation for the president.
6. In order to accomplish the goal of the simulation (the oral presentation of the report to the chair of the board), participants in the simulation will take part in briefing sessions, meetings, interviews, preparation of written reports, writing of interoffice memos, debriefing sessions, one-to-one meetings, informal communication, and oral presentations.
7. The simulation ends when the president makes the final presentation to the chair of the board.

This, then, is a brief synopsis of what happens and what you will be taking part in during the simulation. All of this takes place within the organizational structure described earlier in the chapter.

Additional Instructions for Participation

Let's talk about some other things you need to know when participating in the simulation:

- In L&L Associates, the chair of the board sets down rules that govern how you and the other students will work with one another in L&L Associates.
- The major rules in the simulation are provided by the organizational hierarchy, as reflected in the job descriptions, organization chart, and chain of command. Who works with whom, who is responsible for what, who talks to whom and about what—all these are part of the job descriptions and the organizational hierarchy. How these jobs are carried out, the norms for behavior, and the corporate culture are established by the chair of the board. The chair may allow input from the other members of the organization.
- Although the majority of class time is allocated to working in the organization, 15 minutes at the end of each work day (class session) will be devoted to discussion periods designed to increase your knowledge as a student of business and professional communication. These sessions are called *debriefings.* During these sessions, the day's experiences will be processed and evaluated.

- Participation in the simulation, like participation in real-world organizations, involves different kinds of activities at different times for different employees. Not everyone does the same thing, nor does everyone do their work at the same time.
- At any time deemed necessary, the instructor may stop the simulation and spend some time to discuss what has been occurring. While this may not take place in your class, it is a mechanism available when the instructor thinks that learning will be enhanced more by discussion than by continued activity.

Requirements and Materials Needed for Participation

The entire class participates in various roles at L&L Associates. Each of you is given a specified role to play and a job description which explains how to participate. The simulation takes approximately 9 to 12 hours of class time. Additional time outside of class may be required.

Your instructor will provide you with the following materials you need for participation in the simulation:

1. A copy of Chapter 3 of this text
2. An L&L employee identification badge
3. An L&L Associates role description card
4. L&L participation forms
5. Signs for the designated areas of the room in which employees are to sit
6. An organization chart for L&L Associates

A simulation is a model of reality, invented for the purpose of learning through experience. We have designed the simulation of L&L Associates so that you can learn through experience. Participating in simulations has many advantages for learning. Let's discuss the most important of these benefits.

Learning by Doing

It is one thing to read something in a book—for example, that newborn infants are fragile. It is another thing to care for a baby. Some organizations sponsor simulation programs for teenagers who want to baby-sit. They practice bathing and changing dolls before they will be expected to care for a real infant. The most valuable part of a simulation is that it allows you to learn about something by doing it. You can read in a book about the flavor of a grapefruit; you *know* what it tastes like from eating it. You can learn what speech preparation is from reading this text; you can learn about doing it in the simulation.

Limiting the Costliness of Experience

Another advantage of participation in the simulation is that mistakes are less costly than learning through experience with the "real thing." Imagine, for example, that medical students had to learn about surgery by operating on real patients without learning anatomy and watching accomplished surgeons first.

Learning from Mistakes

In simulations, you can make mistakes and learn from them. In this situation, failure in and of itself becomes a learning experience. Having realized the consequences of your actions, you can try again. If you are simulating a sales presentation and the presentation does not work, you can learn from your experience without losing your job. In a real-life situation, a critical mistake in making a sales presentation might indeed result in the loss of one's job!

Learning About Yourself

Finally, by participating in L&L Associates you will learn about more than just organizations: you will learn about yourself and how you behave in such a context. You will get to see yourself in action, and you will have the opportunity to use what you learn in order to improve yourself as a communicator.

SUMMARY

In this chapter we have introduced you to L&L Associates, a fictitious company designed to illustrate concepts in this text and to serve as a simulated organization if your instructor decides to use it that way. Throughout the remainder of this text, we will use L&L Associates to provide examples of the ideas we discuss.

L&L Associates is a complex organizational structure consisting of three divisions: the production division (which produces information packages and/or services for clients), the finance division (which handles all corporate financial management), and operations (which deals with all internal workings of the organization, including its internal and external communication functions). Much of our discussion centered around a subdivision of operations: the corporate communications department. As in any complex organization, communication must follow the chain of command specified by the organization chart.

L&L Associates is a company in the business of producing health-related information and services for clients who engage the company for some specific project. For example, in the last year, L&L produced materials on how to quit smoking for the National Association of Smokestoppers, as well as a videotape on substance abuse for use in towns and cities across the nation. Thus, the common purpose of L&L Associates is to develop information and services that satisfy clients and produce a profit for the company.

Some of the main positions at L&L on which we focused include the chair of the board of directors, the company president (CEO), the executive vice president of operations, the vice president of operations, the manager of the corporate communications department, the project heads, and group members. The current task in which all of these people are directly or indirectly involved is the preparation of the president's annual speech to the board of directors. To carry out this and other tasks, employees at L&L engage in all of the types of communication activities discussed in this text: group meetings, interviews, speeches, and day-to-day interaction.

CHAPTER 3 ACTIVITIES

Most of the activities associated with this chapter are embedded in the L&L Associates simulation. The following are suggested as role-play activities in which you might apply the kinds of skills you can use in the simulation.

1. Write a brief description of L&L Associates and the roles in the organization. Identify which of the jobs you would like to have and what you think would be the learning advantages associated with that job.
2. Call a local stockbroker's office and find out how to get materials on annual reports issued by three large companies. Think of what you, as part of a group working on an annual oral presentation, would use from these materials.
3. Read the material on oral presentations in Chapters 8 and 9. What kinds of things do you think you would need to know about if you were preparing a speech for an annual report to be presented by someone else?
4. Work with three other students. Have a meeting on the question "Shall we use the L&L Associates simulation in class?" Write up a brief summary report of the meeting.

CHAPTER 3 NOTES

1. Linda C. Lederman and Lea P. Stewart, *Lindlee Enterprises: An Organizational Simulation,* Dubuque, IA: Kendall Hunt, 1986.
2. Daniel Katz and Robert Kahn, *The Social Psychology of Organizations,* New York: Wiley, 1966.

PART II

COMMUNICATION ACTIVITIES IN THE ORGANIZATION

CHAPTER 4

Fundamentals of Interviewing

Communication is the goal of many forms of activity in the organization. One important communication activity is the interview. In this chapter we will discuss fundamentals of interviewing, and in Chapter 5 we will examine types of interviews that you are likely to experience in the organization. We will focus primarily on the role of the interviewee, although we will include some information useful for developing skill as an interviewer.[1] We will begin by providing a definition of an interview, and then we will discuss the importance of interviews in organizations. Next, we will examine the components of the interview process and the basic format of the interview. As we go along, we will use L&L Associates to provide some specific examples of the kinds of interviewing you'll be learning about.

DEFINITION OF AN INTERVIEW

We define an interview as *a communicative process, involving two parties, in which a predetermined, public purpose guides the interaction.* Let's examine this definition in more detail.

Interviewing is one aspect of the communication process we described in Chapter 1. All of the elements of that process—mutual influence, exchange of verbal and nonverbal symbols, and intentionality—are present in the interview. Later in this chapter we will discuss the components of the interview process to elaborate these ideas.

Interviews involve two parties, the interviewer and the interviewee. Note that we did not say that the interview involves two *people;* the fact is that interviews may involve several people. In an employment interview, for example, you may be interviewed by two or more people at the same time. At L&L Associates, a project group may conduct an informational interview to gather material for the president's speech they are helping to prepare. Although there may be more than two people, there is only one *interviewer* party and one *interviewee* party.[2]

The interview process is guided by a predetermined, public purpose. The interviewer always approaches the interview with a planned purpose. He or she needs to obtain information about a specific content area in order to use that information in a precise way. The journalist, for instance, has the purpose of collecting information for a story. The supervisor conducting a disciplinary interview may have the objectives of informing the employee of the specific problems with his performance and the associated penalties that will be imposed. In L&L Associates, for example, the manager of the corporate communications department might interview the project heads to get an update on the project's development.

Note that there can be more than one purpose for an interview. Also note that there can be both public and private purposes. Either the interviewer, the interviewee, or both may have *private* purposes they keep hidden from the other party. For example, the interviewee may take part in the employment interview to practice her interviewing skills even though she has no interest in working for that company. The interviewer may already have selected a candidate for a position, but he may go through the process of interviewing more applicants to demonstrate to his boss that he conducted a thorough screening. There are undoubtedly a variety of private purposes operating in the interview process, as there are in other communication situations. An interview always has a *public* purpose, too, which is the explicit objective of the interview. This purpose is always known by the interviewer. The interviewee may or may not be aware of this purpose in advance but is usually informed of it at some point during the actual interview.

What occurs in the interview is guided by the public purpose, although private purposes influence the interaction as well. The interaction consists primarily of the asking and answering of questions. Generally, the interviewer carefully plans many of the questions in advance so that all of the questions are relevant to the specific purposes of the interview.

THE IMPORTANCE OF INTERVIEWS

When people think of interviewing, they usually think first of the *employment interview.* Clearly, the employment or selection interview, as it is called, is an important type of interview; it is the one you must succeed at in order to become a member of an organization. In the L&L Associates simulation, for example, your instructor may choose to use selection interviews to determine assignments to the various roles in the company. This would be one way of using a simulation to give you firsthand experience with interviewing. Like any employment interview, this would also provide the opportunity for the interviewer to learn about you and for you to learn about the interviewer and the job situation. The employment interview is vital from the point of view of the organization because hiring mistakes can be extremely costly. As a member of an organization, however, the selection interview is only one of many types of interviews that you will experience.

Organizations have procedures for evaluating the performance of employees. Those procedures typically involve a *performance appraisal interview*. Skill at this type of interview can enhance your relationship with your supervisor, lead to improved job performance, and demonstrate your overall competence and maturity as an employee.

For employees in some positions, *information-gathering* and *investigative interviews* may become an important part of their jobs. At L&L Associates, employees conduct information-gathering interviews in order to develop the materials needed for the president's speech or some other aspect of the project under way. Organizational problem solving requires an investigation into the nature of the problem and how it might be solved. One major activity that is used in fact-finding is the interview. As we will discuss in Chapter 6, group activities frequently involve fact-finding, and one form the group's fact-finding may take is the interview. Thus, although your position in the organization may not require investigative interviews, groups to which you are assigned may require skill at this type of interview.

Unfortunately, employees encounter problems of a variety of types both within and outside the organization. Many employees experience either *counseling* or *disciplinary interviews* as a result. Organizations today tend to be concerned with the worker as a total person. It is not uncommon to see employees jogging or doing some other form of exercise during their lunch break, using facilities provided by the company. In addition to providing exercise facilities to help employees maintain their physical health, companies often make counseling available to assist workers in maintaining their mental health. Thus, some employees will be involved in counseling interviews. Others will find that disciplinary interviews await them. In either case, the interview focuses on personal problem solving, and skill in these types of interviews is certainly beneficial, if not a necessity.

When we enter organizations, we typically expect or hope for advancement. The development of a career involves planning, both for the immediate future and for the more distant future. Such planning often occurs in the form of a *career development* or *objective-setting interview.* Success at this type of interview can make the difference between effective and ineffective planning, which has consequences for your career and for the organization.

A final type of interview which you are likely to experience is the *exit interview.* In today's society it is rare indeed for an individual to stay with the same organization for all of his or her working life. Typically, a person changes jobs several times, working for a number of different organizations and perhaps in different parts of the country. Effective handling of the exit interview may leave you and the employer with positive feelings about one another. You may want to work for that organization in the future, or your position in another organization may necessitate contact with your former employer. From the point of view of the organization, effective exit interviews provide valuable information about why employees have chosen to terminate their employment, information which may help the organization reduce the costly problem of employee turnover.

As you can see, a variety of types of interviews take place in the organization. Employees at all levels are involved in interviews throughout their stay with an organization—from the selection interview through the termination or exit interview. Thus, skill at interviewing is important to your success as a member of a business organization. In the next section we will take a look at the components of the interview process.

COMPONENTS OF THE INTERVIEW PROCESS

We will be discussing five different types of interviews in Chapter 5. However, there are some features that interviews have in common, so our purpose in the rest of this chapter is to discuss the interview in general. We will begin by examining the interviewing process; then we will discuss two basic approaches to interviewing. We will then consider the structure of the interview and the types of questions used.

In Chapter 1 we defined communication as a process, and we emphasized that as a process, communication is dynamic and ever-changing and involves both intentional and unintentional sending of messages. As a type of communication, the interview is also a process. By examining the four components of the communication process as they apply to interviews, we can gain a fuller understanding of that process.

The Communicators

In the interview there are typically two communicators, with clearly defined roles of interviewer and interviewee. As discussed earlier, occasionally there are two or more interviewers with one interviewee, or there can be more than one interviewee with one interviewer. We mention this because you may experience situations in which this occurs, and you will need to try to adapt your communication to that situation. We have already mentioned the concept of adapting to a communication situation, but we will reemphasize it here. To adapt to the situation means to observe that situation and the people in it and choose communication behaviors that are appropriate. Let's say you are interviewed by one main interviewer and then are given a second interview to which your interviewer has invited other interviewers. You will need to adapt your behavior to take those additional interviewers into account. For example, you will need to attempt to establish rapport with the additional interviewers. To do this, you might decide to initiate some small talk with them at the beginning of the interview. You might also direct questions to them, and you can use eye contact to include them as you respond to questions. You should not completely neglect the person who originally interviewed you, however. You can include her with eye contact and by making references to points that came up in that first interview.

Both the interviewee and the interviewer are influenced by their past experiences, attitudes, values, and backgrounds, and they cannot shed those aspects of themselves when they come to an interview. This may have positive or negative effects on the interview process. We are all aware of discrimination that takes place in the hiring process because of interviewer bias against women or blacks or Hispanics or elderly people or college students or handicapped individuals or overweight people; the list is endless. Interviewees can also form negative impressions of organizations because of biases. If the interviewer represents a group of people about whom the interviewee has a negative stereotype, the interviewee may not want to work for that particular company. Stereotypes can work in positive ways, too, in that an interviewee or interviewer may form good impressions because the other belongs to a favored group of people. Our point is that these aspects of individuals will influence the interview process, and we cannot overlook them when we are trying to assess what happened during an interview.

The Context

Like any other communication event, interviews occur in a context. They take place at a particular time in a specific location, and these aspects of the context influence what happens. In Chapter 1 we discussed three general aspects of the setting that affect the process in any communication situation: purpose, time of day, and place. In this section we will examine these as they relate to the interview process. In addition, we will focus on two other features of the interview context: events that precede or follow the interview, and the perceptions of the two parties.[3]

The physical closeness between the interviewer and the interviewee afforded by this seating arrangement suggests a more informal interview situation.

of either or both the interviewer and interviewee.[5] One of the parties may have had a problem at home or an argument at work that morning or may have to deal with a crisis later that day. Approaching holidays can affect a person's mood in positive or negative ways, too. These unrelated events can have a powerful effect on the interview process even though neither party recognizes their influence. As the interviewee, you need to attempt to establish rapport with the interviewer, regardless of the interviewer's state of mind. This means either initiating small talk or being responsive to the interviewer's attempts at casual conversation. It also means displaying interest in the interviewer by maintaining eye contact; being nonverbally responsive (nodding when you agree or understand, smiling occasionally, and leaning forward); and taking an active role in the interview (asking questions and elaborating your answers).

Perceptions of the Situation The final aspect of the context that is important is *how the interviewer and interviewee perceive the situation.*[6] Their perceptions are influenced by all of the other features of the context we discussed; by aspects of themselves, such as attitudes and experiences; and by the nature of their relationship, as we will discuss in the next section. One individual may see the situation as formal and threatening, and the other may perceive it as casual and neutral. The important point is that how people perceive situations affects their behavior. If, for example, the interviewee perceives the performance appraisal

Exhibit 4.1 FEATURES OF THE INTERVIEW CONTEXT

1. Type of interview
2. Time of day and week
3. Place
4. Events unrelated to the interview
5. Interviewer and interviewee perceptions of the situation

interview as hostile and threatening, he may behave very defensively during the interview or may be reluctant to express important feelings.

Exhibit 4.1 summarizes the factors that influence the context of the interview: the type of interview, the time of day and week, the place in which the interview occurs, events unrelated to the interview, and the perceptions of the interviewee and interviewer. These are not independent aspects of the context. Rather, they interact to influence the process.

The Relationships

The third component of the interview process is the *relationship between interviewer and interviewee.* The nature of the interviewee-interviewer relationship differs from interview to interview. In many interviews that relationship may be noninterpersonal at the outset and may remain that way. The two parties may not have had any previous contact and thus respond to each other in their social roles rather than as unique individuals. They treat one another as interviewer and interviewee.

In other interviews, the relationship may change. It may become more interpersonal, or it may be more interpersonal at the outset. For example, in a performance appraisal interview the interviewer and interviewee may have a long history of working together. Indeed, they may have established an informal relationship, as we discussed in Chapter 2 (an informal relationship may involve socializing outside the organization). What they know about each other as unique individuals will influence their behavior in the interview process. If the interviewer knows that the employee does not handle criticism well, she may withhold some criticism or may be very careful about phrasing it in a nonthreatening way. The more we know about the other, the easier it is to tailor our communication to that specific individual.

At L&L Associates, employees often have had previous contact with the other party in the interview process. Sometimes these people are close friends. Although this presents an advantage in that the employees know a great deal about each other, it sometimes can make it more difficult for employees to perform their roles effectively. They may feel awkward being interviewed by a friend. However, once an interview is under way, employees usually begin to feel more comfortable. This experience often happens in the business world: people have previous knowledge of others with whom they deal in interviews, and this knowledge can affect the interview process in various conscious and unconscious ways.

What is unique about the interviewer-interviewee relationship is that it is often brief but intense.[7] It is brief in the sense that the relationship may last only as long as the interview itself. This is true for many interviews, although within the organization, interviewee and interviewer often must maintain a working relationship. The relationship is intense in that the interviewer must get to the heart of the interview fairly quickly. As we develop social relationships, we usually take time to get to know one another. We stay at surface-level topics for some time before progressing to more personal subjects. In the interview, the two parties must get to the specific topic quickly. When that topic is not personal, as in the case of most information-gathering interviews, getting to the point is not a problem. When the interview focuses on more personal issues, as in the case of a performance appraisal or disciplinary interview, approaching the topic can be awkward for both parties.

As the interviewee, then, you will often have little time to "warm up" to the interviewer or the topic. That's why it is important to prepare yourself for the interview, to anticipate possible topics and think about what you have to say about them. Your interviewer will begin making judgments about you immediately. By being prepared, you stand a better chance of making a favorable impression and of communicating your ideas clearly and in the way you intended.

In any interview, particularly in the organizational context, there is generally a sense that the relationship is superior-subordinate. Typically, the interviewer is in the superior position: he controls the time and place of the interview, initiates and terminates the interview, and directs the questions. Selection interviews, exit interviews, disciplinary interviews, performance appraisal interviews, and investigative interviews usually involve this kind of relationship between superior and subordinate. The extent to which the interviewer and interviewee perceive their relationship as superior-subordinate will affect their behavior and, consequently, the interview process. For example, the interviewer may try to maximize the distance between himself and the interviewee in order to maintain a strong sense of a superior-subordinate relationship. That, of course, will influence the interviewee's behavior in the interview, or at least his perceptions of the interview.

The Messages Exchanged

The final element of the interview process is the *exchange of messages.* As in any type of communication, messages may be intentional or unintentional in the interview, and they may be verbal or nonverbal. How messages are interpreted affects subsequent messages. For instance, if the interviewee perceives a remark made by the interviewer to be sarcastic, she may respond sarcastically or defensively. This can occur whether or not the interviewer's comment was intended as sarcastic. When we communicate with others we have a tendency to believe our interpretations of messages to be correct, and so we act on our interpretations.

Interviews involve question-answer sequences; we will discuss types of questions used in the interview process later in this chapter. We will also examine effective ways of answering questions in this chapter and in Chapter 5.

These four components of the interview process—the communicators, the context, the relationships, and the messages exchanged—are interdependent. To develop your skills as an interviewee, you need to be aware of how these components set up a cycle of influence. You need to adapt your communication as required by the process, but you cannot adapt if you are not aware of influences on the process. Our purpose in discussing the interview process was to help you develop increased awareness of those aspects of the interview to which you need to adapt.

TWO BASIC APPROACHES TO INTERVIEWING

It is fairly common practice to distinguish between two basic approaches to interviewing: directive and nondirective. In this section we will discuss these two approaches, a combined approach, and how you as an interviewee must adapt to the approach selected by the interviewer.

Nondirective Approach

Sometimes interviewers want to do as little talking as possible; they want the interviewee to control what is talked about, in what order, and for how long. In these cases, interviewers choose a *nondirective approach,* in which they allow the interviewee to control the discussion. (Many counselors and therapists use a nondirective approach because they want their clients to talk about what is important to them, what is bothering them, and how they feel about matters. Since the counselor doesn't know what problems a client is having until the two have met, the nondirective approach is especially useful early in their interaction.)

Supervisors may choose a nondirective approach for handling performance appraisal interviews because they want the employee to discuss his own performance and areas in which improvement is needed. This can make the atmosphere of the interview less threatening for the employee; it can improve the relationship between supervisor and employee; and it can give the supervisor valuable information about how the employee sees his performance.

The major advantage of the nondirective approach is that the interviewee is free to talk about what concerns him. Moreover, the nondirective approach may help relax the interviewee, who will then open up more.

A disadvantage of the nondirective approach is that the employee may not talk about topics that the interviewer thinks are important. Also, since the interviewer does not control the pace of the interview, it may take a long time for the purpose of the interview to be accomplished.

Directive Approach

In the *directive approach,* the interviewer controls the topics and pacing of the interview. The interviewer initiates the interview, asks questions about specific topics, asks further questions when the interviewee has not answered a question sufficiently, and closes the interview. Many interviewers choose this approach because it maximizes their control over the interview. Disciplinary interviews and selection interviews are frequently, although certainly not always, conducted this way.

One advantage of the directive approach is that the topics the interviewer thinks are important will be discussed, and they will be discussed at great length if the interviewer chooses to pursue them. A second advantage is that the interviewer can control the pace of the interview so that it accomplishes its purpose in the time allotted. Finally, the directive approach puts less responsibility on the interviewee, which may appeal to many interviewees. For instance, interviewees may be reluctant to comment on their job performance or to mention areas in which they need improvement for fear of bringing up negative points that the supervisor had not thought of. So the directive approach may appear safer from the point of view of the interviewee.

A disadvantage of the directive approach is that the interviewee may not have the opportunity to talk about what he or she thinks is important. As a result, the interviewee may leave the interview feeling frustrated or dissatisfied. Second, the interviewer who uses the directive style may appear to employees to be autocratic and unwilling to listen. When employees perceive interviewers in this light, they may be reluctant to open up and give honest responses to questions.

Combination Approach

Although we have talked about two distinct approaches to interviewing, it is likely that interviewers frequently use a combination approach. Two communication researchers, Craig Tengler and Fredric Jablin, found that recruiters conducting employment screening interviews in a university placement center generally began with a directive approach and moved to a more nondirective approach.[8] These interviewers tended to ask more closed questions (those requiring one- or two-word answers) early in the interview and more open questions later.[9] Tengler and Jablin find this especially interesting because employment interviewers tend to make their decisions about applicants in the initial four to seven minutes.[10] Apparently, at least some interviewers are making those judgments on the basis of very limited information, because the closed questions they ask early in the interview do not provide much new information about applicants.

Other interviewers may begin with more open questions to see what topics the interviewee brings up, then become more directive in pursuing those topics. The effective interviewer adapts to the demands of the situation and to the interviewee, being directive when necessary and nondirective when it improves the interview. For example, an interviewer who begins a disciplinary interview with a nondirective approach to see how the employee feels about the problem may have to switch to a directive approach if the employee skirts the issue.

Adapting to the Interviewer's Approach

As an interviewee, you will need to adapt to the approach of the interviewer. Students have often returned dismayed from employment interviews in which the interviewer used a nondirective style. One student reported that an interviewer simply said, "You have 30 minutes. Talk." The student was unprepared for a nondirective style and was lost as to what to say. He had a difficult time adapting to the nondirective style, and as a consequence, his performance in the interview suffered. He needed to discuss those aspects of himself and his background that would best demonstrate that he was qualified for the position. For instance, he should have described details of his work experience not provided on the résumé. He could have discussed specific skills that made him a desirable applicant. In order to take advantage of the situation, the student should have been prepared for the possibility that the interviewer would use a nondirective approach.

As you prepare to enter any interview situation, then, it is important that you prepare for both directive and nondirective approaches. Prior preparation will make it easier for you to adapt to the approach selected by the interviewer and to adapt to changes in that approach during the interview. As Tengler and Jablin found in their research,[11] sometimes in selection interviews the interviewer begins by being very directive but later switches to a nondirective approach. You need to be very familiar with the information included on your résumé so that you can answer closed questions that ask for facts. At the same time, you need to be ready to elaborate on your experiences and education. For other types of interviews, too, you need to be familiar with the facts and ready to elaborate on them. For instance, in the performance appraisal interview it is important that you be prepared with information about your strengths and weaknesses so that you can provide specific instances of both. You also need to think about your own views of your performance in case the interviewer chooses to be nondirective. Careful preparation is the key to being able to successfully handle both approaches or a combination approach.

THE STRUCTURE OF THE INTERVIEW

The interview is often regarded as having three parts: the opening, the body, and the closing. What is involved in each part can differ from one type of interview to another, but some of the purposes of each part are common to all types of interviews. In this section we will look at those common aspects.

Opening

Most interviewers use the *opening* of the interview to try to establish rapport with the interviewee. The interviewer wants the interviewee to relax and feel free to talk. In order to accomplish this, the interviewer frequently begins with small talk or gives information about herself and the topics and purpose of the interview. When the interviewer and interviewee are well acquainted, as is often the case in the organization, the interviewer still may engage in casual conversation to ease into the interview. In most interviews, then, you can expect that the interviewer will try to get you to relax and will try to establish rapport.

You should be prepared for this as an interviewee. Sometimes people feel that the interviewer is "up to something" when she begins with small talk, but the interviewer is usually trying to get you to relax before asking you more difficult questions. So use the opening as an opportunity to get "warmed up" and to establish a relationship with the interviewer.

Some interviewers, however, choose to get right down to business. You also need to be prepared for this interviewer, although this situation is less likely to occur. If the interviewer moves right into the interview with little or no opening, it may indicate that he is in a hurry. Take this as a cue to keep your answers as concise as possible without sacrificing the quality of your responses. If the interviewer asks you to elaborate on your answers, then do so. The lack of rapport building in the opening of the interview may have been the result of some factor other than the interviewer's haste.

Body

The main portion of the interview is the *interview body,* which is composed primarily of questions and answers. We will discuss types of questions and how to respond to them in the next section of this chapter. As an interviewee, you should know that the effective interviewer will have a plan for the body of the interview, not just a list of random questions to ask. That plan is referred to as the *interview schedule.*[12]

Interview schedules can range from loosely structured to highly structured. In the loosely structured interview schedule, the interviewer plans what major or primary questions to ask. This kind of schedule gives the interviewer the greatest flexibility in conducting the interview. As the interview schedule becomes more and more structured, the interviewer has less flexibility—all questions that will be asked are determined in advance and may even be precisely worded. The interviewer simply follows the list of questions, not deviating from the schedule.

For most if not all of the interviews that you will experience as a member of an organization, the interview schedules (if they are used) will be loosely or moderately structured. Employment interviewers, for example, rarely ask a specified list of questions without deviation; they need to find out as much as they can about each individual they interview. Asking only standardized questions is not likely to produce the kind of information they need. Instead, the interviewers tend to listen to responses and then ask questions that call for elaboration of answers (these questions are known as probing questions, which we will discuss later).

Frequently, interviewers plan a *sequence* of questions they want to ask in the body of the interview.[13] They may, for instance, organize their questions according to topics. An interviewer conducting a performance appraisal could organize her questions into the following topics: positive aspects of the employee's performance, negative aspects of the employee's performance, problems encountered by the employee in trying to do the job, and areas in which the employee will try to improve during the next year. By planning a specific sequence of ideas, the interviewer will give a sense of order to the interview. This helps the interviewer keep track of what information has already been obtained and what still needs to be obtained. It also makes it easier on the interviewee, who can think about one issue at a time. The interviewer whose questions jump around can confuse the interviewee.

However, as an interviewee, you need to be prepared for either case. If the interviewer seems to be following a plan, do your best to stick to the topic. If the interviewer is asking you about previous job experience, don't talk about other issues until you have completely discussed the topic at hand. If the interviewer does not seem to be following any plan but instead is asking random questions, try to finish discussing a topic before you move on to a new one. Try to give very complete, thorough answers to the questions raised; sometimes interviewees give a brief answer, expecting to have an opportunity to elaborate, but you may not get that opportunity. You will have to pay careful attention to the interviewer's questions in order to determine which approach the interviewer is using.

Closing

An interview ends with the *closing.* The interviewer generally uses some method to end the interview on a positive note, particularly when he has to maintain a working relationship with the interviewee. One technique that is often used is to ask the interviewee if she has any questions. In many interviews, the interviewer will give you a chance to ask questions or determine the topics at the end of the interview. You should be prepared to take advantage of this opportunity. Prepare questions ahead of time, if possible. And be sure to ask the questions that have come to mind during the interview. Sometimes interviewees do not expect to be able to ask questions, and they prepare none. When in doubt, prepare some questions. Just because they are prepared doesn't mean you have to ask them if you decide they are irrelevant or if they have already been answered during the body of the interview.

Just as the interviewer is trying to close the interview on a positive note, so should you. You never know when you will need to talk to this interviewer in the future, so it is best to try to maintain a positive relationship. Smiling, expressing appreciation for the interviewer's time, and shaking hands are all ways of ending the interview in a pleasant manner.

TYPES OF QUESTIONS

Interview questions can be categorized three ways: open versus closed, primary versus secondary, and neutral versus leading.[14] In this section we will look at these three categories of questions so that you can recognize them and respond appropriately. (Keep in mind that the three categories overlap; for example, one question could be classified as open, primary, and neutral, another as closed, secondary, and leading. This will become clearer after we discuss the three categories.)

Open Versus Closed Questions

Open questions are general, leaving room for a wide variety of answers. "How do you feel about your job performance?" and "Why have you sought counseling?" are open questions. The interviewee has a great deal of flexibility in answering open questions, but remember, questions can differ in the degree to which they are open. The most open questions provide the greatest flexibility. The question "Tell me about yourself" is very open and leaves room for a wide range of answers. "What did you like about college?" is also an open question, but it is less open than "Tell me about yourself" because the range of possible answers is more restricted.

Closed questions limit the answers that are possible. Like open questions, closed questions can differ in the degree to which they restrict response options. "Which do you like better, blue or red?" is a highly closed question, compared to "What is your favorite color?" A *bipolar question* is also a closed question; it limits the interviewee to two options, often to the options of "yes" or "no." "Did you meet the deadline?" is a bipolar question, as is "Which do you like better, blue or red?"

In answering open questions, you have a great deal of flexibility. This can be an advantage or a disadvantage. In an employment interview, for example, the open question allows you to focus on the most positive aspects of yourself. However, if you are unprepared for open questions like "Tell me about yourself," you can flounder around, offering a very incoherent answer. You can also stumble into an area that you would rather not bring up, but once you do it, it may be impossible to retreat. For instance, if you mention that you changed colleges three times, you cannot retract that statement. This may open up a new area of questions that focus on a less positive aspect of yourself.

The best way to handle open questions is to prepare for them. Although you cannot know precisely what questions you will be asked in any type of interview, you can think of questions or topics that are likely to come up. If you have been called in for a disciplinary interview, for instance, you can anticipate the issues that will be brought up by the interviewer, and you will be prepared to deal with them.

A second suggestion for handling open questions is to keep them focused on a topic. Don't wander from topic to topic, treating each only in general terms. The best strategy is to focus on a specific area and provide details about it. For instance, if in a performance appraisal interview you are asked what problems in the workplace are making it difficult for you to do your job, pick a few points and elaborate on them. Don't jump from problem to problem, providing little or no detail.

Closed questions are typically easier to answer because you don't have to figure out in which direction you want to take your response. However, closed questions, particularly bipolar questions, force you to choose between alternatives. Neither option may be acceptable to you in some cases. Then it is better if you refuse to choose and instead explain the alternative you would prefer. In deciding to do this, of course, you must analyze the situation and the interviewer to determine whether this is appropriate. If you decide that it is not, you can still refuse to choose one of the alternatives and accept the consequences. If you decide that it is appropriate to explain your own preference, you can go ahead and offer your alternative. Let's look at an example to clarify this situation.

Suppose you are involved in an exit interview and an interviewer asks you, "So tell me the truth. Why are you leaving? Is it the salary or your co-workers that you are unhappy with?" You may not be leaving for either of the two reasons presented in the bipolar question, so you have to figure out how you'll respond. Since you are leaving the organization, you may decide that you can say whatever you'd like, so you decide not to pick one of the alternatives presented. Instead, you put forth your real reason or reasons for leaving. On the other hand, you may be concerned with leaving a positive impression of yourself. You sense that the interviewer is convinced he has isolated the only two possible reasons and is likely to get defensive if you do not choose one of the two options. So you may decide to choose one of them, but then elaborate on an additional reason for leaving.

Primary Versus Secondary Questions

In addition to being categorized as open or closed, questions can be classified as primary or secondary. *Primary questions* are the main questions asked, those that bring up a topic and can stand alone.[15] "What are your career plans for the next five years?" and "What goals have you set for yourself for the next year?" are primary questions. They make sense on their own.

Secondary questions are also called *probing questions* because they are designed to get more information about a topic that has already been introduced or an answer that has been given. "Why did you select that goal?" and "What else do you have in mind for your future?" are probing questions. There are many times when an interviewee's response is too brief, too vague, incomplete, or irrelevant, and the interviewer asks a secondary question to elicit more information.

If you do a good job of answering primary questions, the interviewer may not need to ask you as many probing questions. A good interviewer will always try to probe vague or incomplete answers, so you need to be prepared for that when you enter interview situations. Being vague won't usually keep the interviewer from asking more questions about a topic. Rather, it is likely to cause her to ask you more questions until you provide a complete or more specific answer. Whether or not you want to provide the information the interviewer is seeking is up to you, but you should be aware of the fact that interviewers will usually probe unsatisfactory answers.

Neutral Versus Leading Questions

Questions can also be classified as either neutral or leading. *Neutral questions* do not pressure the interviewee into supplying a particular answer.[16] "What are your greatest strengths?" and "How did you get interested in accounting?" are neutral questions. "Where are you from?" is both neutral and closed.

Leading questions pressure the interviewee into providing a particular response. "You oppose the new plan, don't you?" and "Wouldn't you rather

Exhibit 4.2 TYPES OF QUESTIONS

Question Type	Examples
1. Open vs. closed	*Open:* "Tell me about yourself."
	Closed: "Where are you from?"
2. Primary vs. secondary	*Primary:* "What are your reasons for leaving the company?"
	Secondary: "Why do you say that?"
3. Neutral vs. leading	*Neutral:* "What is your opinion of the new policy?"
	Leading: "You don't like the new policy, do you?"

work third shift?" are leading questions because they imply that a certain answer is preferred by the interviewer. When that pressure becomes quite extreme, the leading question is referred to as a *loaded question.*[17] "How many jobs have you been fired from?", "How long have you been stealing supplies from us?", and "Are you going to support that unfair, incoherent new policy?" are loaded questions—it is quite clear that they pressure the interviewee.

As an interviewee, you need to be aware of leading and loaded questions so you do not fall into the traps they set. Remember that you make the choices about what to say, on the basis of your analysis of the interviewer, the situation, and your own goals and needs. If you are aware that you have been asked a leading question, you can think about possible ways to respond to it rather than automatically answering the question in the way the interviewer prefers. For instance, you may choose to suggest a rewording of the question. If the interviewer asks, "Are you going to support that unfair, incoherent new policy?" you might reply by rephrasing the question itself, asking, "Do you mean, do I support the new overtime policy?"

As we mentioned earlier, questions can be categorized in all three ways. "What do you like about your job?" is a primary, open, neutral question. It is not important for you to categorize every question asked of you in an interview situation. This discussion has been designed to acquaint you with ways to classify questions and ways to deal with different types of questions. Exhibit 4.2 summarizes the types of questions and provides examples of each.

SUMMARY

In this chapter we have focused exclusively on the interview process as it takes place in organizations. Interviews are a prevalent communication activity in organizations, and as an employee, you are going to experience a variety of types of interviews.

The four components of the communication process are, of course, present in interviews. The first component is the communicators. In the interview process, there are typically two communicators, and their past experiences, values, attitudes, and biases affect their perceptions of one another and their behavior in the interview. The second component is the context, which comprises the type of interview, the specific time of day and week, the place, events unrelated to the interview, and the interviewer's and interviewee's perceptions of the situation. The context significantly influences the perceptions of the interviewer and interviewee and their behavior in the communication process. The third component of the process is the relationship between interviewer and interviewee. In most interview situations, the interviewer is in the superior position, and as a result, the interviewee must follow the lead of the interviewer. The fourth component is the intentional and/or unintentional exchange of messages. The messages are influenced by the other three components, and the other components are affected by the messages exchanged.

Interviewers generally approach the interview in either a directive or a nondirective fashion, although some may use a combination approach. The interviewer who controls the process—initiating topics, determining the pacing of the interview, and so on—is using the directive approach. The interviewer who allows the interviewee to initiate topics and control the pace of the interview is using the nondirective approach.

The interview has three main parts. In the interview opening, the interviewer typically tries to establish rapport with the interviewee and get him or her to relax. In the main part of the interview (the body), the interviewer asks questions and provides information as needed. In the last part of the interview (the closing), the interviewer's objective is to wrap up the interview, to deal with any last questions the interviewee may have, and to end on a positive note.

Interviewers use a variety of types of questions: open or closed, primary or secondary, and neutral or leading. These categories overlap. Which types of questions the interviewer uses depends upon the specific interview situation. As an interviewee, you need to be ready to handle a variety of types of questions.

CHAPTER 4 ACTIVITIES

1. Make an appointment with someone in your campus career placement center to discuss the employment interviewing process. Use this as an opportunity to discover how the placement center works, what recruiters look for in applicants, and how recruitment interviews are conducted.
2. Make a list of the types of interviews you have participated in (employment, information gathering, college entrance, scholarship, performance appraisal, disciplinary, counseling, exit). For each one, if you can recall, write your impression of how you performed. What conclusions can you draw?

3. If you have participated in any interviews recently (within the last four to six months), answer the following questions in regard to one of them:
   a. What type of interview was it?
   b. At what time of day and week did it take place? What influence did the timing have on you? On the interviewer?
   c. Where did the interview take place? What was the setting like? How did this influence you?
   d. Did anything happen that day that affected your performance in the interview? What happened, and how did it affect you?
   e. How did you perceive the interview situation as you were going into it (was it threatening, casual, formal, important, evaluative, etc.)? How did you perceive it after the interview was over? Did your perceptions change?
4. Fill in an example for each of the types of interview questions listed below. Be sure to use examples different from the ones provided in this text.

   *Open:*____________________

   *Closed:*____________________

   *Primary:*____________________

   *Secondary:*____________________

   *Neutral:*____________________

   *Leading:*____________________

   *Loaded:*____________________

CHAPTER 4 NOTES

1. There are several good books that focus on developing skill as an interviewer. See, for example, Charles J. Stewart and William B. Cash, Jr., *Interviewing: Principles and Practices,* 5th ed., Dubuque, IA: Brown, 1988; and James G. Goodale, *The Fine Art of Interviewing,* Englewood Cliffs, NJ: Prentice-Hall, 1982.
2. Stewart and Cash, p. 3.
3. Ibid., pp. 30–32.
4. Ibid., p. 31.
5. Ibid.
6. Ibid., p. 32.
7. Ibid., p. 3.
8. Craig D. Tengler and Fredric M. Jablin, "Effects of Question Type, Orientation, and Sequencing in the Employment Screening Interview," *Communication Monographs,* vol. 50, 1983, pp. 245–263.

9. Ibid., p. 262.
10. Ibid., p. 248.
11. Ibid., p. 262.
12. Stewart and Cash, p. 46.
13. Ibid., p. 45.
14. Ibid., p. 59.
15. Ibid., p. 63.
16. Ibid., p. 67.
17. Ibid., p. 69.

CHAPTER

5

Types of Interviews

In the organizational context, you are likely to experience a variety of types of interviews, from the selection interview to the exit interview. The types of interviews differ in their objectives, and each presents unique challenges. Being a skillful communicator in interviewing situations, then, means having the ability to adapt to the many types of interviews you'll encounter in the organization. Chapter 4 examined fundamentals that apply to all kinds of interviews. In this chapter we will discuss five types of interviews, including their objectives, important issues involved, and your role as an interviewee. Let's look at five kinds of interviews: employment, performance appraisal, information gathering, disciplinary, and exit.

EMPLOYMENT INTERVIEWS

Objectives

The *employment* or *selection interview* is just one part of the hiring process, although it is an important part. You may have already experienced the employment interview. Even if you have only had part-time jobs, you probably were interviewed, however informally. In some ways we can regard the employment interview as the most important type, because it is usually a prerequisite for entrance into an organization. If your class is participating in the L&L Associates simulation, your instructor may require employment interviews for the various positions in the organization. This means that at L&L Associates, as in any other organization, one of the key factors in determining the position you get—if you get hired at all!—is how you handle the employment interview.

We can look at the objectives of the employment interview from two points of view: the objectives of the interviewee, and those of the interviewer. As the interviewee, your objectives include (1) making a positive impression of yourself in order to be offered a position and (2) gathering information about the organization so that you can make a decision about whether or not you want to work for it.[1] The first objective is often very obvious to people. They are there to get a job. But it is important that you recognize that you must try to collect information about the organization so that your decision whether to work there or not is an informed choice. That is why it is smart to prepare questions about the organization and ask them during the interview. The more you find out about the company, the better you will be able to decide whether you will "fit in." In Chapter 2 we explained the concept of organizational culture and the importance of understanding the rules, values, and norms of that culture. In the employment interview you may be able to begin to get a sense of what the culture of that organization is like and what will be expected of you. Fredric Jablin, a communication researcher who has conducted many studies of the employment interview process, believes the selection interview plays an important role in communicating expectations about the job and the organization.[2]

The interviewer's objectives include (1) gathering information about the applicant in order to make an informed decision regarding hiring and (2) providing the applicant with information about the organization.[3] Just as the interviewee is trying to create a positive impression of himself or herself, the interviewer is trying to project a favorable image of the organization.[4] One of the reasons people say they fear employment interviews is that they know they are being evaluated. It is important that you recognize that you are also making evaluations—you are evaluating the interviewer and the organization itself. Thus, the evaluative aspect of the employment interview is two-sided, not one-sided, as people often think.

Important Issues

One of the most important issues you need to be aware of is that employment interviews are influenced by federal laws. A number of laws have been enacted to try to prevent discriminatory hiring practices: the Civil Rights Act of 1964, the Age Discrimination in Employment Act of 1967, the Vocational Rehabilitation Act of 1973, the Vietnam-Era Veterans Readjustment Assistance Act of 1974, and others.[5] Because of these laws, it is illegal to discriminate against job applicants on the basis of sex, age, race, religion, national origin, or color or because of a handicap or veteran status.[6] The implication of this for the employment interview is that questions seeking information in these areas are potentially illegal. The candidate who believes that the selection process has been discriminatory can file suit with the government against the company.

As an interviewee, you need to be on the alert for questions that appear to probe for information in the areas of race, religion, national origin, and so forth. You are not obligated to answer these types of questions, but if they are asked, you will have to make a decision during the interview about whether or not you will answer them. If, for example, the interviewer asks about your marital status, you should choose whether or not you will answer the question, because it is potentially discriminatory. Employers cannot discriminate in hiring certain people because they prefer married people or because they prefer unmarried people. But the question may still come up in the interview. As the interviewee, you should prepare yourself to handle these questions in case they are raised.

You have several options for dealing with these kinds of questions. First, you can decide to answer them honestly. If you choose this option, you should realize that your responses may evoke the interviewer's biases and may lead to discrimination. Second, you can handle such questions by asking the interviewer why she needs that information. If she asks you whether you are married, for example, you might reply, "Is marital status a job qualification?" or "Why do you want to know?" You risk angering the interviewer or putting her on the defensive; on the other hand, she might be impressed with your assertiveness. A third option is simply to say, "I prefer not to answer that question." You again run the risk of alienating the interviewer. All choices have potential negative consequences, so you have to select the option that is right for you. Learning how to handle these situations takes experience. Participating in employment interviews can provide you with experience in handling this type of question.

The Role of the Interviewee

Preparation The best way to increase the probability that you will perform effectively in the employment interview is to prepare thoroughly. Preparation for the employment interview must be extensive and careful. There are several areas to consider when you are preparing for the interview:

1. *Self-analysis* The first step in your preparation is to analyze yourself. By this we mean that you need to know what your career goals are, your likes and dislikes, your skills and your shortcomings, and where you are willing to locate. If, for example, you are interviewing for the position of vice president of operations at L&L Associates, you need to know what makes you a better candidate for that position than for

other positions in the organization. The more you know about yourself and what you are seeking in an employment situation, the more effectively you will handle the interview. One reason is that you will be able to answer the types of questions asked, which typically focus on areas such as these. If, for example, the interviewer asks, "What are your long-term career goals?", you will have a very difficult time answering unless you have thought a great deal about yourself in relation to a career. Another reason a careful self-analysis helps in the interview is that you will have a better idea of what to ask the interviewer about the organization and the position. If you know that potential for advancement is important to you, you have an area about which you should inquire.

2. *Résumé preparation* The second step in your preparation involves the writing of a résumé and various cover letters. A résumé is a summary of your education, experience, and interests, which you send to potential employers. A detailed discussion of résumé writing is beyond the scope of this text, but there are some excellent books available.[7] Here we simply want to stress that the résumé does not get you hired. It is designed to get you an interview. Therefore, it should not only briefly summarize your education, experience, and interests; it should also create the best possible impression of you.
3. *Research of various organizations* The third step in preparing for employment interviews is to research each of the organizations to which you will be applying. Your goal is to learn as much as you can about each organization. Being prepared in this way has two advantages. First and perhaps most important is that the information allows you to make an informed decision about whether or not you want to work for a particular company. For example, as you research a company, you may discover that you do not want to relocate there and may decide not to apply. Second, by doing research you can demonstrate to the interviewer that you are a serious candidate who is sincerely interested in the organization. Interviewers do not want to waste their time on casual interviewees, people who are just looking around. In a study of selection interviews, Lois Einhorn found that "all the successful interviewees [those whom interviewers rated more favorably after the interview than prior to it] expressed desire to work for the specific organization with which they were interviewing."[8] They also made it clear that they had done research on the organization.[9] If you demonstrate a lack of basic knowledge about the company, the interviewer is likely to assume that you are not very interested in the organization.

   In researching an organization you should try to find out about its products or services, locations, financial status, major competitors, future plans, history, and reputation.[10] One way to locate this information is to write to the company and ask for a company brochure. In addition, college campuses usually have a career placement center with a library of information about organizations. Finally, you can use the resources of a college or city library.

4. *Practice answering questions* The fourth step in interview preparation is to think about and practice giving answers to questions that are likely to be asked. It is a good idea to rehearse answers out loud because you may discover that you have trouble expressing certain ideas. You are likely to be asked questions about your education, experience, and career plans and choices and about the specific position for which you are applying. If you have done your self-analysis and have carefully prepared a résumé, you should be better equipped to answer questions in these areas. Exhibit 5.1 presents types of questions interviewers often ask.

Thorough preparation in these four areas—self-analysis, résumé and cover letter preparation, research of the organizations to which you are applying, and preparation for specific questions—will improve your chances for a successful employment interview. In fact, a lack of preparation is likely to

Exhibit 5.1 QUESTIONS OFTEN ASKED BY INTERVIEWERS

Interviewers will ask questions about choices you have made:

- Why did you choose to major in ______ in college?
- Why did you choose to go to ______ for college?
- Why are you interested in this company?
- Why are you seeking a position as ______?

Interviewers will also ask questions about future plans:

- What do you see yourself doing in five years?
- What are your goals for the future?
- Do you plan to further your education?

Interviewers are likely to ask questions about you as a person:

- What are your strengths and weaknesses?
- What motivates you?
- What type of work do you like?
- Are you willing to relocate? Do you like to travel?
- What have you liked and disliked about your previous jobs?
- What did you like and dislike about your college experience?

Interviewers will ask you about the specific position for which you are applying:

- In what ways are you qualified for this position?
- Why should I hire you for this position?
- What specific experiences have you had that have prepared you for this position?
- In this position you are likely to encounter the following situation. How would you handle it?

doom you to failure, particularly if you are inexperienced at employment interviews.

Participating Although we cannot give you a step-by-step procedure for how to behave in an employment interview, we can suggest some guidelines for effective participation (summarized in Exhibit 5.2). These guidelines are derived from research done on the selection interview process. Although there are no guarantees that following these guidelines will bring you a successful interview outcome, doing so will increase the likelihood of such an outcome.

1. *Be active.* It is important that you be an active participant in the interview. Although the interviewer takes the lead in many respects (he or she indicates where you should sit, controls the time and place of the interview, indicates when the interview has ended, and so on), that does not mean that you should be passive. In the study mentioned earlier, Einhorn found that successful applicants were more dynamic than unsuccessful candidates—speaking rapidly, smiling frequently, gesturing, using active verbs, and initiating comments.[11] Einhorn also found that successful applicants talked more than unsuccessful applicants,[12] a result supported by Tengler and Jablin.[13] Einhorn concluded, "The successful applicants, in essence, played active roles in the interviews."[14]
2. *Be specific.* You should be specific and give details when answering questions. For example, don't say, "I have leadership qualities" and then stop talking. Explain what you mean and give specific instances in which you demonstrated leadership qualities. If you state a like or dislike, say why you feel that way. Don't make the interviewer have to keep probing to get information from you. Besides, by providing details, you are able to give the interviewer more information about yourself that can help create a positive impression. Einhorn's study revealed that successful applicants elaborated their answers and used a variety of supports to substantiate their claims.[15] The types of supports we discuss in Chapter 8—statistics, examples, definitions, comparisons, and others—are appropriate for the employment interview.

Exhibit 5.2 GUIDELINES FOR EFFECTIVE PARTICIPATION IN EMPLOYMENT INTERVIEWS

1. *Be active.* Initiate comments; ask questions; smile; use active verbs; gestures; and speak as much as possible, but stay on the topic.
2. *Be specific.* Provide support for your claims; elaborate on your answers; offer information rather than waiting for the interviewer to probe for details.
3. *Project confidence.* Maintain eye contact; lean forward; smile; gesture; be active.

These can and should be used to support your claims that you are qualified for the position.

3. *Project confidence.* You should try to project an image of confidence throughout the interview. The successful applicants in Einhorn's study projected a confident and professional image by maintaining eye contact, leaning forward, and occasionally interrupting interviewers and by taking an active role in the interview.[16] Other studies have yielded the same results.[17] It is natural to feel nervous about the interview, but by making a conscious effort to control your behavior, you may be able to project confidence in spite of your nervousness. Thorough preparation for the interview may help alleviate some of that nervousness.

If your instructor requires employment interviews in class, use that as an opportunity to practice your interviewing skills. Try to prepare by self-analysis and rehearsal of probable questions. In the interview, apply the three guidelines for effective participation listed in Exhibit 5.2. It may take some practice before you can apply them easily.

PERFORMANCE APPRAISAL INTERVIEWS

Objectives

Organizations need a mechanism for evaluating the performance of employees. That mechanism frequently involves a written evaluation and a *performance appraisal interview* between employees and their supervisors. Each organization has its own version of the performance appraisal process. Consequently, the objectives of the performance appraisal interview can differ from organization to organization. However, there are several objectives that are likely to be involved. Michael Sincoff and Robert Goyer suggest the following objectives for the performance appraisal interview:[18]

1. Review the employee's job performance in light of job responsibilities, goals set by the employee, and job standards.
2. Discuss the employee's strengths and weaknesses in job performance.
3. Discuss problems encountered by the employee in doing his or her job and consider solutions to those problems.
4. Develop plans for improvement of job performance.
5. Identify the employee's needs for training and development and discuss long-term career goals and training needs.

Goodale suggests an additional objective for the performance appraisal interview:[19]

6. Discuss and communicate administrative decisions, such as salary increases, transfers, and promotions.

As you can see, the objectives of the performance appraisal interview are not restricted to an evaluation of the employee's performance. They are broader than that, covering problems the employee encounters on the job, employee training needs, plans for improving job performance, and more. Knowing this can help you prepare properly for a performance appraisal interview, as we will discuss shortly.

Important Issues

The quality of the method used to appraise an employee's performance directly affects the interview process. Exhibit 5.3 illustrates a performance appraisal form. Unfortunately, methods of appraisal are far from perfect, because they often involve a high degree of subjectivity.[20] As a result of this subjectivity, employees may believe that they have been treated unfairly, and indeed, they may have been.

Why are performance appraisal methods subjective and open to criticism? One answer to that question is that most jobs involve duties that are not concrete and quantifiable. For example, if your job involves creating advertisements, your performance should not be assessed simply on the basis of how many ads you produce in a given time period. The quality of those ads and your creativity and skill in creating them are also aspects of your performance, and these aspects are far more important than how many ads you came up with. But creativity, skill, and quality are not quantifiable. As a consequence, when your performance is evaluated, someone must use judgment. This is where the subjectivity comes into play and why employees may feel that they have been evaluated unfairly. Organizations often use rating forms that attach numbers to subjective criteria in order to try to correct this problem. For instance, you might receive ratings on a scale from 1 to 5 for the quality of your ads and for your creativity and skill. Although this may help improve the situation somewhat, you can see it only creates the illusion that subjectivity is not involved and that these aspects of your job performance are quantifiable.

As an employee in an organization, you should be thoroughly acquainted with the appraisal system used. In addition, you need to be aware of its shortcomings. If you believe you have been rated unfairly, you should speak up about it. Sometimes people see their ratings, but because of this illusion of objectivity, they don't question those judgments. Other people simply are afraid to speak up. If you sincerely believe that your evaluation is unfair or discriminatory, it is important that you pursue the matter—salary decisions, promotions, and other "goodies" are handed out on the basis of performance evaluations.

Exhibit 5.3 PERFORMANCE APPRAISAL FORM

PERFORMANCE REVIEW FORM

Employee______________________ Position______________________

Period from ______________ to ______________

	Unsatisfactory	Satisfactory	Excellent
1. Written communication skills			
2. Oral communication skills			
3. Ability to meet deadlines			
4. Attendance record			
5. Ability to accept criticism			
6. Ability to set goals			
7. Ability to devise plans and follow them through			
8. Relationships with other employees			
9. Ability to adapt to new policies and procedures			
10. Ability to follow instructions			

Evaluator______________________ Signature of Evaluator______________________

I have read and understand the above review of my performance.

Employee's Signature______________________ Date______________

As we discussed in Chapter 2, it is important to use the formal lines of communication. Thus, if you have a problem with your performance review, you should try to speak to the person who did the rating—usually your supervisor. You should tell him that you'd like to discuss your performance appraisal. When the two of you meet, you need to identify the specific areas where you need clarification. A good strategy may be to begin by asking questions, such as "Why was I given a rating of 'below average' on dependability?" Listen to the supervisor's response; you may discover that he can point to a number of specific reasons that justify the ratings. If, however, you are not satisfied with his explanations, you should state your disagreements and provide evidence for your opinions. You need to provide specific details to support your claim that you deserve a higher rating on dependability. For instance, you might present the fact that you missed only three days of work or that you were never late during the past year. If your supervisor is unwilling to alter the ratings and you still feel strongly that the ratings are inappropriate (and you have some support for your opinions), you might want to speak to your supervisor's boss about the issue. You can also use your contacts in the informal network to find out how others have handled similar situations, and with what outcomes.

Another issue of importance is that appraisal methods should not be discriminatory. The laws that we mentioned when discussing employment interviews pertain to more than the selection process. An organization must not discriminate against individuals in making promotions or salary decisions, either. And since those decisions are made on the basis of performance ratings, methods of appraisal must not be discriminatory. Goodale suggests that appraisal methods that evaluate employees on the basis of personal traits or characteristics have great potential to be discriminatory.[21] (These methods rate employees on such things as initiative, maturity, personality, and so forth. Not only are these abstract concepts, but for many types of jobs it is not clear that they are directly relevant to one's job performance.)

The Role of the Interviewee

Preparation You can and should prepare for the performance appraisal interview. Although each organization has its own system, your supervisor may have a brief meeting with you about a week or so before the interview to go over the procedures with you. This will give you a better idea of how to prepare. You may or may not see the written evaluation prior to the meeting, and you may or may not be asked to complete a self-assessment. In any case, prior to the meeting, you must evaluate your own performance. What have you done well, and in what areas do you think you need improvement? Although it is difficult, you must try to be as honest as possible. This is not the time to be humble about your accomplishments, nor is it the time to overlook weaknesses.

As you consider your performance, think about whether or not it meets any previously agreed-upon standards or goals. If you did not meet all of the standards or goals, which ones did you fail to meet? Which did you satisfy, and which did you exceed? You should also consider problems you have encountered in trying to carry out your job. Do you have sufficient resources? Sufficient personnel and time to get jobs done well? Are there any working conditions impairing your job performance, such as excessive noise, unsafe conditions, or inadequate space? You are not trying to come up with excuses for poor performance; rather, you are trying to identify *solvable* problems that could lead to improved performance over the next rating period.

In addition to considering how well you performed and identifying the obstacles you faced, you should also think about plans for improvement. In what ways do you plan to improve, and how will you try to implement those plans? Finally, you should think about your long-term goals and plans and assess whether or not you are making progress toward those goals. Is there training you need that would help advance you toward those goals?

Note that by planning in advance, you can take an active role in the performance appraisal interview. Your salary and career are at stake. It does no good to simply be a passive recipient of whatever praise or criticisms the interviewer hands out. The interviewer cannot know what problems you face in doing your job and may not know the best ways to solve those problems. Our point is that it is *your* job and career, and thorough preparation allows you to be an active participant in the appraisal process.

Participating Although you need to be prepared, you do not have to go into the interview with all the answers. The interview should involve a cooperative effort to solve problems, set goals, and develop plans. Be open to the suggestions of the interviewer, remembering, of course, that she is your supervisor and as such can ultimately impose decisions. If your attitude is one of cooperation, it is more likely that her attitude will be similar.

With thorough preparation, the interview is more likely to be a positive experience. In addition, you can help make the experience worthwhile by following these suggestions:

1. As difficult as it may be, try not to get defensive. Jack Gibb noted that when people become defensive, rather than supportive, their communication tends to display six specific characteristics: evaluation (instead of description), control (instead of problem orientation), strategy (instead of spontaneity), neutrality (instead of empathy), superiority (instead of equality), and certainty (instead of provisionalism).[22] Exhibit 5.4 summarizes these characteristics and provides examples of each. You should avoid displaying these features of defensive communica-

tion in the appraisal interview. No one likes to hear criticism, and your supervisor may not be tactful in presenting it, but you gain nothing from displaying anger or defensiveness. Assert yourself if you have something to say, but yelling at your supervisor will not produce a positive evaluation. In fact, on your next evaluation you are likely to see "Cannot accept criticism."

2. Take an active role. Express your opinions and ideas, and support them with specific examples and details. If you can support your opinions, your position is likely to be taken more seriously. If you need clarification of a rating, ask for it.
3. Rather than spending too much time justifying past performance, try to keep a solution-oriented focus. Raise questions about how you can improve and try to work out a specific plan for improvement.

Studies have found that supervisors who encourage employee participation in the appraisal process are seen as helpful and constructive by those employees.[23] Unfortunately, your supervisor may not view the interview as an exchange of ideas. He may see it as a one-sided situation in which he, the supervisor, presents information to you, the employee. If this is your supervisor's approach, you might approach him at some time other than the performance review period to discuss the interview process. Explain that you think it could be beneficial if you could add to the performance assessment and suggest solutions to some problems. Be specific about how you'd like to see the process changed, but be open-minded to the supervisor's ideas. You may be able to convince him that your active participation in the process would be constructive.

Exhibit 5.4 CHARACTERISTICS OF DEFENSIVE AND SUPPORTIVE COMMUNICATION

Defensive Communication	Supportive Communication
Evaluation. Being judgmental ("Your work is careless").	*Description.* Refraining from judgment ("Your reports contain many mistakes").
Control. Forcing one's way on others ("I don't care what you want—I want it done my way").	*Problem orientation.* Looking for mutually satisfying solutions ("How should we do this?").
Strategy. Being manipulative; telling an employee she can have input but then not using it.	*Spontaneity.* Being honest; telling an employee that she can't give input, and why.
Neutrality. Being indifferent ("I don't care how you feel about it").	*Empathy.* Being concerned ("I understand how you feel").
Superiority. Treating others as inferior ("What would *you* know?")	*Equality.* Respecting others as equals ("What is your opinion?").
Certainty. Being closed-minded ("There's only one right way").	*Provisionalism.* Being open-minded ("What are some alternatives?").

INFORMATION-GATHERING INTERVIEWS

Objectives

The major objective of the *information-gathering interview* (also called a *fact-finding* or *investigative* interview) is to gather information. This is a very broad category; the focus of many types of interviews is information gathering. Our focus will be on the fact-finding interview. As a member of an organization, you are likely to have to collect information for reports on various topics. At L&L Associates, this is a type of interview that occurs quite frequently. We will also be shifting our focus in this section from you as interviewee to you as interviewer. This is one type of interview in which you may find yourself in the interviewer role as a new member of an organization.

Important Issues

William Donaghy points out that one of the major issues in interviewing is finding the right people to interview and getting their permission to conduct the interviews.[24] John Brady states in his book on interviewing, "Interviewing has been compared with the fine art of salesmanship—and the first thing that a salesman needs is a list of potential customers."[25] The interviewer needs a list of potential interviewees. The key is to find someone who has the information that you need and who is willing to grant you an interview.

The topic you are investigating will limit the list of potential interviewees. Suppose, for example, that you have been asked to prepare a report on *telecommuting*—that is, the practice of having employees work at home on computers linked to the company's mainframes rather than having them report to an office each day. Who should you interview about that topic? You could interview individuals who have taken part in a telecommuting program, individuals in organizations that are currently involved in such a program, and individuals who have directed or implemented a telecommuting program. Moreover, you might want to interview one or more scholars who have studied telecommuting. Although you have several options, the list of potential interviewees is not unlimited.

Once you have located individuals to interview, you need to obtain their permission. Although not everyone will be willing to be interviewed, you'll find that most people are willing if they are approached in a courteous manner. You should call them well in advance and let them know who you are, with what organization you are affiliated, what you want to talk about, and how much of their time you need. People are likely to refuse if you treat them unprofessionally or if you make them suspicious of your intent.

A second issue is the research the interviewer must do prior to the interview. Before taking someone's time, the information-gathering interviewer must do a great deal of homework. For the report on telecommuting, you would need to research the topic prior to the interview. There are plenty of journal articles and book chapters on the subject, and you should do some reading. By doing research prior to the interview, you as the interviewer can gain sufficient background about the subject to know what questions to ask. An interviewer who is totally unfamiliar with a topic cannot ask good questions.

The Role of the Interviewer

As the interviewer, you need to prepare an interview schedule. Your schedule should probably be moderately structured, meaning that you should plan your primary questions in advance of the interview. You need to organize those questions, perhaps by grouping them into categories or topics. You take your list of questions to the interview and use them as a guide. Remember that these are only your *primary* questions. As the interviewee responds, you will need to ask secondary or probing questions in order to get the interviewee to elaborate and clarify answers.

An information-gathering interviewer usually must conduct the interview on the interviewee's territory. This is not the case for most types of interviews. The interviewer in this type of situation is asking for time and cooperation from the interviewee, and as a result the interviewer does not have the control that is typical in other interviews. Keep that in mind as you conduct information-gathering interviews. If you act as though the interviewee owes you time and information, he may refuse to cooperate. To open the interview, you must let the interviewee lead, although you should still try to establish rapport and provide an orientation to the interview, as in any other interview opening.

In conducting the interview, you must listen carefully to the interviewee's responses. Beginning interviewers often worry so much about what they are going to say that they do not listen well. It is only by careful listening that the interviewer can know what probing questions to use and what responses are worth pursuing. If the interviewer does not listen, the interview may be very choppy, because questions will not flow naturally from the responses of the interviewee.

One of the important tasks of the interviewer is to record the interview. This can be done either by taking notes or by using a tape recorder, although you will have to get permission to use a tape recorder. There are some people who will not allow an interview to be recorded electronically, so you need to be good at note taking. If you are going to use a tape recorder, make sure that it is functioning. Imagine your dilemma if you take no notes and discover later that the machine did not record any of the interview! If you choose to take notes, try to write as little as possible during the interview so you can devote your attention to the interviewee. When the interview is over, rewrite your

Employees often conduct information-gathering interviews within the company when they are involved in fact-finding projects.

notes, filling them in from memory. Before you prepare your report, you can always call the interviewee to check the accuracy of your facts.

In closing the interview, you should show your appreciation for the interviewee's time and cooperation. Remember, she did not have to grant you the interview. You might want to make arrangements to show the interviewee what you have written so she can check for accuracy, or you might want to arrange a phone call for the same purpose. You might even want to ask if you can call her if you need further information as you are writing your report. Whatever you decide to do, you are trying to end the interview on a positive note so the interviewee does not regret having granted you an interview.

DISCIPLINARY INTERVIEWS

Objectives

As Goodale defines it, a *disciplinary interview* is "a discussion between an employee and his or her immediate supervisor to correct the employee's failure to perform at an acceptable level. Usually it is triggered by a specific incident in which the employee's performance is unacceptable."[26] Unacceptable performance can take many forms. The employee may not meet deadlines, may

Exhibit 5.5 OBJECTIVES OF THE DISCIPLINARY INTERVIEW

1. To identify the nature of the unacceptable performance
2. To discuss causes of the unacceptable performance
3. To formulate a specific course of action to correct the situation

make a serious error in performing a task, may fail to perform required tasks, may be absent too much, and so on.

The purpose of the disciplinary interview is to define and communicate the nature of the unacceptable performance, to examine causes of the poor performance, and to decide on a specific course of action in order to correct the situation.[27] Exhibit 5.5 summarizes these objectives. Employees who are called in for a disciplinary interview do not necessarily know what they did wrong. That must be established during the interview. Perhaps the employee violated a policy of which he was unaware. Informal norms and rules for behavior are part of an organization's culture, as we discussed in Chapter 2, and these are not always clearly communicated. In such cases, employees may not realize that their behavior was unacceptable.

Once the problem is defined, the next objective is to discuss causes of the problem. There may be circumstances beyond the control of the employee that produced the unacceptable performance. For example, an employee may fail to perform a required task because she simply was never told to do that task.

The final objective is to plan a course of action to correct the situation or to prevent future problems. If the employee has been absent too frequently, a plan to correct that problem must be agreed upon. If no solution is specified, the problem may continue in spite of the interview.

Important Issues

We hope you never have to experience a disciplinary interview, but it is best to be prepared for it. An issue you should consider if called in for a disciplinary interview is whether or not you are actually capable of performing your job in an acceptable manner. Sometimes people convince an employer to hire them for a specific position even though they are not fully qualified for that job. As a consequence, they have difficulty on the job. You need to consider if that is so in your case, because if it is, you may find yourself faced with many disciplinary interviews—or you may find yourself out of a job.

A second issue is whether or not you believe the disciplinary interview is justified. You may be the victim of discrimination, in which case you should seek legal advice. Chances are that the interview is justified, although that does not mean that you are the direct cause of the situation. Company policies are not always communicated clearly, and many problems result from circumstances out of your direct control. So try to be as nondefensive as possible in trying to assess whether or not the disciplinary interview is justified.

The Role of the Interviewee

You may or may not be made aware of the specific reason for the interview in advance. If you are, you should try to prepare by thinking about the situation and what caused it. If you do not know why you are being disciplined, there is not much you can do to prepare except to try to evaluate your recent performance.

In the interview itself, you should try to remain cooperative, as difficult as it may be. Remember, it does not do any good to fly off the handle. In fact, it may only make the interviewer feel more justified in disciplining you. When we discussed performance appraisal interviews, we identified characteristics of defensive and supportive communication (see Exhibit 5.4). Your goal should be to avoid defensive communication behaviors.

Be willing to admit it if you did something that was unacceptable. You and the interviewer will search for causes for the unacceptable performance, but in some cases the problem can be identified as the result of a conscious choice you made. You should be willing to accept the responsibility for that choice.

In those cases where the problem was not directly your fault, such as when a policy was not communicated, do not allow the interviewer to pin the problem on you. Stand up for your rights, but do so without yelling or name-calling. Explain what you perceive to be causes of your poor performance and why those causes are not within your control. As always, give specific examples to support your position. Suggest solutions for eliminating those causes; if they are not dealt with, you might find yourself in another disciplinary situation.

Even if the problem is your fault, try to suggest solutions to the situation if the interviewer gives you a chance. In any case, you will be asked to correct the situation or prevent future problems. If you cannot accept the solution offered, you had better try to come up with another solution and offer it to your supervisor. If you leave the interview without a clear solution or one that you can live with, you are setting yourself up for future problems.

EXIT INTERVIEWS

Objectives

An *exit interview* takes place between a representative of an organization and an employee who is leaving. The employee may have made a decision to leave or may have been asked to leave. We can consider objectives of the exit interview from both the employer's and the employee's points of view.

Employer's Viewpoint From the employer's point of view, there are three objectives in an exit interview. First, and perhaps most important, the interviewer is trying to ascertain the employee's reasons for leaving (if the employee is leaving voluntarily).[28] Employee turnover is extremely costly and disruptive to an organization. Exit interviews can provide valuable insight into the reasons for turnover because employees may be more honest in stating their reasons for leaving once they have terminated their employment. A second objective is to create a feeling of goodwill toward the company.[29] A third function the interviewer can fulfill is to complete the process of termination during the interview, by obtaining a forwarding address, settling any accounts, and explaining how company benefits will be handled.[30]

Employee's Viewpoint The objectives from the interviewee's point of view are similar. First, the interviewee can clarify his perceptions of the organization and provide specific reasons for leaving.[31] The employee may want to do this if he strongly believes that there are problems with the company that need to be addressed. He may also be interested in maintaining good relations with the organization. His specific reasons for leaving may not reflect any company shortcomings, and he may want to communicate that. The interviewee's second objective is to find out what benefits are forthcoming and what information the organization will provide to prospective employers.[32] Finally, the employee can use the interview to clear up any remaining questions, such as when he will receive his last paycheck.

Important Issues

As Goodale points out, the issue of whether the employee is leaving voluntarily or has been asked to leave has a significant impact on the exit interview.[33] The interview will have a very different flavor in each case. There will be no discussion of the employee's reasons for leaving if she has been terminated by the employer. And clearly the employee is likely to be much less cooperative if leaving is not a voluntary decision. As an interviewee in an exit interview, whether your leaving is voluntary or not, you will need to decide the extent to which you will disclose information to the interviewer. If you have been asked to leave, you probably should not verbally abuse the organization to the interviewer. If you do, you may feel better for the moment, but you are probably going to regret it later. You can preserve your sense of dignity by effective handling of the exit interview.

If you are leaving voluntarily, you still want to consider how much information to disclose. By being too honest about the organization's shortcomings, for example, you may damage the relationship you have had with your former employer. That employer may then be less positive later on when called on as a reference for you. Use your best judgment, rather than just assuming that anything goes since you are leaving anyway. Make effective choices on the basis of your analysis of the interviewer and the situation.

The Role of the Interviewee

Before you enter the exit interview situation, prepare for the interview by thinking about your reasons for leaving, your perceptions of the organization, and the questions you want to ask about benefits and so forth. The interviewer may not address all of your concerns, and it is difficult to think of them on the spot. You don't want to leave the interview and then realize that you forgot to ask some important questions. Make a list of your questions in advance and bring them to the interview.

Once you enter the situation, state your opinions and support them. The interviewer who is not very skilled may try to persuade you that you are wrong about the organization or that another organization you are about to join is no good. You do not have to defend your choice to leave or your choice of a new employer.

During an exit interview, the interviewee should attempt to create a positive impression, because future employers are likely to contact the organization.

Be sure that your questions about benefits and other issues get answered. Don't leave the interview unsure of something because you didn't ask the interviewer for clarification. You have the interviewer's time and attention now, but you may not be able to get answers easily later, when you are no longer associated with the organization.

Finally, remember that future employers may contact the organization for information about you. So you want to be courteous in the interview and leave a positive impression of yourself. Regardless of the circumstances of your leaving, this should be your goal. If you were asked to leave, remember that it was not the interviewer's decision to terminate you.

SUMMARY

In this chapter we have focused exclusively on five types of interviews you are likely to experience as an organization member. We examined the objectives and the important issues involved in interviews used for employment decisions, performance appraisal, information gathering, disciplinary action, and exit from the organization, and we have discussed your role in each type of situation.

The employment interview is the gateway to the organization. Success in the employment interview depends in part on thorough preparation. You need to conduct a self-analysis to determine your career goals, your likes and dislikes, your strengths and weaknesses. Your preparation also involves writing a résumé, researching the organizations with which you'll be interviewing, and practicing your answers to questions you are likely to be asked. In the interview itself, you must be active and specific, and you must try to project confidence.

The objectives of the performance appraisal interview include a review of the employee's performance, a discussion of problems faced by the employee, and the development of a plan for improvement. In handling the performance appraisal interview, you as the interviewee should avoid the characteristics of defensive communication and should take an active role in the interview. It is your performance and your career, so if you have suggestions and opinions, assert them.

The information-gathering interview is a useful tool for collecting information needed for reports. Finding the right people to interview and obtaining their permission is one of the obstacles you may face as an interviewer. Prepare for the interview by researching the topic and preparing a well-organized interview schedule. One of the decisions you will have to make is how to record the interview: will you take notes or use a tape recorder?

Disciplinary interviews are designed to identify the nature of the employee's unacceptable performance, to examine causes, and to develop a specific plan to correct the situation. As an interviewee in such a situation, you need to be willing to accept responsibility for your own performance. If you made a mistake, admit it. If, on the contrary, your inadequate or unacceptable performance was caused by factors outside of your control, be prepared to discuss those factors and suggest solutions.

When you leave an organization, you may be called to an exit interview. From the employer's standpoint, the purposes are to discover your reasons for leaving, to create a feeling of goodwill toward the organization, and to complete any necessary paperwork or details. From the point of view of the employee, the exit interview serves as a vehicle for expressing feelings about the organization and reasons for leaving and to settle any remaining issues, such as final pay and forthcoming benefits.

CHAPTER 5 ACTIVITIES

1. Go to the career placement center on your campus to see what resources it has and what services it offers. There may be a library of materials on a variety of careers and organizations. Browse through the materials to get a sense of what is available. See if any videotapes on the employment interview process are available through the center; watch the tapes for pointers about preparing for and handling the interview.

2. The best activity related to material in this chapter is to participate in the various types of interviews. Your instructor may arrange for the class members to conduct one or more types of interviews. If these are videotaped, watch your tape and write a self-evaluation, identifying your strengths and weaknesses.

3. Locate a member of the community who is in a career that interests you. Arrange to conduct an information-gathering interview with that person to find out what that career entails, what qualifications are needed, and what job opportunities are available.

CHAPTER 5 NOTES

1. Michael Z. Sincoff and Robert S. Goyer, *Interviewing,* NY: Macmillan, 1984, p. 111.
2. Fredric M. Jablin, "Organizational Entry, Assimilation, and Exit." In *Handbook of Organizational Communication: An Interdisciplinary Perspective,* Fredric M. Jablin, Linda L. Putnam, Karlene H. Roberts, and Lyman W. Porter (Eds.), Newbury Park, CA: Sage, 1987, pp. 679–740.
3. Sincoff and Goyer, p. 111.
4. Ibid.
5. James G. Goodale, *The Fine Art of Interviewing,* Englewood Cliffs, NJ: Prentice-Hall, 1982, pp. 40–41.
6. Ibid., p. 43.
7. See, for example, Richard Nelson Bolles, *What Color Is Your Parachute?* Berkeley,

CA: Ten Speed Press, 1981; Melvin W. Donaho and John L. Meyer, *How to Get the Job You Want,* Englewood Cliffs, NJ: Prentice-Hall, 1976.

8. Lois J. Einhorn, "An Inner View of the Job Interview: An Investigation of Successful Communicative Behaviors," *Communication Education,* vol. 30, 1981, p. 221.
9. Ibid.
10. Charles J. Stewart and William B. Cash, Jr., *Interviewing: Principles and Practices,* 5th ed., Dubuque, IA: Brown, 1988, p. 151.
11. Einhorn, p. 227.
12. Ibid., p. 224.
13. Craig D. Tengler and Fredric M. Jablin, "Effects of Question Type, Orientation, and Sequencing in the Employment Screening Interview," *Communication Monographs,* vol. 50, 1983, pp. 245–263.
14. Einhorn, p. 227.
15. Ibid., p. 223.
16. Ibid., p. 227.
17. These studies are reviewed in Jablin, "Organizational Entry," p. 691.
18. Sincoff and Goyer, p. 129.
19. Goodale, p. 67.
20. Ibid., pp. 73–75.
21. Ibid., p. 75.
22. Jack R. Gibb, "Defensive Communication," *Journal of Communication,* vol. 11, 1961, p. 141.
23. Ronald J. Burke, William F. Weitzel, and Tamara Weir, "Characteristics of Effective Employee Performance Review and Development Interviews: Replication and Extension," *Personnel Psychology,* vol. 31, 1978, pp. 903–919.
24. William C. Donaghy, *The Interview: Skills and Applications,* Glenview, IL: Scott, Foresman, 1984, p. 211.
25. John Brady, *The Craft of Interviewing,* New York: Vintage Books, 1976, p. 6.
26. Goodale, p. 151.
27. Ibid., p. 154.
28. Sincoff and Goyer, p. 157.
29. Ibid.
30. Ibid.
31. Ibid.
32. Ibid., p. 158.
33. Goodale, p. 169.

CHAPTER 6

Working in Groups

In today's business organizations, one person cannot take responsibility for making major decisions about complicated matters. That is why people work together in groups. The committee is the main instrument for decision making and problem solving. People also work together in task forces and project groups and at conferences. For example, at L&L Associates, the main enterprise is working on the projects that clients bring to the company. Project groups hold frequent meetings to discuss the current projects, and employees at L&L spend a large part of the workday in meetings or group activities of one kind or another.

The members of a group are chosen in order to bring in a wide range of expertise and to bring various points of view together so that the number of ideas can be maximized. The group is a vehicle for bringing ideas into focus and for synthesizing conflicting opinions into a consensus. Executives use the work of groups as a basis for their decisions. Groups also help evaluate programs and policies, organize activities, and reconcile conflicts.

The main advantage of group decision making is that it exposes conflict and facilitates constructive criticism. By bringing together a great many experts with different interests and conflicting ideas, the group can arrive at a solution that will minimize potential problems within the organization. Furthermore, when group members represent differing points of view, the chances are lower that a disgruntled minority will resist the solution when it is implemented.

In this chapter we will explain the kinds of groups that organizations use for problem solving and decision making. We will describe how they work and define the tasks they are likely to perform. We will also explain how to work effectively in groups.

TYPES OF GROUP MEETINGS

There are many types of group meetings in the modern organization. Conferences and committees are the most common types of meetings. Besides these, there are a number of newer kinds of meetings, which are becoming more familiar to organization members. These include quality circles, employee assistance groups, and mediated meetings.

Conferences

Conferences are called when someone in the organization needs information or ideas on an ad hoc basis. A *conference* is actually a one-time committee, to which people are invited because they have necessary information or because they have some interest in the decision to be made. Conferences can involve two or more people. The interview, which we discussed in Chapters 4 and 5, is a type of two-person conference.

A conference is not just a casual get-together, although it may be formal or informal. It may be scheduled in advance and meticulously planned, or it may be called on the spur of the moment to deal with some emergency. If the conference is to be successful, there must be some kind of formal charge, a statement of the problem to be solved at the conference. For example, an executive can call her comptroller and her attorney for a conference about stock issues. A marketing manager can call in various salespeople to confer with him about a possible sales campaign. A personnel manager can meet with union representatives and various supervisors to get information about how employees are responding to a new benefits package. At L&L Associates, the vice president of operations is likely to hold both planned and spontaneous conferences with the manager of corporate communications.

Committees

Most organizations use committees to do some of their work. *Committees* are groups of people who have specific responsibilities and hold regular meetings. Committees are rarely informal. They are usually integral, ongoing components of the corporate organization. A finance committee might be charged to do periodic reviews of the financial status of the organization. A "watchdog" committee may have the responsibility to seek out fraud and mismanagement. A personnel committee might hold regular hearings for aggrieved employees.

Standing committees are established either by organization bylaws or by executive decision. Their responsibilities are assigned to them by the executive. They are also instructed on the nature of the reports they must present, and they are given regular deadlines for reports. Ad hoc committees are called together to deal with special circumstances. They differ from conferences in that they are usually required to meet several times in order to fulfill their charge.

Quality Circles

One special kind of group that has become popular in many contemporary organizations is the *quality circle.* Quality circles were first employed in Japan; they have been adopted in the United States by companies interested in improving group morale.[1] Quality circles consist of supervisory personnel, staff members, and production employees, who are brought together either on a regular basis or for some specific purpose. They are designed to facilitate sharing of expert information and to sensitize supervisors and employees to each others' needs.

Quality circles are especially useful when there may be conflicts in perspective. The purpose of participation in quality circles is to analyze and solve work-related problems that cut across levels of the hierarchy of the organization. For example, one travel agency formed a quality circle to deal with the problem of duplication of work effort that appeared when the agency began using computerized systems for making travel reservations. The circle consisted of travel agents (who made the reservations and therefore had firsthand knowledge of the way various computer reservation systems worked), managers (who had the broader picture of where these activities fit within the rest of the company's activities), and upper-level executives (who had various degrees of responsibility for, and knowledge of, issues that were not part of the responsibilities of the managers or travel agents). By bringing together the three groups, it was possible to restructure company work policies in order to take full advantage of the computerized reservation systems.

Quality circles are a rapidly growing feature of modern business organizations. They offer the advantage of providing a formal structure for bringing together people of diverse status to address problems in the organization. There are some problems, however, since participation in problem solving carries some presumption that what the group decides will be taken seriously. Quality circles are often used for "cosmetic" features. Once potential participants discover that their contributions are not taken seriously, they are not likely to participate effectively in subsequent meetings.

Employee Assistance Groups

Employee assistance groups are used in organizations to provide therapy and support for employees with problems that interfere with work performance. Drug addiction, alcoholism, compulsive gambling, and other kinds of psychosocial problems can affect the way work is done. Such problems can be economically and efficiently handled by employee assistance groups. Often, these groups are provided as an employment benefit. Employee assistance groups are available at L&L Associates, which is committed to the health of its employees.

It is important to understand, however, that the operation of an employee assistance group is very different from that of a task group. Employee assistance groups deal with individuals' problems, while task groups are designed to deal with problems that affect the organization in general.

Mediated Meetings

Advances in technology have made it possible for groups to meet via electronic connections. *Teleconferencing* links individuals through television monitors, allowing people at various locations to simulate face-to-face meetings. People

The videoconference is one type of mediated meeting that takes place in organizations.

can deal with important issues without having to travel long distances to be in the same room together. In L&L Associates, you might have the opportunity to participate in a simulated teleconference with clients, and you can explore the effects—positive and negative—the mediation has on the exchange of messages.[2]

Computer-mediated communication is also used as a kind of nominal group technique so that employees can exchange information and ideas relevant to important problems in the organization. (Nominal group technique—see pages 125 and 144 for further discussion—is used when face-to-face contact might result in deleterious conflict. Participants record their ideas in writing, to be read by other members. Comments are also exchanged in writing.) Computer-mediated communication is asynchronous. Participants can post their notes to a bulletin board or send them to other members. Immediate response is not necessary; members can comment at their convenience. Such asynchronous meetings tend to remove pressure to engage in combat over controversial issues. We will discuss computer-mediated communication in more detail in Chapter 11.

REASONS FOR MEETINGS

Meetings are held for a great many reasons. The overriding urgency is to bring together people who represent various interests in the organization and to combine the talents of people with differing expertise. Exhibit 6.1 summarizes various reasons for meetings, which are discussed in the sections that follow.

Formal and Ritualistic Meetings

Most organizations hold meetings for *formal* or *ritualistic purposes,* such as reports to stockholders, a presentation of the annual budget, or a "kickoff" for a sales campaign. For example, at L&L Associates, the president's speech to the chair of the board serves a ritualistic purpose. Although the contents of the speech vary from year to year, what makes it ritualistic is that the presentation is an annual event and that certain specific protocol must be adhered to if the

Exhibit 6.1 REASONS FOR MEETINGS

1. Ritual
2. Problem solving
3. Fact-finding
4. Briefing
5. Policy setting
6. Program planning
7. Training
8. Decision making

occasion is to be successful. It is an instance in which not only the substance of the message, but also its form, matters.

Those who attend these meetings are mainly spectators. The few speakers, who are usually top officials of the company, have specific agendas to follow and prepared messages to present. In stockholders' meetings, there may be a routine casting of votes, but except in very rare cases, decisions have been made in advance. Formal meetings are an important part of an organization's culture (a concept we discussed in Chapter 2). Participants often remember them as important occasions because these meetings can provide a sense of unity. If the executives who conduct the meetings prepare carefully, they can use the time to impart important messages to those who attend.

Problem-Solving Meetings

Problem-solving meetings bring people together in order to find solutions to the organization's problems. At L&L Associates, for example, in working on the materials for the president's speech, employees will hold many problem-solving meetings as they hit snags in the development of ideas. Standing committees may be charged with continuing investigations of company routines and practices. Some committees may regularly evaluate programs and make recommendations for improvement. Product review committees examine the quality of the company's product, the effectiveness with which it is being marketed, and possible challenges from competitors. When organizations are confronted with emergency problems, task groups may be called together to make decisions about actions for the company to take. Decisions made by problem-solving groups are generally not binding on the organization. These kinds of groups make recommendations to the executive.

Problem-solving meetings should proceed through a format known as the *standard agenda.*[3] There are five phases in the standard agenda.

Phase 1 This phase of the standard agenda involves understanding the group's charge. The group receives and reviews its instructions, which include an identification of the problem or condition to be examined, a list of limitations on the group's activity, specification of the person or persons to whom the group is to report, and a deadline by which the report must be presented. The group commences its work by examining the charge to make sure everyone understands it.

Phase 2 Phase 2 of the standard agenda is fact-finding. The group obtains as much information as it can about the problem it must consider and evaluates this information in order to decide what components of the problem can and must be changed. During this phase of discussion, the group may revise its charge, in consultation with the charging authority. Most problem-solving groups are given considerable support during fact-finding. Professional staff members may be assigned to them; they often have access to company records and materials; and they are usually able to secure the services of consultants and experts to advise their work.

Phase 3 In phase 3 of the standard agenda, the group sets criteria for its solution, describing the situation as it would look if the problem were solved. For example, a company might charge a group to investigate falling sales figures in a particular territory. During fact-finding, the group may examine sales records, interview sales personnel, and study the activity of competitors in the area. They may also check whether customers in the area have needs that the company is not meeting. During this criteria-setting phase, the group may decide to specify a sales increase goal, say, ten percent during a specific time period. The group must then examine limitations on its activity. For example, there may be budget restrictions that limit expenditures in the territory; legal restrictions unique to the area in question; and practical limitations, like an inability to deal with the activities of competitors.

Phase 4 In phase 4, the group puts together a solution. The solution may be the inspiration of one person in the group, or it may be painstakingly put together so that each component addresses one feature of the complicated problem the group is trying to solve. Most groups are responsible for dealing with the practical aspects of their proposals. That means preparing a budget. However, the group is usually given the support of specialists during this phase of the activity. The final step in phase 4 is the preparation of an evaluation plan for the proposal. This requires the group to set up time lines for its operation and to provide for periodic reviews to assess how well the proposal is working, should it be accepted.

Phase 5 The last phase of problem solving is the preparation of the final reports. Usually this is governed by the requirements of the organization. For example, if the group was charged to prepare a proposal for an external funding agency, the form of the final report is governed by the agency's specifications. In any case, most problem-solving groups attempt to make their final written proposal appear attractive, intelligible, and literate. They may include arguments on behalf of their proposals and discussion of why various other alternatives were rejected.

Variations of Problem-Solving Meetings

Fact-Finding Meetings Some meetings are restricted to *fact-finding.* The groups are charged with investigating a problem or situation and presenting a report on the important facts and issues. The results of the investigation are used to advise those who make subsequent decisions about matters of policy and administration.

Briefings At *briefing sessions,* individuals or groups provide interested and concerned personnel with important information. For example, the project groups at L&L Associates meet for briefings to provide them with information they need in order to prepare the president's speech. Participants at briefings are customarily permitted to ask questions and to raise issues regarding the importance of the information to their daily tasks. Briefings can be organized to orient employees to new tasks; to explain changes in company policy, such as modifications of employee benefits; or to provide technical updates on scientific or financial matters.

Briefings are usually well prepared. Oral reports are backed up with visual aids, handouts, and other supporting materials, which we will discuss in Chapters 8 and 9. Care is taken to ensure that the information presented is accurate and detailed and that experts are present to handle questions.

Policy-Setting Meetings Some problem-solving groups are requested to consider overall policy of the organization and propose additions and revisions. Such groups are usually made up of executives and their advisors and consultants. Participants must be familiar with the operation of the organization. In order to do an effective job of policy making, the group must anticipate the effect of policy changes on every aspect of the organization's operations.

Program-Planning Meetings A final type of problem-solving group devotes its attention to planning meetings. These groups are charged to set up a formal program, such as the annual stockholders' meeting, a training session, a quality circle, or a retreat. It is their task to take the objectives specified for the meetings and devise a program that has a good chance of achieving those objectives. Their procedures may follow the standard agenda. Their charge, however, is limited to implementing someone else's program or solution to a problem.

Problem-solving groups of various types are related to one another. A fact-finding group may develop a compendium of information for another group that is charged with making a decision relevant to some serious problem. The same set of facts may be referred to a policy-making group. Every decision made by groups within the organization can be the topic of a briefing session or a formal meeting. Administrators need to establish a meticulous liaison between the various groups performing important tasks so that the groups do not duplicate their work or interfere with one another.

Training Sessions

Groups are also used extensively for employee orientation and training. New employees must learn what tasks they are to perform and how to do them. Technical innovations often require retraining of personnel whose job it is to operate equipment. Employees often need to learn specialized skills if they are responsible for tasks such as word processing, operation of duplicating machines, or processing of company forms. Individual, one-on-one training is expensive. Effective training usually involves more than one employee at a time and generally requires some kind of shared experience. Organizational training is a specialized form of education which relies heavily on small-group interactions.

Decision-Making Meetings

People come together in the decision-making meeting in order to arrive at some conclusion and, often, determine some course of action. It is in these meetings that plans are made and the implementation of previously determined plans is decided on. These meetings do not fulfill their purpose unless a decision is arrived at—even if the decision is not to decide!

Participants in these meetings may have the authority to empower the decisions arrived at, or they may report to someone with authority who will either give the final approval or rubber-stamp the decision. At L&L Associates, the president holds a decision-making meeting with the other executives in which they decide how to approach the annual presentation to the chair of the board.

As you can see, groups meet for a variety of purposes. The types of groups used in an organization depend on what kinds of problems it encounters in its day-to-day operations. The operation of any group is dependent on the skilled performance of the employees who make up its membership. Later in this chapter we will focus on effective behavior of members of small groups.

THE NATURE OF SMALL GROUPS IN THE ORGANIZATION

People have a tendency to be idealistic when they consider group operations. They tend to believe that by participating in group processes they have a hand in determining the outcome. When a group is legitimately established to do useful work, this is quite accurate. Occasionally, however, groups are used to rubber-stamp executive decisions or to create the illusion of democracy. When groups are used for these purposes, they are injurious to employee morale. Regardless of whether the group is doing real work, however, there are six dynamics associated with small-group activity. Let's consider these dynamics of small groups.

Group Climate

Climate is an abstract term used to refer to the general way in which the people in a group work with one another. A *cohesive climate* means that group members try very hard to get along. This is often useful, although when members try too hard to get along, they may surrender their individual ideas in the interests of harmony. The situation can lead to what is called *groupthink,* as we will describe later. Groupthink generally results in ineffective decisions.[4]

Group Norms and Pressures

When people work together over a period of time, they tend to develop *norms,* or regularities in the way they deal with one another. These are "rules" for behavior, and people who violate them can seriously interfere with the operation of the group. Therefore, groups exert pressure on members to conform to norms. These pressures toward uniformity serve two functions: they enable the group to move in the direction in which it wants to go, and they allow the group to maintain itself.

Norms are not legislation, however. They are social habits developed by the members of the group as they work together. Consequently, they can be modified by individual or mutual decision. It is very important for group leaders to observe how members work together. When work is not being done well, the leader often must intervene to help the group develop new norms for their interactions.

Each of us has our personal norms, values, and needs. When we interact with others in a group, we must balance our own social habits against the group norms. On the one hand, we try to avoid sacrificing individuality to group pressure. On the other hand, we want to fit in, so we allow ourselves to learn how the group does things we can go along with. In fact, going along is one way to get along. However, this is not always helpful to the group. For example, most people find themselves uncomfortable when they must disagree with others, so they tend to avoid conflict. But in group processes, conflict is important. People are appointed to groups because they are *likely* to disagree. It is from reconciliation of different points of view that the best solutions flow. Consequently, it is often important to try to establish norms for disagreement within the group. This is best done by establishing in advance some ways to resolve conflict when it arises.

Another problem that affects group norms is that people tend to bring along all of their previous experience in group membership when they participate in a new group. It is hard to adopt the norms of a new group, because we have already learned techniques in our families, social groups, therapy groups, or other task groups. To the extent that a new member wants to feel part of the group, he or she tries to behave as other group members do. Simple imitation, however, is often not enough to provide the kind of learning necessary to be a collaborative member. Members may make many mistakes before they take on the habits necessary to handle group norms well. The atmosphere or climate that prevails in the group helps members decide how far they wish to go in sacrificing their earlier habits for those of the new group.

Individual and Group Goals

Participation in small groups involves a balance between the individual's motives and the group's goals. Individuals have motives for joining groups, and they have needs that they expect to fulfill through their participation in those groups. At the same time, groups have specific goals that they must accomplish. Individual members must recognize that in the organization, the group's goals must generally be given priority over anyone's personal needs. However, the group must also make an attempt to satisfy the individual members in order to reap the benefits of their contributions. Dissatisfied members are not likely to be as productive as they could be.

Group Structural Properties

The *structural properties* of a group are those qualities of organization within the group itself. Although we often like to think of group members as being equally powerful (able to influence others), that is simply not the case. A power hierarchy develops within a group, and it affects who communicates with whom and how much a particular member communicates. More powerful members tend to talk the most and to receive the most communication.[5]

Why do some members become more influential than others? In the organizational context, this occurs because groups are often composed of employees from different levels in the hierarchy. Those in higher-status positions in the company are likely to be powerful group members. Other members often defer to these people simply because of their positions in the organization. Other people develop power in the group because of their expertise in the topic to which the group is addressing itself. Members who work particularly hard and devote a lot of their energy and time to the group may also become influential. Regardless of the reasons in a particular case, it is clear that groups develop power hierarchies that influence how members work together.

Task and Social Dimensions

Groups operate on two levels. One level is the *task dimension*—how the group goes about accomplishing its job-related purpose. The other level is the *social dimension*—how the members feel about and relate to one another as people. Although some groups focus more on one dimension than the other, both dimensions are operating in all groups. In the workplace, however, the task dimension is generally emphasized more than the social dimension. The success of a task group depends in part on how well its leader and members handle their personal relationships with one another. When a task group becomes a social setting, members may make personal connections that eventually get in the way of the group process. There is no way to prevent members from having personal relationships with each other, but the emotional content of those relationships should not interfere with clear thinking and honest expression of ideas. When members get very close to each other personally, they may control themselves excessively in order to avoid the appearance of disagreement with people they like. By the same token, when individuals develop hostilities to each other, their personal antagonisms might interfere with sensible discussion.

Group Members' Roles

The most effective way to prevent personal feelings from interfering with group processes is to encourage members to play task-related roles. Group members tend to develop particular patterns of behavior, which then become expected of them; these are called *roles.* There are two main categories of roles: task roles and social or maintenance roles. Task roles can be further divided into those associated with group processes and those associated with the content of the discussion. Effective group process alone will not result in a quality solution, nor will emphasis on content without concern for process. Both kinds of roles must be synthesized so that the group will proceed systematically and intelligently in its consideration of the problem which represents its task. Let's examine the types of roles group members can enact.

Task Roles *Task roles* are sets of behaviors that are designed to assist in the accomplishment of the group's goal. There are two types of task roles: process roles and content roles.

1. *Process roles* There are a number of tasks that must be performed in order to keep the group process going. Some members are charged with these *process roles.* One of the most important is *record keeping.* Someone in the group must be designated to take charge of records. While most corporations provide secretarial help to task groups, someone must be responsible for supervising the secretarial work (which in-

cludes keeping minutes of meetings, maintaining records of information considered by the group, keeping members posted on agreements and commitments, and managing the flow of information in and out of the group).

Leadership is a second important process role (it is also, in part, a group maintenance role). Much of the work of leadership involves making sure that the procedures used by the group are effective and efficient. The leader is also responsible for coordinating the contributions of individual members, for delegating tasks, and for many other behaviors that enhance the group's process. Leadership is discussed in detail in Chapter 7.

Information management is another process-related role that must be assumed by members in a modern task group. Decision support systems demand considerable technical knowledge and skill on the part of group members. In order to integrate data acquisition, storage, and retrieval using computerized data bases, members must be familiar with computer terminals and information storage systems. In most cases, such specialized process roles require personnel who are trained in both the details of the group's task and the technology needed for the support systems. Most groups in industry receive this kind of personnel support from management. These personnel are not members of the group, but ancillary to it. They are assigned to serve the group. Their work is generally supervised by the group leader, who consults with the members about deployment of support workers.

2. ***Content roles*** Some group members, if not all of them, need to take on content-related roles—they must contribute ideas to the group and evaluate those ideas. *Content roles* include a variety of behaviors, but all involve contributing to the ideas and information used by the group in accomplishing its task. Offering opinions, introducing the group to new information, providing evidence that supports or rejects a particular proposal, summarizing the discussion, and disagreeing with ideas are all examples of content roles.

Social or Group Maintenance Roles We have pointed out that social interaction is peripheral to the actual work of a task group. However, there is no way to escape the fact that when people work together, they develop social connections which must be honored. *Social* or *group maintenance roles* are behaviors that encourage a cohesive group climate and effective working relationships among members. Group members are responsible for treating one another courteously, ensuring that everyone has an opportunity to participate, and seeing that interpersonal friction is kept to a minimum. Group maintenance roles include encouraging other members, making supportive comments, mediating in conflicts, and any other behaviors that maintain harmonious relationships. People who like one another usually enjoy working together, and when people work well together they learn to like one another. When you have a job to do, however, you may find that you have to work with people who would otherwise not be your friends. It is not unusual in organizations to hear someone say, "I don't have to love the guy; I just have to work with him." But when you work with someone, your relationship must be at least civil, and members who play social roles help maintain cordial group relations.

We already noted that in addition to being a task role, leadership is a group maintenance role. The group leader often acts as a mediator of disputes, "traffic director," and conciliator. Leaders who overlook the importance of effective working relationships among group members are not likely to bring the group to successful completion of its task. This aspect of leadership will be discussed in more detail in Chapter 7.

EFFECTIVE PARTICIPATION IN WORK GROUPS

To participate effectively in work groups, you must (1) be able to identify the role(s) you need to play in the group, and (2) participate in the decision-making process. Let's talk about both of these requirements.

Identification of Appropriate Roles

Individual members have a great many options for their behavior. Exhibit 6.2 lists some of these options and indicates their contributions to the group.

Participation in the Decision-Making Process

After you determine the most suitable behaviors by reviewing the roles listed in Exhibit 6.2, your next step is to consider how groups arrive at decisions. We have already discussed the standard agenda for group operation. Although the sequence of steps that groups follow to arrive at decisions can differ, there are a number of activities that groups must engage in. The standard agenda illustrates what those activities are. By familiarizing yourself with the standard agenda, you can participate effectively in the decision-making process. Let's review the components of the standard agenda.

Phase 1 The group specifies its problem, defines its terms, and makes sure it understands what is expected of it. Throughout this phase, the group has the option to redefine its problem and its goals in consultation with the authority that established the group.

Phase 2 The group identifies what facts are needed and collects them. During fact-finding, the group must make a decision about whether it will work on

Exhibit 6.2 MEMBERSHIP BEHAVIORS

1. *Productive behaviors.* The following behaviors contribute directly to task accomplishment:
   a. A member can comment on the statements of other members of the group. This helps the group clarify and evaluate each contribution.
   b. A member can present factual information. This helps the group collectively obtain the information it needs to do its job.
   c. A member can question the accuracy, relevance, or timeliness of factual information.
   d. A member can make suggestions and encourage analysis in order to facilitate mutual understanding.
   e. A member can express opinions about any matter before the group.
   f. A member can encourage quiet members to participate and discourage those who talk too much.
   g. A member can seek compromise and reconciliation between members who are in conflict.
2. *Leadership behaviors.* The task of the leader is often assisted by members who help by making leadership-type contributions. The following are leadership behaviors:
   a. A member can encourage consensus.
   b. A member can propose alternatives so that the group does not succumb to groupthink.
   c. A member can help assign tasks and make sure that work is equitably distributed.
   d. A member can help the group meet its deadlines and stay on schedule.
   e. A member can provide summaries and reviews to ensure that all members are sufficiently informed about what is going on.
   f. A member can use personal authority and expertise when necessary.
   g. A member can help to create an open and nonjudgmental climate.
3. *Supportive behaviors.* The following behaviors help to sustain goodwill and cooperation among group members:
   a. A member can show interest in the contributions and ideas of others.
   b. A member can perform assigned tasks willingly.
   c. A member can express loyalty to the group and its goals.
   d. A member can support the leader's decisions.
   e. A member can listen intelligently and critically to others.
   f. A member can show trust in his or her colleagues.
   g. A member can help defuse tensions by displaying humor or talking in a conciliatory fashion.
4. *Digressive behaviors.* The following behaviors tend to retard the operations of the group and generally should be avoided:
   a. A member can respond with excessive emotion.
   b. A member can tell personal stories and share irrelevant information.
   c. A member can make excessive demands for information or spend too much time talking.
   d. A member can interrupt others or seize other members' turns to talk.
   e. A member can carry on personal socializing during work time.
   f. A member can tell jokes or try to draw attention to his or her personal performance.

symptoms of the problem, causes of the problem, or both. The group reviews the problem on the basis of the facts it gathered. Once again it may be necessary to revise the problem, depending on the new information the group discovered.

Phase 3 The group specifies its goals. This is a very sensitive part of the process. The group must be careful not to confuse goals and solutions. A *goal* is a statement like "We will improve sales by ten percent." A *solution* specifies the ways and means by which the goal will be achieved. Groups have a tendency to stop with the goal statement, but to do so means that the job is not complete. During this third phase of the standard agenda, the group also explores its constraints and limitations. It discovers what it must do and what it cannot do.

Phase 4 The group pulls together a solution, develops an implementation plan and budget, and explores the objections that might be raised against the proposal. It is also useful during this phase of the standard agenda to compare the solution selected with alternatives which have been rejected, in order to show the comparative advantages of the chosen course. The group must also check its solution against its goals and limitations in order to ensure that there is a chance of achieving the goal without violating any of the limitations.

Phase 5 The group prepares the final report. Customarily, staff personnel are provided to handle this matter; the staff is directed by the group leader or a committee charged with supervising production of the final report.

As a member of a group, you can help to work through these steps by taking an active part in the process. To do that, you must understand these steps in the decision-making process as well as adopt effective roles. In the next section we will focus on how to communicate effectively in the work group.

Effective Communication in Groups

It is safe to say that the quality of the communication in any group is a major factor in determining the quality of the group's decisions and actions.[6] It helps when members are effective communicators. They must be able to engage in interpersonal communication, manage their nonverbal behavior, and be able to present speeches when necessary. In addition, they must be attentive to the official roles and status of both their fellow members and the leader.

When an employee and his supervisor are both members of the same group, it may be difficult to avoid talk that could jeopardize their relationship outside the group. It can be very difficult to disagree with one's supervisor, even when it is necessary to do so. By keeping discussion focused on content, however, group members can keep tensions to a minimum. Members must concentrate on communicating clearly. They must be sure they are understood

Exhibit 6.3 COMMUNICATION SKILLS IN GROUPS

1. Providing information
2. Analyzing and evaluating information
3. Listening
4. Questioning
5. Participating
6. Thinking as a group (synergy)

and that they understand what others say to them. Group members need to develop the six communication skills listed in Exhibit 6.3, which we will discuss in the next section.

Providing Information The group needs to have information in order to operate. Members must communicate information that the group needs, and in a way that is useful to the group. Members who withhold information, perhaps because they feel shy or resentful, impede the progress of the group. The group depends on its members to provide necessary information. Group members are appointed on the basis of a presumption they have something worthwhile to contribute.

Analyzing and Evaluating Information Providing information alone does not make you an effective communicator in the group. You must also help to analyze and evaluate information presented by others. Information cannot be accepted uncritically. Sometimes facts are erroneous or inconsistent. Sometimes authorities must be questioned. It is important to evaluate each fact to see if it (1) relates to the problem, (2) is accurate, and (3) is timely. One of the most effective ways to participate in the assessment of the information presented to the group is to offer supporting evidence, when you have it, and contradictory evidence, when you are aware of it. You must also be willing to allow others to critique your information. It is most helpful when members make their contributions tentatively, with the understanding that everything said is open to question.

Listening Effectively Group members need to listen effectively. In all communication situations, the ability to listen effectively contributes to a good outcome. To be a good listener demands that you pay attention to what is going on and try to withhold comments until you are sure of what the speaker is saying. Good listening means actively seeking to understand and evaluate ideas.

Good listening is a complex and important group membership skill. Good listeners may not initially be as visible as good talkers, but if you are a good listener, your impact on the group process will be important. Ideas must be heard and understood if they are to be useful to the group. Effective listening

Group members must listen carefully when others make suggestions or offer ideas.

can also enhance the quality of the relationships among group members. People feel discouraged and angry when others do not listen to their ideas. By making the effort to listen, you can help maintain the morale of group members.

Questioning Related to the ability to listen effectively is your ability to ask good, appropriate, and timely questions. Group discussion is a cooperative process. The presumption is that no one member has the whole truth. Thus, it is important to question every contribution. Your questions are designed to make sure that information is complete and accurate and that opinions are based on evidence, not personal prejudice. Furthermore, good questions are a sign of good listening. They encourage speakers to continue making effective contributions.

Participating Effective members are *willing participants.* It is easy to drift off and become a spectator of the group process. To be a good member, you must participate—offer opinions, make suggestions, assess alternatives, and so on. Since your contributions are always tentative, there is no threat involved in participation. Everyone's ideas will be questioned. Everyone will contribute something to an effective solution. Your skills in critical thinking are of no value if you do not express your criticisms. The knowledge you have will not help the group unless you say what you have to say. While it is important to think before you speak, it is also useful not to think for too long.

Thinking as a Group (Synergy) *Synergy* means that group members produce more by working together than they could produce by adding their individual efforts. It is the give and take that occurs within the group that makes the process of discussion so exciting. Members can see how their collective effort produces an outcome far beyond what individual effort could achieve. When synergy exists, the group is able to "think" as a unit. Your success in small-group communication depends in part upon putting your own personal goals aside and working toward what is best from the group's perspective.

Special Techniques for Group Participation

Your effectiveness as a group member will be improved if you are able to manage some of the special techniques that facilitate good discussion. In this section we will examine brainstorming and devil's advocacy.

Brainstorming *Brainstorming* is a process in which members of the group are encouraged to generate as many ideas as they can without censoring or prejudging them. The process is designed to generate a wealth of information and ideas the group can discuss later. It is important to withhold criticism at first, in order to avoid inhibiting other members during brainstorming. As members begin to call out their ideas, they encourage other members to participate. Brainstorming is designed to help the group generate ideas, so you need to feel free to offer whatever ideas come to you. At L&L Associates, this technique is often used. The company needs creativity from its employees as they prepare health-related information packets, and brainstorming helps release creativity in group members.

An alternative form of brainstorming is called *nominal group technique.* In this method, members write out their ideas after careful consideration. Everyone's work is submitted and considered by the other members, and the ideas gathered become part of the group agenda.

Devil's Advocacy *Devil's advocacy* is based on the premise that some conflict is good for a group. If ideas are accepted uncritically, the group may slip into groupthink and miss its opportunity to generate effective solutions. The devil's advocate raises contradictory issues and criticizes popular positions in order to make sure that all ideas are given an equal hearing. Sometimes the person taking this role will say, "Let me play devil's advocate for a moment." This statement communicates good intentions, letting others know that the devil's advocate is not just trying to be disagreeable.

Pitfalls to Avoid in Order to Maximize Effectiveness

To be an effective group member you must not only consciously adopt appropriate behaviors. You also need to avoid some common pitfalls. Let's discuss the two most common problems, which are groupthink and problem people.

Avoiding Groupthink *Groupthink* occurs when a group seems to have a shared vision of its invulnerability and omnipotence and members appear to believe that their decisions are beyond question.[7] This produces a false sense of security and optimism. There is an illusion that the group is safe in all its decisions. Thus, members do not think they have to criticize ideas. They are satisfied to congratulate each other on how well they are doing. Groups that emphasize the importance of being cohesive can fall into the trap of groupthink. Members of such a group care more about getting along than about the task at hand.

The net effect of groupthink is that it imposes pressure on members not to participate. Faulty decisions come about when group members do not raise the questions they should raise, when they see everything so much alike that they lose their ability to ask the important critical questions.

Groupthink presents certain symptoms.[8] First, there is a shared vision that members of the group accept: that they are somehow invulnerable, that they are really somehow beyond question. This allows the group to engage in unwise risk taking.

Second, the group makes collective efforts to rationalize its behaviors or decisions in order to dismiss warning signs that might otherwise lead members to reconsider their assumptions. The group ignores information that might

Group members must ask critical questions and voice their disagreements to avoid the pitfall of groupthink.

contradict its decisions and does not fully explore the alternatives to decisions about to be made.

Third, there is often an unquestioned belief in the group's inherent morality. Group members are inclined to think that they don't need to consider the ethical, legal, or moral dimensions of their behavior and decisions.

Other symptoms include stereotyped views of anyone who might oppose what the group wants; pressure—often direct and powerful—on group members to yield to the group's mind-set; and a variety of devices the group engages in to try to counter all objections, both from within the group itself and from those outside the group.

In order to avoid falling into the trap of groupthink, you always need to function as a critical evaluator of ideas. You should always assess the situation rather than automatically buying into whatever the group explores. Trusted associates outside the group can also help you assess the degree to which your group may be falling into the pitfall of groupthink. At any rate, someone must interrupt this flow of high ego present in a group suffering from groupthink. The member who has the courage to dissent, object, and question is very important in helping the group avoid this pitfall.

Problem People Sometimes groups are ineffective in the ways in which they make decisions; sometimes there are people in the group who are troublesome. As a group member, you need to make sure that you aren't one of these *problem people.* It is always easy to spot defects in others. Our own defects are often more difficult to see. Try applying the communication style spot check in Exhibit 6.4 to assess yourself as well as other group members.

If you find any of these tendencies in yourself, then you must work to correct them. When you observe these problems in others, you need to help the leader deal with the problem people. Individuals must do their share in convincing problem members not to disrupt the group process.

Exhibit 6.4 COMMUNICATION STYLE SPOT CHECK

The following are the most common problems to watch out for in yourself and others when participating in groups:

1. Dominating the group
2. Talking too much
3. Talking too little
4. Blocking progress
5. Focusing on the negative
6. Personalizing commentaries and decision making
7. Listening too little
8. Failing to keep up with the process unfolding

The group depends on its members to manage their participation. It is fairly easy to train group members in the group process. They can be taught about how to manage an agenda, and they can understand quite clearly what is expected of them as a group. But since the group process demands that individual behaviors be synthesized, each member must take personal responsibility for his or her contributions.

SUMMARY

In this chapter we have focused on group activities in organizations. We began by talking about the ways in which organizations bring people together to work in groups. The main advantage of group decision making is that it brings together employees with different expertise, opinions, and ways of looking at problems.

There are many types of group meetings in the modern organization. For example, conferences and committees often involve a small number of people brought together for a specific purpose. Other kinds of meetings are also part of the ongoing operations of many contemporary organizations—for example, quality circles, employee assistance groups, and mediated meetings like teleconferences.

We described the purposes of many different types of meetings that take place in the organization. For example, we looked at ritualistic, problem-solving, fact-finding, policy-setting, program-planning, and decision-making meetings, as well as briefings and training sessions. The purpose of a meeting influences what constitutes appropriate behavior on the part of meeting participants.

As a member of an organization, you will need to understand the dynamics of small groups because those dynamics greatly influence group outcomes. Groups develop a particular climate, norms for behavior, structural properties, and task and social dimensions. Also, groups involve a balance of individual and group goals, and members tend to take on a variety of task-related and group maintenance roles.

Effective participation in work groups requires that members be able to identify the roles they need to play and that they participate effectively in the decision-making process. There are many productive task-related, supportive, and leadership behaviors that members can engage in. They should, however, avoid digressive roles, such as socializing and joking when the group is trying to work.

To help the group engage in effective decision making, members need to understand the five phases of the standard agenda, which is a step-by-step problem-solving procedure that goes through five phases: understanding the charge, fact-finding, setting criteria and limitations, discovering and selecting solutions, and preparing and presenting the final report.

Since the quality of a group's output is greatly affected by the quality of communication in the group, it is important that the members develop effective communication skills. In order to be effective, group members need six primary communication skills: providing information, analyzing and evaluating information, listening, questioning, participating, and thinking as a group (synergy).

We also examined some additional special techniques that groups can use. Brainstorming is designed to generate as many ideas as possible without critical evaluation of them. Devil's advocacy is another special technique group members use to try to stimulate critical evaluation of ideas.

There are two common pitfalls that entrap groups if they are not careful. The first is groupthink. Groups that experience groupthink are likely to make faulty decisions because there is tremendous pressure on members to conform and go along with the prevailing ideas in the group. A second pitfall is problem people. Groups sometimes have members who may talk too much, dominate the discussion, talk too little, block progress, focus on the negative, personalize commentaries, listen too little, or fail to keep up with the group's process. Group members need to be on the lookout for these tendencies in themselves and others and must attempt to correct them.

CHAPTER 6 ACTIVITIES

1. Select some campus group that meets regularly and observe one of the group's meetings. Observe each of the following:
   a. The purpose of the meeting
   b. The group's dynamics:
      (1) Does the group appear to be cohesive?
      (2) Is there a power hierarchy? Can you describe it?
      (3) What norms seem to be operating in the group?
      (4) To what extent does the group focus on task and social dimensions?
      (5) What kinds of roles do members play?

2. Identify three groups to which you belong and list the roles you think you fill in each of those groups. What similarities and differences do you observe? Why might that be?

3. Select some group to which you belong and use the communication style spot check in Exhibit 6.4 to assess your behavior and that of the other group members. Are there any problem people in your group? Do you seem to display any of the problem behaviors? If there are problem people, what can you do to help the group deal with them? If you are a problem person, what can you do to improve your small-group communication?

CHAPTER 6 NOTES

1. See W. G. Ouchi, *Theory Z,* Reading, MA: Addison-Wesley, 1981, or T. J. Pascale and A. Athos, *The Art of Japanese Management,* New York: Simon & Schuster, 1981.
2. On the advantages and disadvantages of teleconferences, see Linda C. Lederman, "Communication in the Workplace: The Impact of the Information Age and High Technology on Interpersonal Communication in Organizations." In *Intermedia,* G. Gumpert and R. Cathcart (Eds.), New York: Oxford University Press, 1985.
3. See Julia T. Wood, Gerald M. Phillips, and Douglas J. Pedersen, *Group Discussion: A Practical Guide to Participation and Leadership* (2nd ed.), New York: Harper & Row, 1986.
4. Irving L. Janis, *Victims of Groupthink,* Boston: Houghton Mifflin, 1972.
5. K. Bach, "Influence through Social Communication," *Journal of Abnormal and Social Psychology,* vol. 46, 1951, pp. 9–23.
6. Randy Y. Hirokawa and Roger Pace, "A Descriptive Investigation of the Possible Communication-Based Reasons for Effective and Ineffective Group Decision Making," *Communication Monographs,* vol. 50, no. 4, 1983, pp. 363–379.
7. See Janis.
8. Ibid.

CHAPTER

7

Leading Groups: Management of Meetings

Part of the job of managing other people in organizations is conducting meetings. In this chapter we focus on what is expected of the person who has the responsibility of leading the meeting in the business setting. As you already know, meetings serve a variety of purposes, and many different types of meetings take place in organizations. Exhibit 7.1 presents a summary of the reasons for meetings outlined in Chapter 6.

A leader brings to the job of conducting any meeting a commitment to that job and a desire to make the session a productive one. The first responsibility of the leader is to plan the meeting. Let's look at what this important aspect of meeting management entails.

PLANNING MEETINGS

Although meetings are everyday occurrences in organizations and it is easy to see how they can take place without much apparent planning, effective leaders know that the best meetings are those which are thoroughly planned. This does not mean that the planning has to be apparent; it means it has to be existent.

Sometimes the leader wants the planning to be apparent. Sometimes he or she does not—the appearance of spontaneity may matter. The critical point is that if you are going to conduct a meeting, you need to do your homework. Good meetings entail planning, regardless of whether that will be obvious to the others who will participate.

There are a number of considerations you need to address in order to be

Exhibit 7.1 REASONS FOR BUSINESS MEETINGS

A business meeting can be held to accomplish any one of the following purposes:

1. Ritual
2. Problem solving
3. Fact-finding
4. Briefing
5. Policy setting
6. Program planning
7. Training
8. Decision making

prepared to conduct a meeting. The most important of these are summarized in Exhibit 7.2, the convener's checklist. Let's discuss each of the steps listed in the convener's checklist.

Type of Meeting

In planning the meeting, you must first determine the type, or what kind of meeting it needs to be. For example, will it be best to conduct a conference or to call a committee meeting? Should you meet in person, or can you get the job done via a teleconference? If you decide to have a conference, would it be best to hold a two-person conference or one in which more personnel are involved? The type of meeting is the first thing you consider when deciding to have one.

The decision on the type of meeting depends upon the purpose of that meeting. From the time you begin to consider calling a meeting and throughout each of the steps we are now discussing, the purpose of the meeting is a critical factor. (Refer back to Exhibit 7.1, which reviews the purposes of meetings.)

Once you have identified the purpose of the meeting, answering the question of the type of meeting to hold becomes easier. For example, when you want

Exhibit 7.2 THE CONVENER'S CHECKLIST

When calling a meeting, you need to take the following steps:

1. Determine the type of meeting.
2. Decide upon the necessity of the meeting.
3. Set a goal for the meeting.
4. Specify the function of the meeting.
5. Identify who needs to be at the meeting.
6. Prepare a game plan to accomplish the goal.
7. Do your homework to prepare for the meeting.
8. Articulate criteria for determining success.
9. Plan an official agenda for the meeting.

to get advice on some issue and you need that advice immediately, holding a conference is better than setting up a committee to meet and report. If the matter is really urgent, it might even be better to get that advice via a teleconference rather than waiting until all of the necessary people can gather to meet in the same place. The type of meeting depends in large part on your definition of the purpose for meeting to begin with.

Necessity of the Meeting

Having determined the purpose of the meeting, and having identified the type of meeting most suitable for accomplishing that purpose under the given set of circumstances, you must next consider whether it is absolutely necessary to hold a meeting at all. This means you must determine whether the purpose of the meeting could be accomplished in some better way rather than bringing people together to meet. You already know that there are times when having a meeting matters, simply for the ritual of meeting. Sometimes even though the purpose of the meeting can as easily be accomplished by means of written communication, bringing the group together serves some ritualistic purpose—for example, simply to remind the individuals that they are a group and their input as a group is important. At L&L Associates, for example, the meeting for which the president is preparing to speak is ritualistic: it is an annual report meeting.

Goal

If you determine that it is necessary to meet in order to accomplish some purpose, the next step is delineation of the goal of the meeting. That is, you must decide what needs to happen in order to accomplish the objective for which you are bringing these people together.

In defining the goal, you are assessing what outcomes are necessary. Sometimes the goal is more clearly definable before the meeting. And sometimes the goal is accomplished simply by meeting, regardless of the actual outcome—as when the president of L&L Associates satisfies the ritual purpose of the annual meeting by giving the annual report. The important thing is to know what matters: if a certain objective has to be accomplished, then a meeting which simply takes time and has people come together is not meaningful.

Specific Function

What function does the meeting serve? As you know, there are a variety of purposes that meetings can serve. Your responsibility as leader is to determine which applies in any given situation. Defining the function, along with defining the goal of the meeting, is part of making sure that the meeting will be planned appropriately.

Who Needs to Be at the Meeting: Personnel

It is critical to decide who needs to be there in order for the meeting to work. If some of the people who need to be at the meeting cannot attend, not only does the meeting fail to accomplish its purposes, but you have also unnecessarily taken the time of those who do attend. It is a waste of time to have to meet again. In planning a meeting, therefore, an effective leader determines beforehand whether there are people who need to be there. If some people have to be there if the meeting is to be meaningful, the leader has them check their calendars to clear the time. Only then does the leader contact the others who are to be invited to the meeting.

Game Plan to Accomplish Goal

There is a purpose to the meeting and a goal that that meeting has to accomplish. The *game plan* is the course of action that is most likely to accomplish those objectives during the meeting. A game plan is not fixed; it is a preliminary design. Naturally, a good leader needs to be adaptable enough to shift gears as the meeting unfolds if a better course of action should become apparent. Sometimes the game plan is embedded in the agenda designed for the meeting. Some subjects are more important to discuss than others, and some subjects are potentially more controversial than others. Part of the game plan is sequencing topics so as to make the most effective use of the time scheduled. Sometimes, for example, this means leaving a controversial topic until late in the meeting so that other business will have been completed.

Preparation for the Meeting: Homework

Homework refers to the kinds of preparation that are done beforehand. Sometimes all the preparation that is necessary is to take into account the considerations we have been discussing in this section. At other times the preparation includes reading background material, reviewing earlier events, or preparing materials to distribute to those who will attend the meeting.

By planning ahead in these ways, the leader ensures that the meeting time will be used effectively. Since time is considered money in the business world—and organization members often spend far more of their time in meetings than they'd like—a well-prepared meeting that does not squander time is a credit to the convener.

Criteria for Assessing Success

In your preparation for a meeting, you must specify what will measure the effectiveness of the meeting: what kinds of outcomes, attitudes, or accomplishments need to come out of the meeting if it is to be considered successful. If the criterion in a given case is to get agreement for some course of action, nothing less than that will do. A measure by which to evaluate the results and decide what to do next is a critical factor in planning a meeting.

Preparing an Official Agenda

The *agenda* is the list of topics for the meeting and the order in which those topics are to be discussed. Exhibit 7.3 presents a sample agenda. Usually the convener distributes copies of the agenda at the meeting so that all participants have an idea of what to expect. When there are supporting materials that go along with some topics—such as documents to read and review—the convener may distribute copies of both the agenda and the documents prior to the meeting and ask that participants read them before the meeting.

As you can see from what we have discussed, the leader goes through a number of preparatory steps when planning a meeting. These all take time, whether the meeting is conducted in a casual manner or not. If you have to conduct a meeting while participating in the L&L Associates simulation, you will have the best results if you attend to all of these planning steps beforehand. Once you have prepared for the meeting, you can turn your attention to what it takes to conduct it.

LEADING MEETINGS

Any work group has *leadership*—those members who influence its direction. Some work groups, like other small groups outside the work organization, give formal titles and responsibilities to their leaders; but some do not, and then the group members simply retain those titles they have outside the group. In L&L Associates, for instance, the title *manager* makes the person who has that job the "leader" in the sense that he or she has authority that others in the project group do not have. But any member of the project group might have leadership in the sense of impact and influence over others in the group.

Group leaders tend to develop certain characteristics as a result of assuming the leadership role. As they conduct the day-to-day meetings of the various groups with whom they have to work, group leaders use a set of special skills that enable them to coordinate the efforts of other individuals in working together toward the accomplishment of the task at hand. In this sense, leader-

Exhibit 7.3 AGENDA FOR A MEETING

AGENDA

Corporate Communications Department Weekly Meeting

May 1, 1988

I. Announcements

II. Report of Vice President of Operations

III. Other Reports

   A. Manager's Report

   B. Project Head Reports

IV. Discussion of L&L Newsletter Proposal

V. Other New Business

ship in the work group is defined by more than just the leader's position in the group.

Leadership includes both a leadership style and leadership functions (the ability to manage the task and maintenance functions of groups).[1] Let's talk about each.

Leadership Style

The way in which the person in charge leads others in organizations is often referred to as *managerial* or *leadership style.* Traditionally, leadership has been viewed in a rather simple light. As summarized by Jack Gibb, the traditional view was that people need to be led, that people perform best under leaders who are creative, imaginative, and aggressive—under leaders who lead.[2]

Social science research into leadership style over the past several decades has produced various descriptions of leadership style. The most common categories for leadership style have usually been labeled as follows: *democratic/participatory* (in which the leader allows the group to determine its own decisions), *autocratic* (in which the leader seeks to impose personal beliefs and solutions on the group), and *laissez-faire* (in which the leader is nondirective).

In more recent years, group dynamics has often been discussed in terms of the metaphor of a team, with the leader characterized as the team manager. As the manager of a team, you as leader must know not only how to manage individuals but also how to manage work groups. This does not mean that you ignore the individuals, but it does mean that part of the set of skills expected of you is an ability to lead groups and to work with them. You will have to lead groups both inside the context of the meeting and outside the formal setting of the meeting, in everyday work circumstances.

Today, leadership style is most often viewed as a complex process that is influenced by many variables in addition to the qualities of the leaders themselves. As we have come to understand that process, we see leadership as an important kind of interpersonal effectiveness—the ability to be competent enough at interpersonal communication to influence other group members. Different people who do similar things have different effects, get different results. Perhaps the most significant way of thinking about leadership style is to identify the ways in which the individual works best at accomplishing her objective: influencing the behavior of those she has to manage.

When we view leadership in this way, it is easy to conclude that there is no such thing as a "most effective leadership style" for all leaders. The most effective style for any manager is the one that is the most natural for that person. Styles that ignore the personality of the leader seem to fail, as do styles that ignore the context (organization) in which the communication occurs and the social norms (culture) of that context. The best advice to give any leader is to be oneself—with one caveat: know yourself well enough to know your strengths and weaknesses as a leader and know how to maximize the former and minimize the latter.

At first reading this might sound easy, and it *is* easier to be who you are than to try to be someone you are not. But telling you to be yourself is not the same as saying "Anything goes" or "All styles are equally effective." Instead, we are saying that in order to be an effective leader, you must assess your own strengths and weaknesses and work on those weaknesses.

The process of making changes in your style of leadership can be effective only when you are willing to invest effort into changing what needs to be changed. To help you discover what you need to work on, Exhibit 7.4 explains a process for improving your own natural leadership style. Linda C. Lederman worked with Brent D. Ruben of Rutgers University on testing this process in leadership training programs. Trainees followed these ten steps as they worked on some of their weaknesses.

Exhibit 7.4 LEADERSHIP STYLE AND SELF-MANAGED CHANGE

Here are ten steps that will help you when you want to improve your own leadership style.

1. *Reframe liabilities into skills to be changed.* The first step in the process of changing leadership style is to identify a skill or set of skills you can work on in order to improve your style.
2. *Examine and assess those skills you want to improve.* Determine the manageability of change. Can it be done? At what costs, and with what benefits?
3. *Monitor your target skills.* Record your observations of two situations.
   a. Record the specific situation (date, time, place, people).
   b. Record the actual behavior (dialogue, nonverbal communication).
   c. Consider what would be a preferred behavior in that specific situation.
4. *Observe an effective model of target skills.* Select someone who has the skills you want and observe the behavioral effectiveness of that person in one situation in which these characteristics are demonstrated.
5. *Determine a manageable goal.* Determine what you can really do and what goes beyond your ability to change immediately. Begin with what you can do—let your success motivate you for further change.
6. *Elaborate on specific performance behaviors to use to achieve your goal.* To make the necessary change, be specific about the behaviors you want to incorporate into your style.
7. *Look for a situation involving the target skill.* Then write two different scenarios for using the skill in that situation.
8. *Implement the most manageable scenario change.* Rehearse the behavior in a low-risk situation. See the outcomes.
9. *Note the consequences and evaluate them.* Decide whether this is a change for the better for you.
10. *Go back to step 1 after you have given yourself time to incorporate change.* Identify another specific behavior or set of behaviors to modify.

Leadership Functions: Task and Group Maintenance

Even after assessing your style of leadership and working to maximize your natural leadership skills, you can still dramatically improve your effectiveness in conducting meetings by working on the two major functions of leadership in meetings: management of the *task function* and management of the *group maintenance* function.[3]

Task Leadership The first order of business for you as the leader of a group is to make sure the group gets its work done—and fast. Just as all groups pressure members toward conformity, groups in the work context exert pressure to get tasks accomplished. Although the group climate may be considered of major importance outside of the organization, productivity and efficiency are the key in the context of the organization.

A group whose members enjoy each other's company so much that they don't get much work done is often referred to as a "happiness for lunch bunch." Such a group is not highly regarded in the organizational setting. The function of the meeting agenda is to help accomplish the purpose of the meeting by setting the group on the right course. There are several important components to the task function of leading the group. They are listed in Exhibit 7.5.

Exhibit 7.5 FUNCTIONS OF THE LEADER

Leaders manage both task and group maintenance functions in the context of the business meeting.

Group task functions

1. Leaders know the purpose of the meeting and implement an agenda designed to accomplish that purpose.
2. Leaders use effective speaking and listening skills to move discussion of the topic along at an appropriate pace.
3. Leaders make sure that all viewpoints get aired.
4. Leaders make sure that all options are given thoughtful consideration.
5. Leaders provide feedback to the group, interpreting the members' actions.
6. Leaders close meetings when goals have been accomplished.
7. Leaders make sure that written records of meetings are kept and distributed where appropriate.

Group maintenance functions

1. Leaders make sure that they encourage participation by all members.
2. Leaders make sure that they develop an atmosphere that is appropriate to the task at hand.
3. Leaders make sure that all group members feel they are part of the group.
4. Leaders make sure that contrasting views can be presented.
5. Leaders make sure that they provide mechanisms for releasing tension.
6. Leaders help members to resolve their differences.

Group Maintenance The second critical aspect of the leader's job is the group maintenance function. At the outset of the meeting, it is the leader's job to introduce members of the group to one another if they are not already acquainted. The leader indicates when it is time to start, initiates the discussion, and encourages group members to participate.

As a leader, you need to be able to help the more quiet group members to talk and to get the more verbal group members to let others speak more. This is called managing the speaking-silence ratio. When and if tensions are evident, it is your job as leader to handle them, just as you must handle any difficult situations that arise. It is part of your job to keep the meeting going, to make sure that the group maintains itself without sacrificing the individuals, and that the individuals get to express personal opinions without sidetracking the group. Exhibit 7.5 summarizes the group maintenance functions for which the leader of a meeting is responsible.

APPLICATIONS: DEALING WITH PEOPLE

As the leader of any group, you are empowered to conduct its meetings. That power can be taken away from you, however, if you do not retain control of the meeting—if you let other group members take control. Let's look at some of the ways in which effective leaders control meetings without making group members feel "controlled."

In addition to your knowledge of yourself and others in groups, effective leadership requires some very fundamental speaking and listening skills. Let's talk first about the speaking skills that the effective leader has.

Special Speaking Skills for Discussion Leaders

You need to master three basic techniques in order to be effective at conducting the meeting: (1) effective question asking, (2) concise and precise use of summaries, and (3) clear use of directives. Let's briefly discuss each.

Question Asking As you know from Chapter 4, the use of good *question-asking techniques* is central to the interview. This skill is also the first technique you need to master for conducting the group meeting. You probably remember that questions can be *open* or *closed* and *directive* or *nondirective.* Effective use of questions is as essential in conducting the meeting as it is in conducting the interview.

Summarizing The second technique to master for conducting the meeting is the use of the *summary.* Summaries help to provide guidance and direction. They reiterate what has been covered and what is yet to be discussed. They also provide the group with a common sense of what has been occurring.

Directiveness The third technique to master is *giving direction.* The leader is expected to move the meeting along. You may wish to do so by asking questions and by providing summaries. Sometimes this simply is not enough and you need to provide the directive—to point out the necessary decision or action.

One of the most difficult things to do as leader is to handle the problem situation: the awkward topic, the person who talks too much, the person who says something inappropriate, the pressures of deadlines. Sometimes the leader must simply choose what seems to be an expedient course for eliminating a difficulty or forging ahead to a conclusion.

Listening and Leading

Truly effective managers of meetings are more than good speakers: they are good listeners. Listening well is a critical tool of the effective meeting manager. Exhibit 7.6 presents the listening style inventory (LSI) and instructions for its use. The LSI is a self-report measure, developed by Linda C. Lederman, which is designed to provide insight into the strengths and weaknesses of your listening skills.

When you have arrived at a score for yourself on the LSI and have placed it on the assessment line, you can judge how effective your listening is by how high your score is. A lower score indicates that you may hear what is said but you do not pay enough attention. A moderate score indicates that you hear and pay attention but are not particularly responsive. A higher score indicates that you go beyond hearing and simple listening: you are actively responsive, you are a good listener.

After measuring your listening skills with the LSI, you can assess your areas of strength and weakness by reviewing the items in the inventory. It is not the score itself that is important: it is the basis for the score. The best listeners are those whose scores are high (4 or 5) on the items in column 1 and low (1 or 2) in column 2. Look to see where you have low scores in column 1 and high scores in column 2. These are areas in which you need to make changes if you want to be more effective at listening.

Naturally, good listening skills apply to most of the communication activities discussed throughout this text. They are spelled out here because listening is an often-overlooked asset of the meeting manager, yet it is one of the most effective tools that a leader can have.

Difficult People

Sometimes leadership of the group requires dealing with difficult people who are members of that group. Difficult people can interfere with effective group progress or decision making. These problem people can prevent groups from

Exhibit 7.6 LISTENING STYLE INVENTORY[a]

Instructions: This measure consists of 24 statements concerning your personal listening style preferences. Read each statement and indicate by circling the appropriate number whether it describes circumstances which *Always* (5), *Usually* (4), *Sometimes* (3), *Rarely* (2), or *Never* (1) occur for you.

	A	*U*	*S*	*R*	*N*
1. I try to wait until others have finished what they are saying before I decide if I understand them.	5	4	3	2	1
2. When people take too long to make a point, I say something to let them know I already understand.	5	4	3	2	1
3. I think it is interesting to listen to most people express their thoughts and feelings.	5	4	3	2	1
4. I am the kind of person who knows what people are saying almost as soon as they begin to say it.	5	4	3	2	1
5. I am the kind of person who gets easily bored listening when I think the subject will be too elementary for me.	5	4	3	2	1
6. I try to wait to make judgments on the meaning of what other people say until they are finished.	5	4	3	2	1
7. When I have other things on my mind, I push them aside when someone else is speaking.	5	4	3	2	1
8. I am the kind of person who thinks fast so I like people who get to the point.	5	4	3	2	1
9. I try to understand what someone is trying to say rather than criticizing the way the person is saying it.	5	4	3	2	1
10. When listening to other people, I find my mind drifting to other subjects.	5	4	3	2	1
11. I nod my head and say "uh huh" or "I see" when other people are talking.	5	4	3	2	1
12. I like the speaker to know I care about what is being said.	5	4	3	2	1
13. When someone else is talking, I use the time to think of what I am going to say when they have finished.	5	4	3	2	1
14. When someone tells me something that is critical about me, I feel hurt or angry even as they say the words.	5	4	3	2	1
15. I have trouble listening when I think the subject matter is going to be too complicated for me to understand.	5	4	3	2	1
16. When I want to say something, I try to wait until the other person is finished and knows I understand what has been said.	5	4	3	2	1
17. When someone is talking, I try to block out other sights and sounds and concentrate on what is being said.	5	4	3	2	1
18. I find myself agreeing or disagreeing mentally with what others say even as I hear them speaking.	5	4	3	2	1
19. When someone speaks to me, I respond without wasting any time to ask any questions.	5	4	3	2	1
20. I listen to try to understand what people really mean, which may not be exactly the same as what they say.	5	4	3	2	1
21. I listen to the tone of voice people use when I really want to know what they mean by what they say.	5	4	3	2	1
22. I get impatient when anyone says something that takes too many words.	5	4	3	2	1
23. I listen to get the gist of something; the rest of the details aren't essential.	5	4	3	2	1
24. I look at someone's eyes and facial expressions to make sure I understand what they mean when they speak.	5	4	3	2	1

Exhibit 7.6 *(continued)*

Scoring the LSI

Step 1. Add up the responses to the items in column 1. Add up the responses to the items in column 2.

Column 1	Column 2
1. __	2. __
3. __	4. __
6. __	5. __
7. __	8. __
9. __	10. __
11. __	13. __
12. __	14. __
16. __	15. __
17. __	18. __
20. __	19. __
21. __	22. __
24. __	23. __
Total in column 1 ______	Total in column 2 ______

Step 2. Compute the following formula:
72 plus total in column 1 = ______ minus total in column 2 = ______

Assessing the LSI Score

Place an *X* on the line below to indicate your score on the LSI.

24	Hearing	56	Simple listening	88	Active listening	120

[a]No part of this listening-style inventory may be reproduced without written permission from Dr. Linda C. Lederman, Department of Communication, Rutgers University, New Brunswick, NJ 08903.

working together effectively, particularly in the decision making in which they engage, because of certain personality characteristics. As the leader of the group, the problem is yours. If you can't handle it, one of three negative consequences will result: (1) the group will get sidetracked and will not accomplish its purpose, (2) the group will accomplish its task poorly, or (3) someone else will handle the problem person and wrest the real leadership from you.

What can you do? In Chapter 6 we suggest that the first thing for you as a group member to do is to make sure that you are not one of those difficult individuals. This is particularly true if you have the responsibility for leadership in the meeting. If you make it hard for others to contribute in any way, then you not only undermine the group—you also undo your own effectiveness as the leader of that group.

Like any other group member, if you find in yourself any of the problem tendencies discussed in Chapter 6, you have a project to work on in the perfection of your own communication skills. But as the leader of the group, you also have a responsibility if there are others who are interfering with group progress. What do you do when the problem person is someone else? What do you do when the dominating people are powerful members of the group? Some individuals gain power through the force of personality, others because of their positions in the organization. A problem person can keep others from actively participating in the group process. More often, the difficulty is that by sheer force of power, the problem person will influence the group to make a poor decision. Sometimes a group member just gets off the track and consumes valuable group time talking about topics unrelated to the group's task. And sometimes a person who wants to make a decision as quickly as possible opposes any extended discussion—even when it is necessary to discuss every option in order to accomplish the task effectively.

Techniques for Dealing with Difficult People There are several techniques you can use to deal with problem people. First, you can talk to the individuals outside the meeting to try to work out the problem privately. Second, you can try to prevent the situation from getting out of hand if you know what to anticipate from group members. Finally, you can use the *nominal group process,*[4] which helps you to analyze the possible cause of the problem at hand and to propose possible solutions to the problem. Let's discuss this process and how you would use it.

Nominal Group Process At the outset, you bring the group members together as if in a meeting situation, but you instruct them *not* to speak to one another. (The nominal group process takes its name from this part of the procedure: if the members cannot speak, they are a group in name only.) Once you have brought the individuals together and have instructed them not to speak, you ask them to write on a piece of paper what they find to be the major causes of the problem being explored. After you have given the group enough time to list the causes of the problem, you ask someone to read one of the things he or she has written down. You write that possibility down, and it becomes the first item on your master list. You go around the group and have the members add their items to the list until a master list has been created. The master list becomes the basis of a discussion in which the task is to get the group to work together in assigning priorities to the identified problem areas.

This process works on several levels. First, individuals in the group take a slow and thoughtful look at all the possible dimensions of the problem before rushing into a solution. Second, group members are allowed organized, creative, and nondefensive sharing of concerns. And third, the group gets started working on something together. Both the process and the product are group oriented.

APPLICATIONS: SPECIAL KINDS OF MEETINGS

In most of our discussion in this chapter, we assume that the meetings you will be conducting are small-group meetings that involve three or more people in face-to-face contact with one another. As discussed in Chapter 6, however, there are other common types of meetings in organizations, and you may also have to conduct them. Let's look at what additional considerations need to be given to leading discussions in these special kinds of meetings.

The Two-Person Conference

A common type of business meeting is the two-person conference. Sometimes a two-person conference takes the form of an interview, as discussed in Chapter 4; sometimes it takes the form of a business meeting, as discussed in Chapter 6. The role relationships are more clearly delineated in the two-person business conference than they are in an interview. You already know a good deal about the dynamics of these conferences from earlier chapters. Here we will focus on your role as leader: What is your responsibility in leading the two-person conference, as differentiated from leading the small group?

The transaction that takes place in the two-person conference, like that in the interview, involves people with different statuses and different degrees of power. Where you are leading the transaction, you are the one with the higher status and power. In order to make effective use of those assets, you need a real understanding of the role of the other person, the subordinate. As the person who has the status and power to make decisions, you need a new range of communication skills.

Your leadership manifests itself from the first. You have the power and status to decide whether to meet or not and when, where, and for how long any meeting will take place. The organizational context provides the sanction initially for your leadership of the conference. When you ask (or tell) a subordinate to have a conference with you, you are expected to set the time and place and plan the agenda for the meeting. Even when it is the subordinate who requests the meeting and you grant the request, you still have control of the meeting. In this case, your control actually manifests itself from the moment you agree to meet. You have the power to say "yes" or "no" to a meeting. The subordinate does not have that same power. The subordinate in L&L Associates, for example, can ask the manager to have a meeting, but the manager can refuse; if the manager requests the meeting, the project team member must agree to meet.

As the leader, you must have the skill to control the channels of communication in the two-person conference, much as you control the agenda in other meetings. In Chapter 4, we distinguished between directive and nondirective interviews; the same principles apply in the two-person conference. You may either be directive (setting the agenda, determining turn taking, and so on) or nondirective (allowing the other to speak at will).

You must decide whether the conference should be conducted in a directive or nondirective manner. The most important consideration is the purpose of the meeting. Is the purpose to gather specific and uncontroversial information, or do you need to probe indirectly in order to find out information that has not as yet been forthcoming? In the first case, it is more effective to be directive, but in the latter, it may be better to be nondirective.

Conducting the Quality Circle Meeting

Another special kind of meeting you may have to conduct is the *quality circle.* As discussed in Chapter 6, the quality circle consists of supervisory staff and production employees. Quality circles address special problems or projects within the organization. You might want to review the section on quality circles in Chapter 6 before reading this section on conducting quality circle meetings.

As discussed in Chapter 6, effective communication is critical to the quality circle, especially because this type of meeting brings together labor and management in otherwise unheard-of ways in the organization. The leader is expected to conduct the meeting effectively.

The leader of the group, whether formally trained in group processes and human communication or not, needs to be able to encourage participation and to recognize the contributions that all group members can make. The leader of the quality circle must therefore be concerned with the dynamics taking place in the group and the effects of those dynamics on the participation of group members. You might want to review the section of Chapter 6 in which we discussed the six dynamics affecting group process.

As the leader of a quality circle, you will be expected to recognize the

Exhibit 7.7 STEPS IN IMPLEMENTING QUALITY CIRCLES

1. Identify the issues to be addressed and the goal of the group.
2. Select the priorities for the group. Determine the issues to address and the sequence in which to consider them.
3. Find out what information is needed to address each of the problem areas or issues.
4. Use the information collected to analyze the problems at hand.
5. Explore the possible solutions.
6. Analyze the advantages and disadvantages of all options.
7. Identify the best solution for the given circumstances.

various skills and resources brought to that group by the individual members, and you will be expected to encourage the sharing of these with the group. Exhibit 7.7 presents steps to follow in implementing quality circles. As you can see, these steps are based on the problem-solving steps discussed in Chapter 6.

Another skill group leaders need, as mentioned above, is the identification and management of any kind of group or individual conflict within the group. Group conflict is more likely in the quality circle than in most other work groups because the quality circle is composed of people whose positions in the organization otherwise cast them in adversarial positions to one another.

Whenever conflict is being handled in the work group, it is important for all members of the group to feel comfortable with the resolution of that conflict. The strategies used most often for conflict reduction involve good common sense, sensitivity to others and their feelings, and a "win-win" attitude (that is, a sense that the best resolutions leave everyone feeling a winner rather than resulting in a winner and a loser). To accomplish this, the leader takes steps to (1) get the conflicting parties to see the conflict as a joint problem, (2) state the problem in such a way as to make it concrete and specific, and (3) generate possible solutions to that problem until arriving at one to which there can be mutual agreement. Sometimes a group that has been through the experience of a well-resolved conflict has more feelings of group cohesion than a group that has had no conflict at all.

A FINAL WORD ON LEADERSHIP: USES AND ABUSES OF POWER

Leadership—the special influence exerted by one individual over others—has fascinated and puzzled people throughout history. In this chapter, we have explored leadership to determine its appropriate boundaries, to understand the unique role of the leader. We have described the leader in the small group as he or she conducts business meetings. In the setting of the meeting, leaders have the power to guide the group in the accomplishment of tasks and to encourage or discourage the individual and group atmosphere. Although the leader is needed to steer the group, the leader must guard against excesses of power that become abuses. The materials provided in this chapter can be used to help you be an effective leader while you enable the others in the group to accomplish their tasks. That is the true use of leadership power.

SUMMARY

In this chapter we have discussed how to conduct meetings and what is expected of you as the person conducting the meeting. We began by talking about the purposes of meetings and how to go about planning meetings. There are nine steps you can take as part of your preparation (these are summarized in the convener's checklist in Exhibit 7.2).

Effective leaders have certain characteristic leadership styles. There is no one style that works for everyone, however. It is possible to improve on natural leadership skills. In Exhibit 7.4 we presented a plan you can use in working to improve your leadership style.

The task and group maintenance functions are also important in a leader's overall effectiveness. The leader's job is to keep the group's attention on the task at hand and to ensure that all individuals contribute their knowledge and skills to the group. The leader is also responsible for managing conflict.

Discussion leaders need to have special speaking and listening skills. The leader must be able to ask the right questions, to summarize the group's progress, and to direct the group toward a decision or action. A listening style inventory was presented in Exhibit 7.6.

Leadership responsibilities also include dealing with difficult people, those who dominate or obstruct other people. One way to control this problem is to use the nominal group process, which focuses the members' attention on group functions.

In addition to conducting small-group meetings, leaders may be responsible for two-person conferences and quality circle meetings. The leader must understand the role of the subordinate in a two-person conference, and the leader needs to have special communication skills in order to keep control of such a meeting. The leader of a quality circle meeting must also be sensitive to the relative power and status the members' roles in the organization confer upon them. Group conflict is more common in quality circles because the members' outside roles are often adversarial.

CHAPTER 7 ACTIVITIES

1. Answer the questions on the listening style inventory (LSI) in Exhibit 7.6 and follow the instructions to assess your listening skills. Talk to a friend who knows you well enough to be honest. Ask your friend's assessment of your listening.
2. Plan a meeting with five to seven classmates about a topic you think is important to the class. Plan the agenda for that meeting and distribute copies to the people at the meeting.
3. Use the agenda you planned in activity 2 to conduct a meeting. After the meeting, talk with participants to evaluate how the agenda affected the meeting.
4. Work on identifying one weakness in your leadership style. Use the steps for self-managed change presented in Exhibit 7.4 to work on that weakness.
5. Role-play a situation in which someone is being difficult in a meeting. Try three different strategies to handle the situation. Evaluate which worked best. Get feedback from others about your actions.

CHAPTER 7 NOTES

1. For a good discussion of leadership, see Joseph Luft, *Group Process: An Introduction to Group Dynamics,* 3rd ed., Palo Alto, CA: Mayfield, 1984; *Leadership and Social Change,* William R. Lassey (Ed.), Iowa City, IA: University Associates, 1971; or Robert Tannenbaum and Fred Massarik, "Leadership: A Frame of Reference," in *Organizational Behavior and Management,* Donald E. Orter and Phillip B. Applewithte (Eds.), Scranton, PA: International Textbook, 1968.
2. Jack R. Gibb, "Dynamics of Leadership and Communication." In *In Search of Leaders* from the series *Current Issues in Higher Education,* no. 5, 1967, p. 55.
3. Lassey, *Leadership and Social Change,* p. 5.
4. For more detail about the nominal group process, see Richard Huseman, "The Role of the Nominal Group in Small Group Communication." In *Readings in Interpersonal and Organizational Communication,* Richard Huseman (Ed.), Boston: Holbrook Press, 1973, pp. 490–503.

CHAPTER

8

Preparing Public Presentations

When we use the term *public presentation,* what comes to your mind? Many people imagine a formal situation, with a speaker standing behind a lectern delivering a prepared message to a large audience. Although this is a type of public presentation, we are using the term much more broadly than that. A *public presentation* is any type of face-to-face or mediated communication in which one or more speakers have the primary responsibility for presenting a message to one or more people. An executive presenting a report to a large group of stockholders is giving a public presentation. So is a supervisor explaining a new company policy to a small group of workers, or the president of a large corporation holding a televised press conference. In L&L Associates, the speech the president is preparing for the board of trustees will be a public presentation. We will develop our definition more fully in the next section of this chapter when we examine types of public presentations.

Presentations are a requirement of many types of jobs, so they take many different forms. As employees move up the corporate ladder, their jobs typically require more and more presentations. But public presentations are not made just by executives. As Adler points out, a survey found that almost half of a group of blue-collar workers reported having given at least one speech. Of those, 31 percent said they had presented four or more speeches.[1]

Unfortunately, there are many people who have virtually no training in making presentations. As a consequence, they are filled with fear at the prospect of speaking to a group. Others are not particularly fearful, but their presentations are less than impressive. Many organizations have recognized the need for proper training of employees and have implemented in-house instruction programs. Goldhaber surveyed 100 businesses, and 54 of his 78 respondents said that their organizations offered speech instruction in some form. And of those 54 respondents, 34 said that their companies offered public speaking instruction.[2] Other companies hire outside consultants to provide speech training to their employees—the companies pay in the neighborhood of $650 per employee for a two- or three-day program.[3] If so many organizations consider training in public speaking to be important, it is clear that you are giving yourself an advantage by working now to improve your presentation skills.

Our primary purpose in this chapter is to provide you with the information you need to begin developing those skills. We will start by clarifying the term *public presentation* and discussing types of presentations common in organizations. We will then discuss six stages of preparation. We will also look at special considerations involved in presenting persuasive speeches. In Chapter 9 we will focus on techniques for delivering presentations and will consider the topic of how to manage fear or apprehension about public presentations.

WHAT ARE PUBLIC PRESENTATIONS?

We have already said that a public presentation is any type of face-to-face or mediated communication in which one or more speakers have the primary responsibility of presenting a message to a group of people. Let's examine that definition so that you can see how a public presentation differs from other forms of communication.

The essential ingredient in our definition is that one or more speakers have the primary responsibility for presenting a message. Although the audience members may respond nonverbally and by asking questions, the speaker is responsible for *managing the situation, presenting information and ideas, and controlling audience response.* This differs from group activity in several ways. In an ordinary meeting of a task force of five members, each person has an equal opportunity to participate. No one individual has the responsibility of presenting a message to the group. All members contribute to, or at least have the potential to participate in, the discussion. However, if one member is charged with presenting a report to the group, that member's report becomes a public presentation because she has the primary responsibility for conveying a message to the others.

By this definition, *it is not the size of the audience* that determines whether a public presentation has taken place. There can be an audience of one, as long as one person (the speaker) is responsible for presenting a message to the other. For example, a salesperson making a pitch to a potential client is giving a public presentation in which there is only one audience member. When you present an idea to your supervisor, you are also making a public presentation. The term *public* implies extended, planned, and sometimes spontaneous discourse made by one person to one or more other persons.

Note also that our definition includes both *face-to-face* and *mediated* communication. Although in most cases public presentations are made to a "live" audience, there are many situations in which the presentation is mediated by communication technology. The most common mediated types are the videotaped presentation and the "live" televised presentation. Teleconferencing, which we discussed in Chapter 6, is also mediated communication. A presentation made during a video or audio teleconference is a mediated public communication.

It is important to realize that a public presentation is oral, even if it is mediated by technology. Sending a message in written form is not a public presentation. A presentation may be written in advance and read, but in order for it to qualify as a presentation the message must be conveyed orally. Finally, we want to clarify that "public presentation" is a broad category. A *public speech* is one subset of that category; the two terms are not equivalent. An employee presenting a proposal for a new product to an executive is giving a public presentation, as is a middle-level manager giving a technical report on the progress of a new project to his superior. The term *public speech* implies a prepared message delivered to a large group of people, such as an address by a keynote speaker at an annual convention. Although a public speech is a type of presentation, we are referring to a much broader communication form when we use the term *public presentation.*

TYPES OF PRESENTATIONS

Public presentations take many different forms. Let's take a brief look at some of the most common types that occur within the organization.

A common situation in which presentations take place is the *supervisory* or *department head meeting.* A supervisor may explain changes in company policy to a group of workers, or a worker may try to persuade a supervisor to try his suggestion. The head of the advertising department may present a proposal to the heads of several other departments at this type of meeting. The possibilities are almost endless for the types of presentations that could occur at supervisory and department head meetings. The project heads at L&L Associates will meet, and some may make formal presentations to the group. The president of L&L Associates will make a formal presentation to the chair of the board, and there are other instances in which managers, vice presidents, or project heads might decide that the best vehicle for presenting material is the public presentation.

For employees at lower levels of the organization, *union meetings* may

There are many types of business presentations that can occur in a variety of settings.

provide a frequent opportunity for public presentations. Meeting participants may make proposals or reports about union or company activities.

It is quite common for people to make *speeches at social functions* such as awards banquets or company holiday parties. Typically this type of presentation is entertaining in tone and content, although it could be intended to motivate or inspire organization members.

Oral technical reports are made at all levels of an organization. They are usually presented to provide factual information.[4] At L&L Associates, this type of report is made frequently, particularly after employees have completed information-gathering interviews and need to report back to their project teams.

Presentations occur at briefing and information sessions. As Adler defines it, a *briefing* is "a short account aimed at helping others perform their jobs."[5] A worker with seniority might brief a new employee on department procedures. A supervisor might brief a group of workers on the functions of a new piece of equipment. These are essentially *information sessions* in which one or more individuals have the responsibility of providing important information in a concise form to other employees.

Our purpose is not to provide an exhaustive list of types of public presentations. Rather, our intent is to demonstrate that public presentations take many forms and that as a result, you are likely to be making presentations when you accept a job in an organization. Many aspects of these presentations will vary—length, size of audience, topic, and formality—and you will need to be skillful at adapting to various speaking situations. As we explain techniques for preparing a presentation, we will emphasize the importance of adaptability.

STAGES OF PREPARATION

In this section we will consider all of the aspects of preparing a presentation. We will treat these aspects as stages in preparation, although you will find that it is not necessary to follow the prescribed order of stages exactly. In fact, you are likely to discover that you must go back to earlier stages in order to improve your preparation; for example, you may discover that you need to do additional research on a particular aspect of your topic. We will discuss five stages of preparation: goal setting, analysis of listeners and situation, generating ideas and supporting materials, organizing ideas, and preparing the introduction and conclusion. Exhibit 8.1 summarizes the stages of preparation.

Stage 1: Goal Setting

Your motivation to make a presentation may come from three sources: yourself, a job assignment, or a request from either an organization member or a nonmember. In the first case, you *decide* to make a presentation. For example, you ascertain that it is necessary to brief a group of new employees on a new procedure in your department, or you have a proposal that you want to "sell" to your superiors. In the second case, you are *assigned* to make a presentation, such as when your supervisor wants you to present a technical report on a project you are involved with, or you want to try to sell a new product to a customer. In the third case, your presentation is the result of a *request.* You may be asked to make a presentation by someone from outside the organization. If you are an electrical engineer, for example, you may be asked to speak about

Exhibit 8.1 STAGES OF PREPARATION

- Stage 1: Goal setting
- Stage 2: Analysis of listeners and situation
- Stage 3: Generating ideas and supporting materials
- Stage 4: Organizing ideas
- Stage 5: Preparing the introduction and conclusion

career opportunities in engineering on "career day" at a local college. Requests may also come from within the organization, such as when a superior asks you to represent the company at an annual convention.

Regardless of how it is that you are motivated to make a presentation, stage 1 of preparation is the same. You must set goals for yourself to guide your preparation. A *goal* is defined as a clear statement of what you want to accomplish by making your presentation. Selecting a goal is like choosing a destination for a trip. Without a destination, how could you possibly plan your route? Speakers must have a sense of what they are trying to accomplish—a destination. Setting a goal gives you that destination. Thus, your first stage of preparation is to write a specific goal statement that will guide you throughout your preparation. Here are some examples of goal statements:

- I will make a 15-minute presentation in which I state and support five reasons why our company should buy a particular type of computer.
- I will speak to my supervisor for 5 minutes to explain a procedure that I think will improve our filing system within the department.
- I will take 20 minutes to explain the new vacation plan to department heads at the next weekly meeting.

Note that in each example, the speaker is specifying what she wants to accomplish by making a presentation. Perhaps the value of setting a clear goal will be clearer if we look at some examples of poor goal statements:

- I will make a presentation about types of computers our company should purchase.
- I will talk to my supervisor about some of my ideas.
- I will explain some changes in company policies to department heads.

These examples simply are not as specific as the first examples, and they leave the speaker with only a vague sense of the purpose or goal of the presentation. There are two major advantages to setting presentation goals clearly. First, the speaker who knows exactly what he hopes to accomplish is more likely to be successful. We all have heard speeches or lectures or reports that didn't seem to make a point. By the conclusion of the presentation we still did not know what the speaker wanted or was trying to say. By setting a goal, a speaker has a focus for the presentation and stands a better chance of making that focus clear to the listeners. If the speaker does not know exactly what he hopes to achieve, the listeners certainly won't know.

The second advantage of goal setting is that it helps the speaker in the remaining stages of preparation. The speaker has a much better idea of what needs to be included and what material is less essential or irrelevant if she has a clear goal statement guiding preparation of the presentation. The first clear goal statement we listed above helps the speaker decide what material she needs to include in her talk—the five reasons and supporting statements for why the company should purchase a particular type of computer. Anything else is irrelevant to accomplishing that purpose. For instance, if while doing research, the speaker finds some very interesting information on the history of computers, she can ask, "Is this information going to help me in accomplishing the goal I have set?" If the answer is "yes," she should include the material in her presentation; if "no," the speaker can save the information for future use.

How do you go about setting a specific goal? You begin with a topic area, which may be very general or quite specific, depending on the job assignment. If your topic is general, you must narrow it down before you can identify a specific goal. If you are interested in introducing your company to teleconferencing, for example, you need to limit that topic to something manageable. Will you talk about types of teleconferencing, or will you do an in-depth report on a specific type, such as videoteleconferencing? If you cannot make that decision, you will need to go through stage 2, in which you analyze your audience and the situation to help you decide. Then you can return to the goal-setting stage.

Once you have identified your specific topic, ask yourself, "Why am I doing this presentation? What is it that I hope to accomplish?" You may have more than one answer to that question; at this point, record all of your answers. For the presentation on teleconferencing you might end up with something like the following:

- I want to inform the department managers about videoteleconferencing.
- I want to persuade the department managers that we should look into the feasibility of setting up videoteleconferencing facilities at our two plants.

If you have identified more than one purpose for the presentation, ask yourself if you can realistically accomplish all of them in one presentation. You may have to answer that question after you have completed stage 2. In general, you should have only one purpose for a presentation. In the example we provide, you would want to select the first purpose, because before you can persuade your company to consider adopting videoteleconferencing, the managers need to know more about it.

Now that you have identified your purpose, you are ready to write your goal statement. Your goal should be a more precise version of your purpose, in which you specify how long you will speak, who your audience is, and exactly what you hope to accomplish. For our example, the goal statement might be

- I will deliver a 30-minute presentation to inform department managers about what videoteleconferencing is, how it can be used, and its advantages and disadvantages.

The more specific your goal statement is, the easier it will be for you to remain focused as you continue your preparation. (Note that at L&L Associates, the president will be making a speech that others have prepared. This is not unusual in an organization. Regardless of who prepares the presentation, those responsible must have a specific and clearly articulated goal.)

Stage 2: Analysis of Listeners and Situation

Analyzing the Listeners In preparing a presentation, it is critical that you consider who will be present when you deliver your message. You do this in order to ensure that your presentation will be appropriate for your listeners. Suppose, for example, that you will be presenting a talk on career opportunities in the health professions to a group of high school seniors. Think of how you would have to change that presentation if you were then asked to speak to a group of junior high students. Finally, imagine that you were asked to speak on that subject to a group of individuals attending an annual convention of health professionals. In each case your presentation would have to be altered in order to make it appropriate for the particular group of listeners you were addressing. We believe that the people who are most effective in their presentations are those who can successfully adapt their message to their listeners. If you think about the teachers you enjoy listening to, one characteristic they are likely to have in common is an ability to convey ideas in a way that you can understand and relate to.

Eugene White proposed a way to analyze the audience for a presentation.[6] Following his method of analyzing listeners, we will consider their *knowledge of the topic,* their *interest in the topic,* and their *position on the topic.* Your task in this stage of preparation is to think about (and, if necessary, gather information about) these three aspects of your listeners.

Knowledge level of your listeners First, you need to have a sense of how much knowledge your listeners have about the subject on which you are speaking. The amount of knowledge your listeners have about your topic can range from none to a great deal. In assessing this aspect of your listeners, try to place them in the appropriate place on the following continuum:

←————————————————————————————→

No knowledge	*Some familiarity*	*Fairly knowledgeable*	*Well-informed*	*Extensive knowledge*

Doing this would be fairly simple if all listeners were alike, but the level of knowledge of individuals may vary widely. Some of your listeners may be at the low end, some in the middle, and some at the high end of the continuum. The challenge to you as a speaker is to try to assess roughly how many of your listeners are in each of the various categories indicated on the continuum and then, of course, to plan your message so that it is appropriate for the largest possible number. The better your assessment, the more success you will have at adapting to the listeners.

In making this assessment, you need to realize that when you do not know the listeners well, you must consider the group as a whole. You make generalizations about your listeners. Usually you cannot know how much knowledge one particular individual has about the topic. (This is not true, of course, if you are speaking to one or more persons with whom you are very well acquainted.) Since it is virtually impossible to give a speech to the "average" person, you must cope with a diverse audience by saying the same thing in several different ways in order to meet the needs of as many listeners as possible.

How do you assess how much knowledge your listeners have about your topic? If the listeners are employees in your organization, you can make your assessment on the basis of your experiences with these individuals, the particular jobs they hold, and what you can find out by asking the appropriate people. Suppose, for example, that as head of the advertising department, you have been asked to speak to a group of managers from the sales department about some new advertising strategies your department has created. Chances are that you have had previous contact with these managers and so have some sense of their knowledge level. Even if you have had no previous contact with them, you can assume that they know a great deal about the product or service being advertised since they are in the business of sales. However, they may not possess expertise on advertising strategies, so you will have to be careful to define or avoid technical jargon. Since these people are *managers* in the sales department, they have probably been in the company for a while or in other sales departments and have undoubtedly worked with employees in the advertising department before. So they are likely to be somewhat informed about advertising strategies, although not as informed as you are. If you think you need additional information about the level of knowledge of your listeners, you can always speak to the head of the sales department about this. He can provide you with information about the people you'll be speaking to.

You can see from this discussion that when you make a presentation within your organization, you probably already possess enough information about your listeners to be able to draw sound conclusions about their level of knowledge. If you do not, you are likely to know people who can provide you with the information you need.

Once you have assessed the knowledge level of your listeners, what do you do with that information? Essentially, you can categorize your audience into one of four types: uninformed, informed, somewhat informed, or mixed. Let's look at how to adapt your presentation to the four types of audiences.

1. ***Uninformed*** When your listeners have very little knowledge about your topic, you must be careful not to use language that is too technical. If you do use technical words, define your terms in language the listeners can understand. Although people may be impressed with how much you know if you talk over their heads, they will not appreciate you as a speaker and they will not understand your message. When your listeners have little knowledge, you must take care to select only a few main points to talk about so that you do not overwelm them with too much new information. When necessary, you must provide the audience with the background they need in order to understand the ideas you will discuss. You can also tell your listeners to stop you if they have any questions about any of the information you are presenting.
2. ***Informed*** You may be confronted with a situation in which most of the listeners have a great deal of knowledge about your topic. In this case, your challenge as a speaker is to provide the listeners with new information or a new perspective on the topic. If you do not do either of these two things, you are likely to leave the audience wondering why you wasted their time. When your listeners have expertise in your subject, you can feel free to use technical language and jargon, as long as you are quite certain that the audience will understand it.
3. ***Somewhat informed*** Your listeners may be somewhat knowledgeable about your topic. When your listeners fall between the two extremes of "no knowledge" and "extensive knowledge," you can assume that they have the basics and can go beyond that. You must be careful to consider whether or not they would be familiar with technical terminology, and you should either define it or avoid it when you are uncertain. It is fairly easy to provide this audience with new information or a new perspective since the listeners are not experts on the topic.
4. ***Mixed*** Speaking to a group in which the knowledge level varies a great deal is the most difficult situation to handle. Your best strategy is to aim for the majority of the listeners. For example, if most of the listeners know very little about the topic, you must avoid technical jargon and you must provide necessary background information, even though some listeners may not need the background. By adjusting your presentation to the level of the majority of the listeners, you stand a better chance of conveying your message to the greatest number of people than you would if you geared your talk to a small segment of the listeners.

Interest level of your listeners In addition to trying to discover how much knowledge your listeners have about your topic, you need to assess a second factor: how interested the listeners are in that topic. If your listeners are very interested in and involved with the subject, your task as presenter is somewhat easier than it would be if your listeners were apathetic. In the latter case, you not only have to present your message—you have to first motivate your listeners to listen to you, to care about the topic. For example, suppose you have come up with what you think is a great idea for a new product your company could produce. When you begin trying to sell your idea to the appropriate people, they do not see the merit of your idea at all. They simply are not interested in hearing about your idea—perhaps it sounds silly to them, or they are too busy with their own ideas, or they think things are fine as they are. Undoubtedly, many creators of innovative ideas have experienced initial listener reactions of doubt or apathy. In a business setting, an idea that represents potential financial risk is not likely to be accepted enthusiastically at the outset. Thus, your challenge as a speaker is to sell the idea and generate interest in it.

Once again, you can think of listener interest in the topic as covering a range.

Apathetic	*Slightly interested*	*Moderately interested*	*Very interested*	*Enthusiastic*

The procedure here is the same as it was for determining the knowledge level of the listeners. You try to assess what proportions of the listeners fall at various points on the continuum. To make this assessment, too, you use what you already know about the audience and you ask appropriate people for more information when necessary. There is one other question that will help you gauge the level of interest of the listeners: Are they attending your presentation voluntarily or did they ask you to speak about the topic to them? If the answer to either part of this question is affirmative, your listeners are likely to be at least moderately interested in your topic. People do not seek out information on a topic or attend a presentation voluntarily unless they have at least some interest in the topic and/or the speaker.

However, everyone has to be motivated to listen to a speech. Even those people who are enthusiastic at the outset must be encouraged. This means that when you prepare your presentation, you must pay attention to ways to keep your audience interested. Apathetic listeners must be excited at the very beginning; their interest must be continually regenerated. A presentation is not like a written document. If people lose the focus of attention when reading, they can always go back and reread the material. If your listeners lose interest while you are speaking, there is no way you can repeat what they missed. Thus, *you must hold their attention all the way through.*

On the basis of your analysis of their interest level, you can label your audience as having no interest, high initial interest, or moderate interest. You will need a different strategy for your presentation for each group.

1. *No interest* When you discover through your analysis that your listeners have almost no interest in your topic, your challenge is to persuade them that they ought to want to listen. This is a common situation for people in sales. Salespeople often have to speak to potential customers who have no initial interest in the product or service. The salesperson's task is to generate interest in the product or service by convincing the customers that they need it. Your best strategy in a situation where your audience is really not interested is to spend some time early in the presentation to show why your listeners should be concerned about your topic. Be able to tell them why they should care, which of their needs or interests you can address, or how they may benefit from what you will discuss. For instance, suppose you have set up an appointment with a college student to whom you want to sell life insurance. The student is young and has very little money, but she reluctantly agrees to listen to your pitch. In preparing for your presentation, you will have to think about how to convince this individual that she *needs* life insurance, that she *can afford it,* and that a life insurance policy carries some *immediate benefits* or advantages. Unless you can convince the listener of this, it is doubtful that you will sell her a policy. In fact, unless you can generate interest in your life insurance policy, it is highly unlikely that the listener will truly attend to all of the facts you try to share about the policy.
2. *High initial interest* In some ways, this is the ideal situation—you do not have to persuade the listeners that they should listen. However, you still need to try to maintain their attention. In fact, because their initial interest is high, your listeners may have very high expectations about your presentation. You can easily let them down if your presentation is dull and lifeless. Therefore, when faced with a situation in which the listeners are initially very interested in your topic, you must build attention-getting devices into your presentation.
3. *Moderate interest* If your listeners have moderate interest in your topic, you should try to generate greater interest by talking about how your topic relates to them. For example, if you must brief a group of employees on a new procedure for a task that is not central to their jobs, they may be only moderately interested at the outset. You should be sure to explain how the use of the new procedure will benefit them in some way, such as by making their jobs easier or by reducing the amount of time they need to spend on the task itself. In addition to showing the listeners why the topic is important to them, you may

want to incorporate attention-getting techniques into your presentation. Remember—when people are bored by a presentation, their minds wander. And when their minds wander, they do not receive your message in the way that you want them to. You must *motivate* your audience to listen.

Listeners' position on the topic The third aspect of your listeners that you need to consider in preparing a presentation is their position on the topic.[7] Generally speaking, people may have a favorable, neutral, or unfavorable attitude toward a topic or issue, although we can again create a continuum of positions.

Hostile	*Moderately unfavorable*	*Slightly unfavorable*	*Neutral*	*Slightly favorable*	*Moderately favorable*	*Extremely favorable*

Just as you did when assessing knowledge level and interest level, you will have to use the information you have about the listeners, or gather information when necessary, to help you assess their positions on the topic. One point to consider is that when people have a lot of knowledge and a great deal of interest in a topic, they typically have strong opinions about it. When people are neutral about an issue, it is often because they have little information about it and do not see it as relevant to their lives. So analyzing your listeners' knowledge and interest levels may help you determine their position on your topic.

To help you adapt your presentation to your listeners' position on your topic, let's examine ways to handle favorable, neutral, and unfavorable audiences.

1. ***Favorable audience*** In some instances, the listeners may be favorable to your subject or proposal. For instance, you may be presenting a report on the success of your company's latest advertising campaign. Or you may be explaining a new and improved benefits package to a group of employees. When your listeners are favorable to what you have to say, you can simply try to maintain their attention and give them a well-organized presentation. If there is some action you want to persuade them to take, you stand the greatest chance of success with this type of audience. You need to be sure to provide them with the details of what you would like them to do. If you have come up with a solution to a problem that has been plaguing your department, for example, you must provide the specifics of how your solution can be implemented and what action is required on the part of your listeners. Otherwise, although they may be favorable to the solution you propose, they may fail to implement it because you have not provided the necessary details for implementation.

2. ***Neutral audience*** Your listeners may be neutral toward your topic because they have little knowledge of the subject, because they do not see how the topic relates to them, or because they simply have not made up their minds as to how they stand on the issue. There are several things that you can do in this situation. First, you should try to persuade your listeners that they should be concerned about the issue by showing them how it affects them in some way. Once you have shown the audience why they should care about the topic, your task is to persuade your listeners that what you are proposing will benefit them.

   For example, suppose that as a worker, one of the tasks you must perform is tedious and that it requires more of your time than you think it is worth. You come up with an alternative way to do the task, but you must persuade your supervisor to allow the change. Perhaps the supervisor is satisfied with the way the task is done and does not perceive the problem or the need for a change. Since your listener is neutral, you must begin by persuading her that the problem is serious enough to warrant attention. You need to show your supervisor that the problem affects her, not just you. Once you have done that (perhaps by explaining how you could be more productive and the department as a whole would benefit if the problem were resolved), you need to show your supervisor how the solution you have come up with will solve the problem and benefit her. Your solution may require more time of your supervisor, so how will you convince her to adopt it? You must show how the benefits of your solution will outweigh the burdens for the *supervisor.* Therefore, you have got to look at the issue from her point of view, persuade her to be concerned about the issue, and then convince her that what you propose is beneficial.

3. ***Unfavorable or hostile audience*** Perhaps the most difficult situation is when your listeners are unfavorable or even hostile to your proposal. If you had to inform employees that their hours or wages were going to be reduced or if you were trying to persuade a group of executives to adopt a plan that would be very costly to the organization, you would undoubtedly face an unfavorable or hostile group of listeners. How would you handle this situation? Let's consider three factors that will influence your presentation.

   First, when people are very unfavorable to an idea, they have a lot of interest in it. Therefore, you do not have to persuade them to listen. Instead, you have to persuade them to listen *to you.* In other words, you must establish that you know what you are talking about and that you are trustworthy. These are the two aspects of *credibility.* In building your credibility as a speaker, let the listeners know that you have researched the topic carefully and have the latest information. Show them that what you propose is advantageous and not harmful to them. Unless you establish sufficient credibility with your listeners, they are not likely to be persuaded to your point of view.

Second, listeners who are unfavorable to your position or topic, will require *sufficient proof* for your proposals. Later in this chapter we will discuss various forms of support or proof that speakers need to incorporate into their presentations. These forms of support not only help maintain listener attention—they also provide evidence for the speaker's claims. In speaking to people who are unfavorable to your proposal, you cannot hope to persuade them unless you have proof or facts for your arguments.

Third, a hostile or unfavorable group of listeners may make counterarguments you need to refute. This means that you will need to consider the reasons the listeners have for not accepting what you are proposing, and then you will need to persuade them that those reasons are unfounded. For example, at L&L Associates, an employee who tries to convince executives to adopt a plan that involves a substantial financial commitment must deal with the counterargument that the plan is too costly. The speaker has to show that the plan is not too costly, that it is worth the cost, or that in the long run it will pay off. It is not a wise idea to leave out discussion of cost, because the listeners will be thinking about it and will raise the issue themselves.

Thus far in describing stage 2 of your preparation we have considered analysis of the listeners and adaptation to them. Exhibit 8.2 summarizes our discussion of listener analysis.

After you have completed your listener analysis, you may need to revise the goal statement you wrote in stage 1 of your preparation. For example, suppose you had set the goal "I will make a ten-minute presentation to the

Exhibit 8.2 LISTENER ANALYSIS

1. *Knowledge* of topic. Audience may be categorized as
   a. Uninformed
   b. Informed
   c. Somewhat informed
   d. Mixed
2. *Interest* in topic. Audience may have
   a. No interest
   b. High initial interest
   c. Moderate interest
3. *Position* on topic. Audience may be
   a. Favorable
   b. Neutral
   c. Unfavorable or hostile

department heads to persuade them to implement my solution to the problem." After conducting an analysis of the listeners, you discover that they are neutral toward your proposal because they do not have much knowledge of the problem. At that point you might want to set a new goal: "I will make a ten-minute presentation to the department heads to inform them of the problem and convince them of the seriousness of that problem."

At L&L Associates, listener analysis is very important. For example, employees need to know a great deal about the chair of the board if they are part of the team preparing the president's message. This single message, to be presented in a ritualistic meeting, is a critical one for the president.

Analyzing the Situation Essentially, this part of stage 2 involves thinking about when, where, and why you are giving a presentation and about how those aspects of the situation affect what you should say and how you should say it. Effective speakers adapt to the listeners and the overall environment of the presentation. Let's look at the aspects of the situation you must consider in preparing a presentation.

Purpose of the situation What is the purpose of the situation in which you will speak? Is it an annual convention of professionals in your field? Is it a monthly department meeting? Is it an annual meeting of the stockholders? It is relatively easy to answer this question, but what is more difficult is determining how the purpose of the situation will affect your presentation. One piece of advice we can give is, make sure that you do not ignore the purpose of the situation. A speaker should not use the situation as an opportunity to express a personal gripe or discuss a favorite topic. One of the authors once attended a graduation ceremony at which the speaker chose to talk about the research project in which she was involved. This was hardly appropriate for the purpose of the situation, which was to congratulate the graduates and provide a sense of passage to the next stage in their lives. If a situation calls for a presentation on company policies and procedures, for example, be sure that you fulfill that purpose. Otherwise you violate the expectations your listeners have for the situation, and this distracts them during the presentation. Rather than listening to you, they sit and wonder when you will address the topic they expected.

Physical location Where you deliver a presentation can enhance or detract from your message. As you prepare to speak, you need to try to minimize those features that will detract from your presentation. There are several aspects of the location that you need to analyze.

1. *Size of the room* We have all attended presentations where it was difficult to hear the speaker or where we could not see the visual aids

the speaker used. If the room is very large, you need to make arrangements for a microphone if you are not able to speak loudly. If your presentation will be very long, you will tire quickly if you have to strain your voice in order to be heard. You also need to think about whether people at all places in the room will be able to see you and any visual aids you might use. If they will not and you cannot change rooms, perhaps you can plan to move around the room. Of course, this depends on whether or not you are using a microphone and whether it is one that allows you to move away from the lectern.

2. *Facilities* You need to check on what facilities will be available in the room and make arrangements for those you need. Are there enough chairs, for instance? Do you need a chalkboard? If there is one, will chalk and an eraser be at hand? What equipment do you need, and is it available? Where and how can you get anything else you need? Is there an easel so that you have a place to display your visual aids? To play it safe, you should always check the room in advance (if possible) and carry vital items with you. Bring chalk and an eraser. It would be a good idea to bring an extension cord if you plan on using any electrical equipment. If you will use an overhead projector, bring a spare bulb—you never know when you will need it. By anticipating potential problems and needs, you can be prepared for the situation and avoid embarrassing moments.
3. *Possible distractions* Some locations afford more privacy and fewer distractions. Some walls are thin, and the audience can hear distracting noises from the next room. Within the room itself, there may be a problem such as a loud air conditioner or a squeaky floor. You need to check the room for possible distracting noises, and if you think the distractions are serious, make arrangements for another location. In addition to noises, there are other potential distractors. If the temperature in the room is too hot or too cold, your audience may have a difficult time paying attention. Uncomfortable seats and poor lighting can have the same effect. You need to try to eliminate any problems in advance. If it is not possible and a room change is out of the question, keeping your message brief will help. And it is a good idea to acknowledge the distraction so that your listeners know that you are aware of it. If you say, for example, "It is very warm in here so I'll try to keep my remarks brief," your listeners will appreciate the fact that you are concerned about them. (Be sure that you do keep your remarks brief, or the audience may be angry that you did not keep your word.)

Time A final feature of the situation that has an important influence on speakers is time. We are referring to the time allotted for your presentation. We cannot emphasize this point enough: stick to the time limit you have been given. Listeners get annoyed and may even become angry if you speak for more than the allotted time. Even if the listeners do not get upset, other speakers may, because you are cutting into their time. Observe the time limit, then, even if it means you have to leave out some information that you consider to be important. Your best strategy is to plan carefully and rehearse your presentation so that you can remain within the time limit without having to leave out information.

You have accomplished several important things by the end of stage 2 of your preparation. You have set a goal or goals for your presentation and have conducted thorough analyses of the listeners and the situation. Exhibit 8.3 presents the details of situation analysis. Perhaps your analysis has revealed that a change in the original goal is necessary. As you continue through the remaining stages of preparation, be sure to keep your goal, listeners, and situation in mind. You must ensure that all aspects of your presentation are appropriate for the listeners and the situation and that all the elements under your control help you achieve your goal.

Stage 3: Generating Ideas and Supporting Materials

Before you can prepare an outline of your presentation, you need to decide what ideas to include. In stage 3 of preparation, then, you generate the main ideas for your presentation and decide what materials you will use to support those main points. This necessitates doing some research on your topic in order to obtain the most up-to-date information and to fill in the gaps in your knowledge. In this section we will discuss how to research your topic, what kinds of supporting materials you need to generate, and how to decide which ideas and supports to include in your presentation.

Researching Your Topic Let's briefly describe some of the sources of information you will use in researching your topic. First, *you* are your most important source of information and ideas. The topic of your presentation will almost always concern the work you do on the job; perhaps it is a project you are completing or a proposal you have made. Consequently, you already have a great deal of information about your topic. Take advantage of this and use what

Exhibit 8.3 SITUATION ANALYSIS

1. Purpose of the situation
2. Physical location
   a. Size of the room
   b. Facilities
   c. Possible distractions
3. Time

you already know as your first source of ideas. Without worrying about the order of those ideas yet, simply list them. You can always add or eliminate ideas later on. At this point, all you are trying to do is discover what you know about the topic.

If you rely on yourself as a source of information and list the ideas you have, you are likely to discover what kinds of additional information you need. You may notice that you will need more recent statistical data to support one of your points, or you may need to obtain more general knowledge about a particular idea. Before you jump into doing additional research on the topic, spend some time determining the kinds of information you are going to need. You can save yourself a great deal of time.

Once you have determined your needs, you can turn to a variety of sources for more information. Your organization possesses plenty of information, much of which is readily available, both in written form and in computer data banks. You need to be able to access those data banks or find someone who can get you the information you need. Computers have made enormous quantities of information easily available, so you should be able to obtain nearly any type of data you need. If the information you are seeking is not available in a computer data bank, you can use the written documents that your organization stores. Policy manuals, technical reports, letters, and memos are just some of the written documents that are useful.

Another valuable source of information is other employees. People with expertise in all kinds of areas are working for your company, people whom you may be able to interview in order to obtain information. We discussed this type of interview in Chapter 5, which you may want to reread if you plan on interviewing anyone to obtain additional information for your presentation. At L&L Associates, project team members interview other employees in the organization to develop ideas for the president's speech.

Finally, you can use published materials as sources of ideas for your presentation. Your local library has a wide variety of books, journals, magazines, newspapers, almanacs, encyclopedias, and other documents that will provide you with needed information on your topic. If you are uncertain about how to obtain needed information, you should ask for assistance from the library personnel.

Developing Supporting Materials In your presentation you will develop main ideas. (You will organize your main points in stage 4 of preparation.) However, a presentation is much more than the enumeration of a set of main points. Each of those main ideas must be developed and supported with supporting materials. In this section we will examine the various types of supporting materials and their functions.

Functions of Supporting Materials Supporting materials serve three primary functions.

1. Supporting materials help you explain or elaborate an idea. Suppose one of your main points is that computer *x* is one of the best personal computers on the market. You need supporting materials to explain what you mean by that. What do you mean by "best"? Do you mean that computer *x* is the least expensive? The fastest? That it has the most memory? Your supports provide the explanation and elaboration of your main idea.
2. Supporting materials provide proof for your assertions. Note that in the example provided above, not only do you have to explain what you mean by "best"—you have to prove that computer *x* is the best. You have to show how the features of computer *x* are superior to those of comparable computers. This requires that you use various supports, such as examples, statistics, and quotations from computer experts. You cannot assume that your audience will automatically accept your assertion.
3. Supporting materials help maintain listener attention. Your supports are the interesting facts, figures, and details that develop your main ideas. Without them, a presentation is a list of undeveloped ideas. During your presentation on computer *x*, your listeners will "tune in" when you provide your supports.

Like all aspects of a presentation, your supporting materials must be adapted to your listeners and the situation. If your supports concerning computer *x* are too technical for your audience or are not relevant to their needs for a computer, then your presentation will be ineffective. The key is to use the analyses you did of the listeners and the situation to help you select the supporting materials that will be most appropriate.

Types of Supporting Materials Let's look at eight types of supports available (see Exhibit 8.4). The last type, visual aids, we will mention only briefly, since we will be discussing them in detail in Chapter 9.

Exhibit 8.4 TYPES OF SUPPORTING MATERIALS

1. Definitions
2. Examples
3. Stories
4. Quotations
5. Statistics
6. Comparisons
7. Descriptions
8. Visual aids

Definitions In a presentation, the speaker is likely to introduce listeners to new words they must know in order to fully understand the topic. For example, all fields have technical jargon; although we do not advocate using jargon to excess, there will be times when you must rely on technical terms. In these instances you need to provide a definition. If you are giving a presentation on computer simulations to an audience unfamiliar with simulations, you will need to provide a clear definition of your subject.

In other presentations, you may not be introducing listeners to new terms, but you may still need to clarify how you are using a specific word. Suppose you are giving a presentation to a client, and you are arguing that you have a high-quality service to offer. Although the client knows the meaning of "high quality," she does not know what *you* mean by that phrase. Spending time defining the term would be worthwhile because it could make the difference in whether or not you close the sale. What constitutes a high-quality service is open to interpretation; therefore, the phrase requires a definition. Your listener analysis should help you determine what the client considers high quality, so you want to be certain that in defining your terms you address the client's needs.

Examples An example is a single instance that develops a general statement.[8] If you make the assertion that product *x* serves a variety of purposes, you need to give examples of those purposes. If you are unable to provide examples to support your generalizations, listeners will think you either do not know what you are talking about or are being deceitful. Suppose that a person in your class says, "I've got a lot of job offers." If he has a difficult time answering when you ask what companies made the offers, what do you think?

Examples are excellent ways to develop ideas and provide proof for them, particularly if they are *real* examples. You can also use *hypothetical* examples, which are things that have not actually occurred but potentially could happen. The advantage of using hypothetical examples is that you can tailor them to the specific group of listeners. The classmate who claims to have had a lot of job offers is a hypothetical example. Hypothetical examples can be somewhat less persuasive because listeners can always say, "But that never happened." Both real and hypothetical examples help maintain the audience's attention, especially if you have drawn on examples that your listeners can identify with.

Stories A story is essentially a more detailed example. Stories grab attention because they create an element of suspense. People want to hear the ending—they want to know how things turned out. There are some important guidelines you need to consider when using stories to support main points. First, the story should make a point that is relevant to your topic and the situation. A story that makes an irrelevant point may confuse listeners as they try to figure out what it has to do with your topic. They will look for a connection that is not there, and they may draw incorrect inferences about how the story relates to the matter you are discussing. Second, the story needs to be adapted to the listeners. The language of the story, the point of the story need to be appropriate for your audience. One of the authors was teaching a public speaking class one semester in which a student incorporated a story into her speech. She told the story exactly as it had happened. The unfortunate part of this is that it involved a great deal of obscene language. In the classroom context, the story was inappropriate, and it made the listeners uncomfortable. The speaker was quite surprised to get this reaction because to her this was a "cool" audience that wouldn't mind her use of language. We tell you this story to illustrate that your stories must be adapted to your listeners. (Imagine how inappropriate it would be if we told you this story and included the actual language the student had used!) And third, when you use stories as supporting materials, you should keep them fairly brief. A long story will make the audience restless, impatient for you to get to the point.

Quotations In the organizational context, you will generally be quoting experts to support an assertion you have made. When we talk about quotations as supporting materials, we are referring to stating word for word what an expert has said or paraphrasing an expert's statement. In either case it is important that your listeners perceive the source you are quoting to be expert. You may have to establish the qualifications of that source. Otherwise, it is no more effective to quote that individual than it is to quote your uncle Harry. The guidelines for using quotations are similar to those for including stories. Make sure the quotation is germane to your topic, that the quotation is appropriate for the listeners and the situation, and that it is not too long.

Statistics Statistics are numbers you can provide to support an idea. Numbers—particularly "bottom line" numbers—are often very convincing in the organizational context. In order to use numbers effectively, you need to have current statistics; that's where your research will help you. You also need to use reliable sources of statistics. Again, if your listeners do not view the source of your statistics as credible, then your numbers will not be persuasive. Try to phrase the statistics in terms that are understandable to your audience. If the members of your audience can handle complex calculations and it is necessary that you report them, go ahead. But most listeners will not have that degree of sophistication, so your goal is usually to state the numbers in simple terms. Most people understand percentages and ratios but do not understand logarithms or mathematical derivations. Finally, if it is necessary to provide listeners with many statistics, it is vital that you use a visual aid to present them. Chapter 9 will provide information about the use of visual aids.

Comparisons Another type of supporting material available to you is the comparison. Comparisons are used to show the similarities among people, things, or ideas. They are especially valuable when presenting your audience with a new idea, because you can help listeners understand the new idea by comparing it to one with which they are already familiar. In introducing an idea for a new product, then, you could compare it to a familiar product.

Descriptions Descriptions serve the function of helping listeners visualize a thing or idea or to understand its components. In a presentation on solar heating systems, the speaker could provide a description of the system and its component parts. Descriptions are often accompanied by visual aids because they assist listeners in picturing the thing being described.

Visual aids As mentioned earlier, we will discuss visual supporting materials in Chapter 9. We list them here, however, so you will remember that these, too, represent supporting materials that are available to help you explain, prove, and maintain attention to your main points.

Choosing Supporting Materials In preparing a presentation, you need to make certain that each of your main ideas is supported. Your goals are (1) to choose a variety of supports, (2) to adapt your supports to your listeners and situation, and (3) to include supports for each main point. First, you should use a variety of supporting materials because individuals respond differently to different types of supports. Some people seem to be convinced only by statistics; others prefer examples; and still others want to hear what the experts say. The greater the variety in your supports, the more listeners your presentation will appeal to. We have already discussed the second idea, adapting supports to listeners and the situation. Failure to do so may render the supports virtually useless. If people cannot relate to the supports, your presentation will not be convincing, nor will the audience pay attention. And third, each point must have supports. Try a couple of different types of supporting material for each main idea. If you have done an effective job of researching your topic, you should have a variety of types of support from which to choose.

Stage 4: Organizing Ideas

At this point in your preparation, you are ready to organize your ideas so that they can be understood. In the process of organizing, you may discover that some of the ideas you have listed do not fit in your outline. You need to cut out those points. Speakers sometimes make the mistake of trying to squeeze every bit of information into a presentation, whether it helps support the goal of the speech or not. If you have written a clear statement of your goal, it will help you determine what to leave in the presentation and what to eliminate. All of the ideas and supporting materials included in your presentation should support your goal. Anything that distracts your listeners from that goal does not belong in the presentation, no matter how interesting it seems. At L&L Associates, since the president's speech is an annual report, there is a lot of material to include. Those preparing the speech, however, must remember to cut out unnecessary ideas.

Keeping that in mind, you are ready to begin organizing your presentation. A presentation has three parts: an introduction, a body, and a conclusion. In the last section of this chapter we will discuss the introduction and conclusion. In this section we will focus on organizing the body of the presentation.

You probably already have a great deal of experience in preparing outlines. Let's review some main points about creating outlines, and then we'll examine the various patterns of organization available to you.

Principles of Outlining In a presentation, all ideas are not equal. Some ideas represent our main points—the key ideas that we want our listeners to understand, believe, be stimulated by, and so forth. Other ideas are actually subpoints that provide support for those main ideas, and still other ideas develop those subpoints. The format for an outline recognizes that ideas carry different weights; symbols used in the outline represent the varying levels of ideas. Thus, the outline looks like this:

I. Roman numerals represent your main points.
  A. Capital letters represent first-level subpoints.
    1. Arabic numerals represent second-level subpoints.
      a. Lowercase letters represent third-level subpoints.
        (1) Parentheses around arabic numerals represent fourth-level subpoints.
          (a) Lowercase letters in parentheses represent fifth-level subpoints.

In creating an outline, you must assign each of your ideas a corresponding symbol. You need to make certain that ideas you include as subpoints actually support and develop your main points. If they do not, they may confuse your listeners and distract them from the main point of your presentation. See Exhibit 8.5 for a sample outline for a presentation.

You can make any group of ideas look like an outline. Consider the following:

Exhibit 8.5 SAMPLE OUTLINE FOR PRESENTATION ON FEATURES OF ORGANIZATIONS THAT INFLUENCE THE COMMUNICATION PROCESS

I. Formal structure directs the flow of communication.
  A. Downward communication
    1. Functions
      a. Job instruction
      b. Job rationale
      c. Providing information
      d. Providing feedback
      e. Ideology
    2. Problems
      a. Insufficient information sent
      b. Wrong information sent
      c. Filtering
  B. Upward communication
    1. Functions
      a. Airing dissatisfactions
      b. Making suggestions
      c. Seeking information
    2. Problems
      a. Distortion
      b. Insufficient information sent
  C. Horizontal communication
    1. Functions
      a. Coordination
      b. Emotional and social support
      c. Problem solving
    2. Problems
      a. Competition
      b. Increased conflict
      c. Specialization
II. Informal communication networks compensate for formal channels.
  A. Definition of informal networks
  B. Functions of informal networks
    1. Emotional and social support
    2. Increase in willingness to cooperate
    3. Increase in member satisfaction
III. Organizational cultures provide guidelines for communication.
  A. Definition of organizational culture
  B. Communication and culture
  C. Adapting to cultures
    1. Listen carefully
    2. Observe others
    3. Fulfill roles

I. Communication flows in three directions in an organization.
   A. Historically, there have been three approaches to the study of organizations.
      1. Authoritarian leadership
      2. Democratic leadership
      3. Laissez-faire leadership
   B. Subordinates often distort information they send to superiors.
      1. Competition in organizations
      2. Lack of information sharing
II. There are two approaches to authority in the organization.

Although this looks like an outline, the ideas make no sense in relation to one another. Our point is that in order to create an effective outline, you must be certain that the points in that outline are *logically related.* It is not enough simply to utilize the format of an outline correctly. In the next section, we will examine six patterns of organization. In preparing your presentation, you need to choose a pattern of organization for your main points so that your ideas have an obvious logical relationship to one another.

Patterns of Organization Let's look at six patterns for organizing ideas. These patterns, which are modified from seven structures developed by Gerald Phillips and Jerome Zolten, are summarized in Exhibit 8.6.[9]

Time For some presentations, your main points represent the steps in a process or the chronology of events. Explaining a new manufacturing process to a group of employees or discussing the history of your organization would necessitate the use of a time pattern of organization. The president at L&L could use a time pattern to summarize the events of the past year for the annual report. The key to using the time pattern is to keep the main points in the proper order—the order that follows logically. If you discuss step 2 first, your listeners will be lost.

Space A spatial pattern is used when the speaker is trying to explain the parts of something, such as a machine or a system. Each of the main parts becomes a main point in the outline. As the speaker, your task is to describe

Exhibit 8.6 PATTERNS OF ORGANIZATION

1. Time
2. Space
3. Classification
4. Comparison and contrast
5. Problem and solution
6. Cause and effect

the relationship of each part to the other parts. The thing you are describing may not exist as a physical object; instead, it may be a system in a more figurative sense. For example, if you were given the task of describing the structure of your organization to a group of new employees, you would describe the organization chart with its various divisions and subdivisions. In this case you would be using a spatial pattern of organization in which the main divisions of the organization represent your main points. Note that it is important to describe the parts or divisions in relation to the other parts rather than as separate entities. If you described them as separate, the employees would not understand the connections between divisions and would not have a good sense of the workings of the organization.

Classification Some presentations focus on types or categories of things, people, or ideas. For instance, you might make a presentation on the types of services your company provides. Such a presentation is best organized by using the classification pattern. Each of the types or categories represents a main point in your outline. If you were giving a presentation on benefits that your company provides, you might organize your speech by types of benefits.

I. Health insurance benefits
II. Life insurance benefits
III. Retirement benefits

There are two important points to remember when using a classification pattern. First, the categories should not overlap. If they overlap, the listeners may confuse the categories. In our outline above, we would not want to include

IV. Hospitalization benefits

because that category overlaps the first one. Second, the categories need to be relatively equal in importance, size, and so on. You would not want to include the following categories:

I. Life insurance
II. Optometric coverage
III. Retirement benefits

The second category, optometric coverage, is not equivalent to the other two categories. It represents a small component of the larger category "health insurance benefits."

Comparison and contrast Another organizing pattern available to you is the comparison or contrast pattern. A presentation may be designed to show similarities or differences between two programs, policies, processes, or objects, or it may focus on both similarities and differences. In these instances you would use a comparison-contrast pattern. For example, if you wanted to persuade upper management that your proposal for a new vacation policy is superior to the present policy, you might want to organize your main points as follows:

New policy:	*Old policy:*
I. Flexibility	I. Flexibility
II. Cost-effectiveness	II. Cost-effectiveness
III. Employee satisfaction	III. Employee satisfaction

Obviously, you would be arguing that your new proposal is more flexible and more cost-effective and that it produces greater employee satisfaction than the present policy. In using this pattern of organization, be sure to talk about the flexibility of your new policy as compared to the old before you move on to discuss the cost-effectiveness of your policy. If you were to present your entire proposal first and then discuss the three points in relation to the old policy, the contrast would not be sharp enough. Listeners may have forgotten some of your points about the proposed policy and may therefore lose the focus of your argument.

Problem and solution You may often be in the position of speaking about a problem and a proposed solution to that problem. This fifth pattern of organization would be appropriate in those instances. How much time you spend describing the problem before discussing the solutions depends on the extent to which your listeners are already familiar with the problem. Sometimes the listeners do not even believe that a problem exists, and your task is first to convince them that one does before you can begin to try to sell them on your solution. On the other hand, if your listeners are acutely aware of the existence of the problem, you may have to say very little about the actual problem, and you can move right to your solutions.

Cause and effect Finally, your presentation may be designed to show the relationship or association between two conditions or events. For example, if management in your company is considering developing a new product line that you think will have positive consequences for the organization, your presentation could be organized using a cause-effect sequence in which you detail the beneficial effects of the new product line.

You may also organize a presentation as an effect-cause pattern, in which you first discuss the effects (some present condition or conditions) and then analyze the causes that produced those conditions. For instance, if sales had dropped for a service provided by your company, your presentation might focus on the possible causes of the decrease in sales.

As a speaker, you have these six patterns to choose from to organize your main points. If you select a pattern that is appropriate for your presentation goal and the ideas you have generated, you will be able to prepare an outline that not only looks like an outline—it lays out your ideas in a logically related order. As a consequence, your listeners will be able to follow your train of thought and will stand a better chance of understanding and accepting your message.

Stage 5: Preparing the Introduction and Conclusion

It is best to prepare the introduction and conclusion of your presentation after you have carefully worked out the outline of the body. Your introduction is designed to provide your listeners with a sense of what is to come, and your conclusion serves to restate main ideas. It is difficult to try to prepare either of them before you have completed the body of the presentation. In this section we will discuss the components of the introduction and conclusion.

The Introduction There are generally five parts to the introduction. Your analyses of your listeners and the situation will help you determine whether each of the five parts is necessary. The first part is the *attention getter.* As a speaker, you need to use some technique to focus the listeners' attention on the topic of the presentation. You are trying to interest the audience in your presentation so that they will listen to it and understand your message. If your listeners have high initial interest this is less of a concern, but if they are apathetic it is crucial that you interest them in the topic. There are a variety of techniques available for getting an audience's attention.

1. *Quotation* Reading a quotation to your audience can be an effective way to grab attention, especially if the quotation is eloquently phrased. Sometimes a person says something in such a unique and interesting way that the language used or the special perspective represented in the quotation enthralls an audience. When using a quotation as an attention getter, be sure that the quotation is both interesting and brief. If it is too long or it is not particularly eloquent, the quotation may be unsuccessful in capturing the listeners' attention.
2. *Humor* People enjoy witty remarks and humorous anecdotes. These can serve as attention-getting devices for a presentation, as long as they are used well. Humor has the potential to grab your audience's attention, but it also has the potential to offend listeners. You must be very careful in your choice of humorous remarks. Be sure that the remarks are appropriate for the audience and the occasion. And equally impor-

tant, the humor must make a point that is related to your topic or the speaking situation. Do not tell a joke about computers if your topic is advertising; your listeners will try to connect the joke to your topic. When they are unable to, they may spend time wondering whether they missed something.

3. *Visual aids* A picture, chart, graph, or other visual aid can be an effective way to capture the listeners' attention. In Chapter 9 we will discuss the effective use of visual aids. You should be sure to follow the guidelines in Chapter 9 when you use a visual aid as your attention getter.
4. *Startling facts* In doing research on your presentation topic, you may have discovered some interesting, perhaps startling, facts. These facts can serve as attention-getting devices. For example, beginning with a statistic that will surprise your listeners will certainly grab their attention. Your listener analysis will help you determine which facts your listeners are unlikely to know. If the audience already knows these facts, you will not succeed in creating an effect of surprise.
5. *Story* Just as a story can be used as supporting material, so it can be used as an effective attention getter. As long as the story is not too long and is relevant to your topic, the suspense it creates can be a very effective means of generating audience interest in your presentation.

This list of attention-getting devices is not exhaustive; rather, it presents some commonly used techniques. If you can think of additional strategies, you should experiment with them. Try various approaches in the classroom, where you are not risking a job or a promotion. You should avoid starting your presentation by saying, "My topic is. . . ." You have undoubtedly heard many speakers use this as an introduction, but if the listeners do not have high initial interest, they are likely to "tune out" when they hear what the topic will be. It makes the presentation sound as if it will be dull from the start.

The second part of the introduction is a statement to establish *common ground.* By common ground, we mean a connection between you, your topic, and your listeners. When people listen to a presentation, they are concerned with how the topic relates to them. You may even have said to yourself, "What does this have to do with me?" as you listened to a speaker. If people do not think the topic is relevant to their jobs or their lives, they are not likely to give it their full attention. For this reason, early in your presentation you want to make an attempt to establish common ground with your listeners. Tell them how your topic is relevant to them, how it will affect them, how they can use the information you provide, and so on. This is especially important if your listeners are not there voluntarily and are apathetic about your topic.

There will be times when this step is unnecessary. If your listeners have sought you out as a speaker because of your expertise on a particular topic, it is likely that they already have an interest in what you have to say. If you are explaining a new procedure to a group of employees who will have to follow the procedure every day on the job, you do not need to establish common ground. You may, however, have to convince them that the new procedure will make their lives easier, not more difficult.

The third component of the introduction is a *credibility-building statement.* When we use the term *credibility,* we are referring to your believability and trustworthiness as a speaker. In other words, your listeners must be convinced that you know what you are talking about and that they can trust you to tell them the truth, to have their interests at heart, and to care about them. If your listeners are people with whom you have a well-established relationship, you do not have to spend time convincing them that you are a credible source. On the other hand, if your listeners are not familiar with who you are, you need to provide them with information to establish your credibility. You can do this by explaining your experience with the topic. For example, "When I worked at company X I was in charge of this manufacturing process" is a statement that lets the listeners know that you have firsthand experience with the topic.

Establishing trustworthiness is not as easy. Attempting to establish common ground with your listeners, as we have suggested, is likely to enhance your credibility. The audience members will sense that you care enough about them to help them see a connection between themselves and the information you are giving.

The fourth task of the introduction is to provide a statement of your *main point.* Your main point is derived from the goal you set at the very beginning of your preparation. If you formulated a clear goal statement, then you know what it is you are trying to get across to your audience. One of the places in the presentation where you communicate this message is the introduction. A clear, concise statement of your main idea will give your listeners a sense of the direction of your presentation. You want the audience to know what your point is early on, so they do not sit there trying to guess what you have in mind.

There are times when it is important *not* to let your audience know what your main idea is until later in the presentation. One such time is when your audience is likely to be hostile to your idea or proposal. In this case, what you as the speaker need to do is take a more indirect approach to the presentation. Rather than stating your main point at the outset, you need to first build some support for your idea. For example, if you are making a presentation to a group of executives, you may not want to state at the outset that you want to suggest a new product the company should manufacture—especially if you think the executives will react very unfavorably to the idea. Instead, you first need to build support for the idea of the company moving into a new product line. Then you need to provide a case for the success of the product line you are proposing, still not stating what your specific proposal is. If you can persuade your listeners to agree that the company should consider a new product line, and if you can convince them that others have had great success with a particular line, you are ready to make your proposal. If you had presented your idea immediately, a hostile group of listeners would not have given your arguments and evidence a fair hearing.

Your listener analysis will help you determine whether to be direct or indirect in stating your main point in the introduction. In most cases, it will be most effective to be clear about your main idea. Sometimes, however, you may need to rely on a more indirect method.

The final part of the introduction is a *preview* of the body of the presentation. Here you are attempting to provide a kind of verbal outline of the presentation. If you are going to speak about the benefits of some software that your department is considering purchasing, end your introduction with a statement such as "There are five reasons why we should buy this software" or "This software has five important benefits." This helps your listeners see where you are going. They know they should listen for five reasons or five benefits. This makes it easier for them to listen, and it also creates the impression that you are very organized.

Remember that the introduction creates the first impression of you. It is therefore important that you be careful in the planning of it. If your introduction is offensive, confusing, dull, or incoherent, your audience will not give their full attention to the body of your presentation, no matter how carefully you have planned it.

The Conclusion The conclusion has two basic parts. The first is a *summary* of the main points of the presentation. You should review your main ideas from your outline—those ideas represented by roman numerals in your outline. The review should be brief, but reviewing is still necessary because your listeners do not have a document to refer to if they cannot remember what all of your main points were. If you discussed five benefits, for example, you need to restate those five benefits in your conclusion in order to remind your listeners of what they are.

The second part of the conclusion is a *restatement of your message.* In the introduction, you let your audience know what your point was, why you were speaking to them. To increase the chances that the audience will remember what your main message is, you need to restate it in the conclusion so it will be fresh in their minds when they leave. The wording needs to be similar to what you used in the introduction, but you should phrase your main point in a slightly different way in order to avoid being too redundant.

Speakers often seem to run out of steam when they reach the conclusion of their presentation. You have probably heard speakers end by saying, "That's it." The conclusion is your last opportunity to leave your audience with a favorable impression of you and your message, so be sure to take advantage of it. Try to be as enthusiastic about your conclusion as you are about your introduction.

PERSUASIVE PRESENTATIONS

When we speak in public, we can attempt to change what people know, what they believe, or what they do. Traditionally, presentations are classified as persuasive or informative. Actually, all speeches contain information and all speeches seek to make some kind of change in the listener. Even a classroom lecturer must persuade her listeners that the information presented is worth having. However, there are times when the explicit purpose of a presentation is to change what the audience believes or to give them good reasons to change their behavior. When giving this kind of speech in an organizational setting, it is important to keep in mind some important persuasive principles.

Persuasive Objectives

There are three persuasive objectives: to influence opinion, to impress, and to actuate. The presentation to influence opinion seeks intellectual agreement. For example, at L&L Associates, the manager of corporate communications could give a presentation in which his objective would be to persuade company vice presidents that his unit is performing effectively. This type of presentation is composed mainly of factual evidence or authoritative opinion, but to be successful the presentation must be adapted to the listeners. It must show why the opinion change is important, both to the individual and to the organization.

The presentation to impress focuses on feelings and desires. The idea is to create a mood and leave a lasting impression on the listeners. In an organization, this kind of speech is often used to boost morale; for example, its goal may be to relax tensions about an impending corporate merger or to get the employees excited about a forthcoming sales campaign.

The presentation to actuate seeks some action from the listeners. Fundraising speeches fall into this category, as do virtually all sales speeches. At L&L Associates, if the vice president of operations delivers a presentation to convince her superiors to make changes in company policies, she is speaking to actuate.

Note that all three objectives are often found in a single presentation. To get listeners to make a donation, for example, they must be convinced there is a good reason to do so and they must be emotionally moved to take out the billfold. Information must also be given; for example, the listeners must be told where to send the money.

Persuasive Appeals

Effective persuasive presentations must be carefully adapted to the audience. One way you can adapt your persuasive message to your listeners is through careful selection of your persuasive appeals. For example, people are concerned with money and goods; with recreation and pleasant experiences; with safety, with status, and with loyalty to the organization, friends, and family. As a persuasive speaker, you must locate the most relevant appeals and use them to motivate the listeners to believe, to feel, or to take action. Conducting the kind of audience analysis we described earlier in this chapter can help you select the appropriate appeals.

Effective persuasive presentations also must be specific. In political campaigns the candidates may have to remain general in their appeals. In business organizations, however, it is usually important that listeners be told exactly what they are to believe or to do. Employees are often quite cynical, and they tend to be skeptical of speakers who deal in glib generalities. Many people understand the power of propaganda and are particularly cautious when they hear someone expressing a point of view that differs from their own.

In order to be truly effective, a persuasive speaker must establish credibility. The speaker's reputation and position are particularly important in persuasion, but the presentation itself can contribute to this authority. Thus, in delivering persuasive speeches, you must take care to be accurate, considerate, interesting, and literate. Any flaw in the presentation will cast doubt on the speaker, which in turn will influence the effectiveness of the presentation. Audiences respond well to speakers who exhibit conviction, integrity, intelligence, and forcefulness. Speakers who show an audience that the cause they represent is personally important to them as well as to their audience are most likely to be effective. It is also important for a speaker to convey the impression of fairness and humaneness. A persuasive speaker cannot prove a point "beyond the shadow of a doubt"; therefore, it is important to make a good impression. A good speaker is not afraid to concede a point, because that will only contribute to the appearance of being ethical and honest.

Persuasive speaking requires the speaker to use fact and opinion and to draw inferences from evidence. Depending upon the evidence, a speaker may make statements with more or less certainty. Subjective statements are verifiable only by the person making them; thus, effective persuaders rely on evidence that can be shared with the audience. People generally do not respond to appeals whose message is "Do this because I say so." Instead, they tend to trust speakers who seem to be saying, "Here are experiences we have in common, and here are the conclusions that logically flow from them."

Responsible use of opinion precludes appeals to prejudice. Responsible opinion is based on current and cogent information drawn from a variety of sources. The speaker should have a store of information and select from it ideas that are relevant to the listeners. With the background information at hand, the speaker will be prepared to answer questions and meet objections. When citing other sources, the persuasive speaker must trust their authority. Above all, the speaker must avoid fallacies the opposition could seize upon. Sweeping generalizations and clichéd appeals to tradition or the American way of life can damage a speaker's credibility.

Obviously, to secure audience agreement or action, a speaker should appeal to the listeners' motives. She is more likely to secure a favorable response if she can show that the idea she is advancing will satisfy some compelling personal wish, need, or desire. Some of the most important needs are for self-preservation, self-esteem, social approval, helpfulness, competition, and acquisitiveness.

Self-preservation stems from the emotion of fear and represents the desire of people to protect themselves from any form of danger. An effective persuasive speaker can show that his proposal would have a beneficial effect on the health and safety of his listeners. Self-esteem represents the desire to develop a satisfying self-image. It is what impels workers to want to do their jobs well and to avoid actions which would endanger the organization and cast blame upon them. Self-esteem may also motivate individuals to be dissenters, to go against the consensus. Effective persuaders attempt to show their listeners that believing or acting in a certain way will enhance their image in the organization.

Social approval is closely tied to self-esteem. People conform to accepted norms of behavior not only because they need to think well of themselves, but also because they want others to think well of them. People seek the approval of others to gratify their own egos. Whatever its basis, social approval is an important motive. It can be used to persuade people to be honest, to work hard, and to be loyal to the organization.

Helpfulness and altruism is stronger in some people than in others, but most people like to believe that what they do is important and useful to others. The psychologist Alfred Adler believed that the desire to do useful work was one of the most important constituents of sanity. Effective persuasive speakers convince their audiences that accepting the ideas advanced would be in the common good.

Many people are competitive. The motivation to compete and win can be used to inculcate team spirit and to get people excited about serving the organization. People are aroused by a challenge; they are impelled to match their strength and intelligence with those of others.

Acquisitiveness is a very important motive. People want more money, more goods, time off, benefits, and other advantages associated with working and competing. Showing audiences that adopting the speaker's ideas will advance their economic interests is a very effective tactic.

The persuasive speech is prepared the same way as any other speech. It differs from other types of speeches only in content. The persuasive speaker must seek an explicit objective, adapt his or her ideas to the audience, and prepare a careful outline that includes many forms of support. It is especially important for a persuasive speech to sustain interest. This can best be done by careful adaptation and a simple outline. A fluent and dynamic presentation is also very helpful, as we will see in Chapter 9.

SUMMARY

In this chapter we have introduced you to the various types of presentations given in organizations, and we have taken you through the five stages of preparation. A public presentation is any type of face-to-face or mediated communication in which one or more speakers have the primary responsibility of presenting a message to one or more listeners. Presentations can take many forms, and most organization members must make presentations in fulfilling the requirements of their jobs.

Regardless of the type of presentation, a speaker needs to go through five stages of preparation. First, the speaker must set a goal for the presentation in order to have a clear idea of what he is trying to accomplish. If the speaker is unclear about the objective of the presentation, planning will be difficult and, in addition, the audience will probably not know what the speaker's point is.

Second, speakers must conduct an analysis of the listeners and the situation. The speaker is trying to assess how much knowledge and interest the listeners have about the topic as well as their position on the topic. The purpose of this kind of analysis is to enable the speaker to adapt the presentation to the listeners and the situation.

Third, the speaker must generate ideas and supporting materials. This includes conducting research on the topic and choosing a variety of types of supporting materials, such as definitions, examples, stories, quotations, statistics, comparisons, descriptions, and visual aids.

Fourth, the speaker needs to create an outline to organize the ideas and materials she has gathered. This involves deciding on the pattern of organization that best fits the ideas the speaker intends to present. The speaker chooses an organizing pattern and orders ideas; topics can be organized in terms of time, space, classification, comparison and contrast, problem and solution, or cause and effect. Which the speaker chooses depends on the main point she is trying to communicate and which pattern best seems to fit the ideas she has generated.

Fifth and last, the speaker plans the introduction and conclusion. The introduction has five basic parts: an attention-getting device, a statement of common ground, a statement to establish the speaker's credibility, the main point of the presentation, and a preview of the contents of the body. The conclusion consists of a summary and a restatement of the main point of the presentation.

Sometimes presentations are explicitly persuasive. In preparing a persuasive presentation, the speaker needs to identify his or her objectives. There are three persuasive objectives: to influence opinion, to impress, and to actuate. Sometimes persuasive presentations involve all three objectives.

Effective persuasive presentations are carefully adapted to the audience through appropriate choice of persuasive appeals. Speakers need to incorporate specific appeals, to establish their credibility, and to appeal to the listeners' motives. Some important motives to which speakers can appeal are self-preservation, self-esteem, social approval, helpfulness, competition, and acquisitiveness.

CHAPTER 8 ACTIVITIES

1. Attend a speech or lecture and listen carefully. Take notes on the following points:
   a. The speaker's goal or purpose. What was the speaker trying to accomplish?
   b. The organizational pattern of the speech. Was it clear?
   c. Supporting materials used. What types were used? Were they effective?
   d. Introduction. Were the five parts evident? Was it effective?
   e. Conclusion. Did the speaker summarize and restate the main point? What kind of impression did the speaker leave?
   f. Overall impressions. Did the speaker appear to be well prepared? Was the presentation clear and easy to follow? Was it interesting?

2. Generate a list of topics about which you could make a presentation. For each one, narrow down the topic and write a goal statement.

3. Conduct a listener analysis of your classmates. Select a speech topic (perhaps one you generated in activity 2) and answer each of the following questions:
   a. How much knowledge do my listeners have about the topic?
   b. How much interest do they have in the topic?
   c. What is their position on my topic?

CHAPTER 8 NOTES

1. Ronald B. Adler, *Communicating at Work: Principles and Practices for Business and the Professions,* 2nd ed., New York: Random House, 1986, p. 254.
2. Gerald M. Goldhaber, *Organizational Communication,* 4th ed., Dubuque, IA: Brown, 1986, p. 352.
3. Adler, p. 255.
4. Goldhaber, p. 349.
5. Adler, p. 351.

6. See Eugene E. White, *Practical Public Speaking,* 3rd ed., New York: Macmillan, 1978, pp. 29–30, 67–75.
7. Ibid., pp. 67–75.
8. Lynne Kelly and Arden K. Watson, *Speaking with Confidence and Skill,* New York: Harper & Row, 1986, p. 190.
9. See Gerald M. Phillips and J. Jerome Zolten, *Structuring Speech: A How-to-Do-It Book About Public Speaking,* Indianapolis: Bobbs-Merrill, 1976.

CHAPTER

9

Delivering Public Presentations

Once a presentation has been prepared, its success depends on effective delivery. Although careful preparation does not guarantee good delivery, a poorly planned message, even if well delivered, is not likely to be effective. It is important that you devote time to both aspects of a presentation—preparation and delivery—if you want to increase the chances that you and your message will be well received.

In Chapter 8 we presented the stages of preparation, up to the point where you have a complete outline with introduction, body, and conclusion. That is not the end of your preparation, however. Additional work is required to prepare for the delivery of that presentation. In this chapter we will discuss the stages of preparing to deliver a presentation. Because it is the delivery of the message that often creates nervousness and tension, we will address the issue of speech apprehension and methods for coping with it. Then we will focus on the actual delivery of the message in the last section of this chapter. Although delivering a presentation can create anxiety, it is also stimulating and sometimes even fun! We cannot convince you of that; you have to experience it for yourself. The course you are taking should provide you with opportunities for delivering presentations, so you can find out for yourself just how exciting it can be to be in front of an audience.

PREPARING TO DELIVER A PRESENTATION

Up to this point in the process, your preparation has consisted of the development and organization of ideas for the introduction, body, and conclusion of your presentation. In this section we will take you through additional stages of preparation that are designed to get you ready for the delivery of your carefully planned message. There are four stages of preparation: deciding on a delivery method, preparing notes, preparing visual aids, and rehearsing.

Stage 1: Deciding on a Method of Delivery

In the classroom context you may be assigned a particular method of delivery to use, but in the organizational environment that decision will be up to you. There are four methods of delivery from which you can choose. We will discuss each of these methods and their advantages and disadvantages (which are summarized in Exhibit 9.1).

Impromptu Speaking *Impromptu speaking* is essentially unplanned, unrehearsed speech. Although there will be times when you are forced to use this method of delivering a message—for example, in an L&L Associates meeting you may be asked to discuss something that you did not anticipate—it is generally not the method of choice. If you have done the kind of planning we discussed in Chapter 8, you cannot use the impromptu method of delivery for your presentation; you are already much too prepared. But if your project head at L&L Associates were to come to you and say, "Brief me on the status of your

Exhibit 9.1 METHODS OF DELIVERY

Method	Advantages	Disadvantages
Impromptu speaking	Natural delivery style. Little time is invested. Audience is less critical.	Lack of preparation can be unnerving. Potential for disorganization. Lack of polish in delivery.
Extemporaneous speaking	Preparation results in clear organization. Can include supporting materials. Flexibility.	Imprecise language. Speaker may forget points.
Manuscript speaking	Precise language. Can time speech in advance.	May increase nervousness. May be dull and lifeless. Inflexibility.
Memorized speaking	Can maintain eye contact.	Potential to forget. Increases nervousness.

project," your oral progress report would constitute impromptu speaking. You would have had essentially no time to prepare. Because you will have to do impromptu speaking, let's examine its advantages and disadvantages and how to handle it most effectively.

Advantages A major advantage of impromptu speaking is that the speaker tends to use a very natural style in presenting the message. Sometimes people become very stiff and awkward in delivering a fully prepared presentation. The spontaneity that impromptu speaking requires can work to the speaker's advantage. The speaker may be more conversational and natural. This is in part due to the fact that the audience tends to be more relaxed and less critical. The audience knows the presentation is being given "off the cuff."

A second advantage is that impromptu speaking doesn't require the time investment that other methods of delivery require, because there is not extensive planning. Obviously, however, the individual has spent time in becoming familiar with the topic, and that is time invested.

Disadvantages The lack of preparation can be unnerving. You may prefer the security provided by careful preparation to the thrill of speaking "off the cuff." For some people, however, this is not a disadvantage, because they do not have time to get too nervous if they are unaware that they will be speaking until the moment of the presentation.

A second disadvantage of impromptu speaking is the potential for giving a disorganized, incoherent presentation without a clear main point. Many speakers tend to wander through a maze of ideas, never leading to a specific main point. Impromptu speaking does not have to result in a disorganized message, but it often does because the speaker did not have time to prepare.

A final disadvantage is the lack of polish in the delivery itself. An unprepared speaker may stumble over more words and may phrase ideas less precisely than a fully prepared speaker would.

Handling impromptu speaking The best way to handle impromptu speaking situations is to try to anticipate them so that you have time to organize your thoughts. For example, if you have been working in the L&L Associates simulation on a project that may become a topic at a staff meeting, organize your ideas about the project so that you could present a coherent update on the project if called upon to do so. If you are asked to speak but are unprepared, you may want to request time to gather your thoughts. You might want to suggest that the chair of the meeting get back to you in a few minutes if you think you need the time to prepare your message. If that is impossible, then as quickly as you can, select a main point to convey. State the point first and then elaborate it as needed. Try to use preview statements, as you would in a prepared presentation. You might say, for example, "We decided to purchase software package X for three reasons. First. . . ." This will not only keep you organized in your thinking—it will help your listeners understand your message.

Extemporaneous Speaking A second method of delivery is *extemporaneous speaking.* This refers to speaking from carefully planned notes. The presentation is not written out word for word, however. Instead, the speaker has a well-prepared outline of ideas and has rehearsed the presentation, but she chooses the exact wording of those ideas during the presentation. Most of your teachers use an extemporaneous method of delivery. They have lecture notes prepared, but they do not read the notes to you. The specific way in which they phrase an idea is generated as they speak. At L&L Associates, employees use the extemporaneous method of delivery most frequently, for the same reason instructors often opt for it: to be prepared enough to cover the important points, but flexible enough to adapt to the needs of the listeners at the moment. We believe this is usually the best method for delivering a presentation because its advantages outweigh the disadvantages.

Advantages First, the speaker is well prepared, so the extemporaneous presentation is organized and clear. The speaker has had the time to carefully prepare an outline of main points and subpoints and to make sure that those points are logically related.

Second, the speaker has been able to prepare supporting materials to help develop and support opinions and ideas. He has had the opportunity to select a variety of supports, to conduct research to obtain additional supports as needed, and to tailor the supports to the specific group of listeners.

Third, the speaker is able to adapt an extemporaneous presentation as the situation and listeners demand. Because the message is not written word for word, the speaker has some flexibility in how he chooses to present it. On-the-spot changes are possible and may even be necessary. Thus, the extemporaneous method of delivery combines careful planning with a certain degree of flexibility and spontaneity.

Disadvantages One disadvantage of the extemporaneous method of delivery is the potential to make inaccurate and ineffective language choices. Because the speaker chooses language as she delivers the message, those word choices are not always the best way to express an idea. Speakers sometimes use the wrong word or a less precise word than they would have had they written the message. A second disadvantage is that speakers may stumble over words and forget points they want to make. This is because extemporaneous speaking requires a speaker to think on the spot.

In spite of these disadvantages, we think you should usually use an extemporaneous method of delivery. With sufficient rehearsal, you can overcome the disadvantages and benefit from the advantages. This method will allow you to be conversational yet organized, flexible yet prepared.

Manuscript Speaking The *manuscript speaking* method of delivery involves reading a presentation that is completely written out ahead of time. At L&L Associates, the president's speech will be a manuscript speech because it will become part of the company's annual report. This means the president will have to read the manuscript without deviating from the printed page. Like all other methods, this method of delivery has advantages and disadvantages.

Advantages First, the speaker is completely prepared. Even the exact language he will use is determined in advance of the presentation. Thus, the speaker can potentially deliver the message smoothly and articulately. When the specific language choices are crucial, the manuscript method of delivery may be most appropriate. In presenting the annual report to the board, the president of L&L Associates will use manuscript delivery for this very reason.

A second advantage of manuscript speaking is that the speaker can time the presentation during rehearsal and will know almost precisely how long it will take to deliver the message. When you give presentations, you will almost always have time limitations that you cannot exceed, as we discussed in Chapter 8. By knowing how long your presentation is, you can avoid the problem of trying to cut material on the spot.

Finally, having the manuscript provides some speakers a sense of security that they don't feel when speaking from an outline. This is not the case for all speakers, however. If you are very apprehensive about speaking to a group of people, the manuscript makes it too easy for you to continue thinking about yourself and how nervous you are. You barely have to think about what you are saying when you read your presentation. If you are speaking from notes, however, and must formulate your words as you go along, you are unable to concentrate on yourself. By focusing on what you have to say rather than how you are feeling, you will be able to relax more.

Disadvantages The first disadvantage of the manuscript delivery method is that it may not help some speakers to relax, even though they think it will. Because they do not have to think about the words being read, speakers who read from manuscripts can continue to focus on themselves throughout their presentations.

The second disadvantage is that reading a manuscript can lead to a dull, lifeless presentation. The speaker must be able to read expressively; otherwise, she may sound monotonous and may become unresponsive to the listeners. You have undoubtedly heard speakers using manuscript delivery who were difficult to listen to. When audience members aren't listening, they aren't understanding the message.

The third disadvantage is the inflexibility of a manuscript presentation. Only experienced speakers seem to be able to deviate from their manuscripts when it is clearly necessary. Less experienced speakers tend to drone on, even when the audience needs a change of pace or clarification of an idea.

If you practice reading aloud and reading for expression, you may become successful at the manuscript method of delivery. Just because the presentation is written does not mean practice is not necessary. Rehearsal is required in order to be able to read the presentation with expression and in order to be able to maintain some eye contact with the listeners. If you intend to use this method of delivery, be sure to double- or triple-space the manuscript to make it easier to read. Also, you have to be careful to use an oral style of writing, writing that is easy to understand when read aloud. In an oral style of writing you use simpler sentences rather than more complex sentences that are difficult for the listener to follow. You also use more transitions between ideas so that listeners can follow the pattern of organization. You need to make clear statements throughout the manuscript—for example, "The first issue is overtime compensation." As you prepare a manuscript, try reading it aloud to a friend in order to find out how it sounds and whether it is clear.

Memorized Speaking The last delivery method you can choose is *memorized speaking.* We will discuss this method only briefly because we advise against its use. This method involves committing the presentation to memory and reciting it. The only advantage to memorization is that the speaker can maintain good eye contact and can present a thoroughly prepared message. Most people cannot handle this method because of the anxiety that is created by not working from notes. The fear of forgetting what to say overwhelms speakers and brings on the very thing they fear. Once a speaker forgets, it is nearly impossible to continue the presentation. Therefore, unless you have an exceptional memory or are required to use this method of delivery, we suggest that you rely on either the extemporaneous method or the manuscript method.

Stage 2: Preparing Notes

Deciding on a delivery method will help you determine what type of notes you need to prepare. For an impromptu presentation, you may have no notes at all, or you might have a couple of ideas you scribbled on a notepad; for a memorized presentation, you will not use notes. In this section, therefore, we will discuss how to prepare notes for the extemporaneous presentation and will provide some suggestions for getting a manuscript ready for the manuscript method of delivery.

Preparing Notes for Extemporaneous Delivery Although some people can speak directly from the outline they completed during preparation, most people need to prepare a new set of notes to make delivery smoother. In this section we will look at several guidelines for preparing your notes. Keep in mind as we discuss these that your primary concern is to develop notes that are useful to you. Notes that do not make sense when you look at them or that are difficult to read will hinder your delivery rather than help it.

Before we can discuss guidelines, we need to mention options you have for your notes. You need to select either index cards or paper. If you do not have a preference, we would advise using 3- by 5-inch or 4- by 6-inch index cards. Cards have several advantages over sheets of paper. Cards are stiff, so they don't rattle and they can be handled more easily than paper. The size of cards also prevents the speaker from putting too much information on them. The problem with paper is that if you put a great deal of information on one sheet, you may be unable to find your place when you look at the paper during the presentation. When you finish with a card, you can slip it to the back of your set of cards. You can do the same with paper, but it can't be done as unobtrusively. Finally, if you end up in a speaking situation in which you do not have access to a lectern, it is much easier to work with index cards. They are small enough to hold in one hand, and they won't flop around and distract your audience.

The following guidelines apply whether you decide to use index cards or sheets of paper. Each of these guidelines is designed to make the process of delivery as smooth as possible.

1. Set up separate cards or sheets for the introduction and conclusion of your presentation and label them clearly. Exhibit 9.2 presents a sample index card for the introduction of a presentation. Note the clear heading indicating that this is the introduction. Putting the introduction and conclusion on separate cards serves as a signal to you. You will know when you are about to move into the body of the presentation, and you will be forewarned when the conclusion is next. This may sound unnecessary, but when delivering a presentation, you will need signals of this kind to help you keep track of where you are in the presentation. This is vital if you discover that you are running out of time and have to cut out parts of the body. You can move quickly and easily to the conclusion because it is on a separate card or sheet with a clear heading.
2. In general, do not write out full sentences on your cards unless you need to read a quotation. If you write out complete sentences, you

Exhibit 9.2 SAMPLE INDEX CARD FOR INTRODUCTION

```
INTRODUCTION
    I. Attention getter: Sales of widgets down
       10 percent.
   II. Common ground: Lower sales affect all of us
       and threaten job security.
  III. Credibility: As general sales manager, I have
       seen this situation before and turned it
       around. Tell 1982 story.
   IV. Main point: We must take action. I have
       several solutions that will work.
    V. Preview: Begin with discussion of causes of
       problem and suggest three potential solutions.
```

may be tempted to read them. (You should select a manuscript speaking style, not extemporaneous speaking, if you want to read your presentation.) Instead of complete sentences, you should put down words and phrases. They should be sufficient to cue you—you'll find out if they do when you rehearse with your notes. You'll discover that some notes have to be rewritten because when you look at them they do not let you know what your next point is. Note on the sample card in Exhibit 9.2 that phrases are used to cue the speaker.

3. Carefully label all parts of the body of your presentation. Your notes need to indicate which are your main ideas and which ideas support those main points. You can use the symbols from your original outline for this. Exhibit 9.3 shows a card with one main point from the body of a presentation. Note that the card contains the first main point, indicated by the symbol I.

   You should also take note of the transition indicated on the card. *Transitions* are words, phrases, and sentences that signal to the listener (and the speaker) when the speaker is moving to a new idea. Transitions also indicate the relationships between ideas. Note the transition the speaker is using in Figure 9.3 to indicate that this is the first main point.

4. Be sure to provide enough detail for the supporting materials you are using. If you are using statistics, list them on the card and label what they represent. If you are using a quotation, put the entire quotation in your notes. If you are using examples and stories, pro-

Exhibit 9.3 INDEX CARD FROM BODY OF PRESENTATION

```
BODY
  Transition: The first feature of an organization is its
              formal structure.
  I. Formal Structure: Directs the flow of communication.
     Three directions: downward, upward, horizontal.
     A. Downward communication
        1. Five functions
           a. Job instruction--how to do specific tasks.
              Example: data entry.
           b. Job rationale--why specific tasks? Example:
              why data entry must follow specific format.
           c. Information--company policies, rules, and
              regulations. Example: retirement benefits.
           d. Feedback--review employees' performance.
              Story: my first performance review.
           e. Ideology--promote identification with company.
              Example: put birthdays in newsletter.
```

vide enough detail about them to enable you to give the audience the whole thing. Supporting materials are an important part of your presentation, so your notes need to help you remember them. In Exhibit 9.3, you can see the supporting materials clearly indicated on the card.

5. Number your index cards or sheets of paper. This is useful in two ways. First, you can quickly and easily correct the order of your notes. Cards are dropped, they fall off lecterns, and so on. This is not a catastrophe if the speaker can put them back in order in a hurry. Second, the numbers at the top of the card can help you with the timing of your presentation. If you have 15 cards and you are on number 5 with only five minutes left, you know you have to quicken your pace or make some snap decisions about which ideas or supporting materials to leave out.
6. Be sure to rehearse with your notes. We will discuss rehearsal later in this chapter, but for now we want to emphasize the importance of practicing with the actual notes you intend to use. You will invariably discover that the notes need to be revised in order to make them more helpful to you.

Preparing a Manuscript If you are going to use the manuscript method of delivery, you need to prepare the manuscript carefully. Once again, your primary concern is with preparing a manuscript that enhances your delivery. A manuscript that is difficult to read and causes you to stumble defeats the purpose of using this method of delivery. Let's look at three guidelines for manuscript preparation.

1. Your manuscript must be typed in order to make it easier to read. With the word-processing capabilities of personal computers, you can use large type to make the manuscript even easier to read. Be sure to at least double-space the document. (Both of these suggestions are designed to enable you to read the manuscript without losing your place.)
2. You need to develop a system of markings to indicate words you should emphasize, where you should pause, and so on. People who orally interpret literature (read aloud to audiences) use these kinds of markings to help them present the reading as expressively as possible. You do not have to use any particular system of markings; what is important is your ability to interpret the markings. You will need to indicate where you should pause to emphasize a point you just made; you will want to mark words to emphasize; and you may want to mark where to speed up, where to slow down, and where to change the mood of what you are reading.
3. You should carefully rehearse your presentation so that you become familiar enough with it to be able to maintain some eye contact with your listeners as you deliver your message. Even a well-read manuscript will not be effective if the speaker does not look at the audience. It is eye contact that helps a speaker engage and involve the listeners in the message.

Stage 3: Preparing Visual Aids

Now that you have selected a method of delivery and prepared your notes, you need to consider whether you need to use visual aids, and if so, what kinds. A *visual aid* is anything that you *show* the listeners to supplement the ideas you are presenting. Visual aids enable the audience members to see what you are discussing so that they can more readily grasp the meaning of what they hear. Some types of visual aids—including tables, graphs, and pictograms—are often referred to as *graphic aids.*[1] In this section we will discuss how to determine whether you should use visual aids, and we will discuss different types of visual and graphic aids and guidelines for their effective use.

Determining the Need for Visual Aids All too often, speakers do not use visual aids when they ought to, or they use aids when they do not need them. In either case it is distracting to the listeners. As you go through your outline and prepare your notes, you need to ask yourself a basic question: "Are there any ideas I will be conveying that would be clearer, more interesting, or easier to grasp if I used a visual aid?" If, after careful thought, your answer is "no," then you should not use a visual aid.

In most presentations, the answer to that question is "yes." If the speaker plans to present statistics as supporting materials, those statistics will be more easily grasped if they appear on a visual aid. When a speaker needs to explain a model, it is much more effective to display the model in some way. In discussing foreign countries, the speaker should identify those countries on a map, particularly if they are not well known.

In general, if you plan to present complicated material, a visual aid may make your presentation much more effective. If you need your listeners to visualize a place or object or system, you should use a visual aid. If you have many statistics to share with your audience, you can present them more easily with a visual aid.

If you think you need to use a visual aid, your next consideration is what type of aid to use. Let's discuss some of the types of visual and graphic aids.

Types of Visual and Graphic Aids There are a wide variety of visual and graphic aids from which to choose. While you are enrolled in a course, you have a great opportunity to practice with a variety of aids in order to broaden your experience. As a student in a course, you have to prepare all of your own visual aids; but when you are employed by an organization, you may have help from people in a graphics department who can prepare these materials for you. Just in case you don't have that luxury in the future, you should experiment with the preparation and use of many types of visual aids.

In the president's presentation at L&L Associates, the use of graphics will be important for two reasons. First, the visual aids will allow for orchestration of the president's manuscript speech. Second, the speech will become part of the company's annual report, and the graphics will be useful in the printed format.

Graphic aids Those visual aids that can be classified as graphic aids can be produced by computers if you have the proper software. Computers can quickly generate graphics that look very professional, so it is always preferable to use such facilities to prepare your graphic aids. If you don't know how, get help from your instructor or from other employees in your organization who know how to use graphics software packages. The time you invest in learning will be well worth the effort. Let's examine three types of graphic aids: graphs, pictograms, and tables.[2]

1. *Graphs* You have seen various types of graphs and you know how useful they can be for illustrating numerical data. There are three major types of graphs. The *circle graph* is also referred to as a *pie chart.*

Exhibit 9.4 presents a circle graph that illustrates a budget. The different-sized pieces of the pie indicate the components of the budget and the percentages of the budget allocated to those components.

Another type of graph is a *bar graph.* Bar graphs are usually used to show comparisons.[3] For example, the bar graph in Figure 9.5 provides a comparison of the sales of experienced versus inexperienced personnel. You frequently see bar graphs that compare quantities of some variable (number of babies born, number of homicides, and so on) for a series of years.

A third type of graph is a *line graph.* The line graph is usually

Exhibit 9.4 CIRCLE GRAPH REPRESENTING A BUDGET

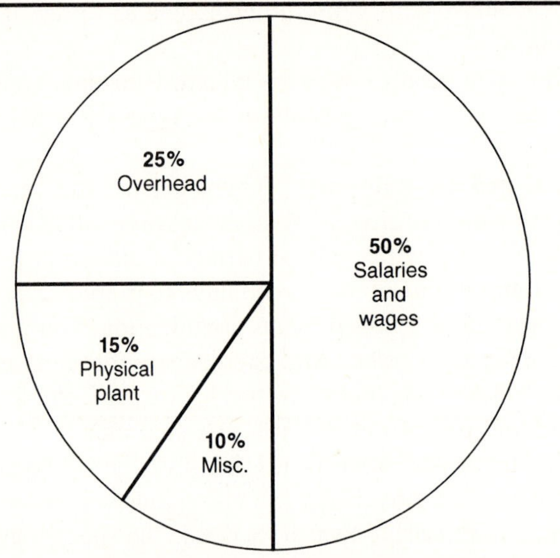

Exhibit 9.5 BAR GRAPH ILLUSTRATING SALES OF EXPERIENCED AND INEXPERIENCED SALESPEOPLE

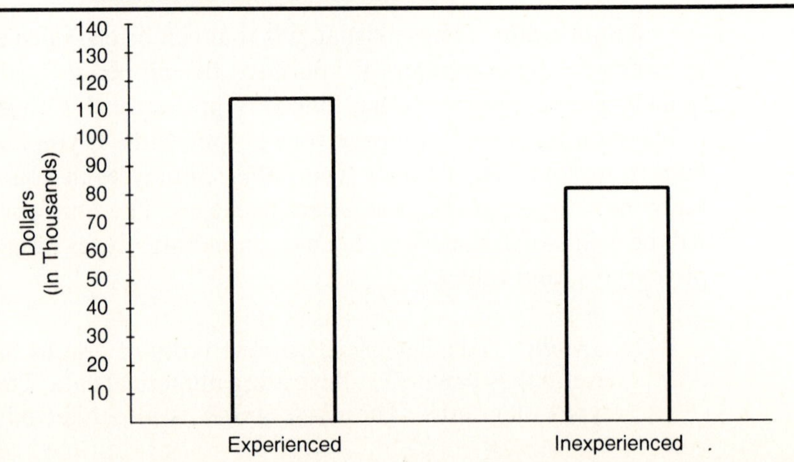

used to show trends, such as changes in traffic fatalities over time or changes in the quantity of sales of a particular product. Exhibit 9.6 is a line graph showing trends in the annual production levels of a company.

2. ***Pictograms*** *Pictograms* (also called *pictographs*) are similar to bar graphs, but they use pictures to illustrate percentages.[4] Exhibit 9.7

Exhibit 9.6 LINE GRAPH SHOWING AVERAGE YEARLY PRODUCTION RATES

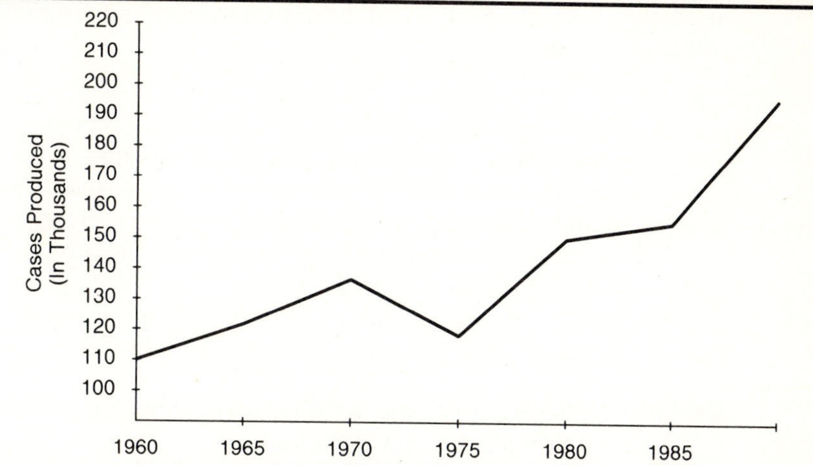

Exhibit 9.7 PICTOGRAM ILLUSTRATING PERCENTAGES OF TYPES OF CARS SOLD IN 1985

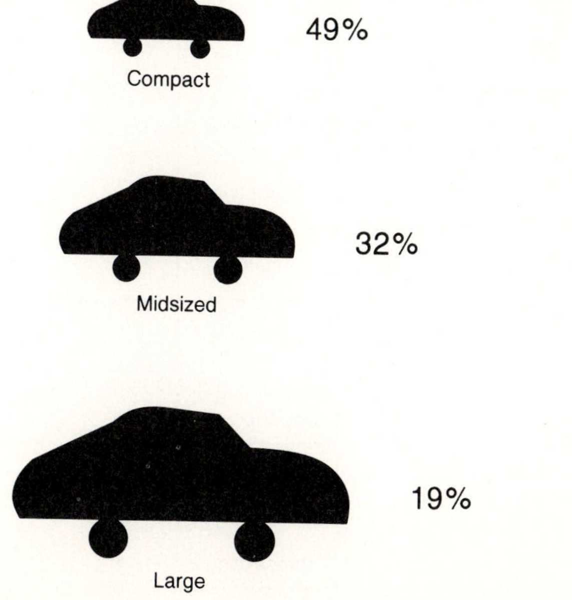

presents a pictogram that shows the percentages of compact, medium-sized, and large automobiles sold during 1985. The addition of the pictures makes this type of graphic aid very easy to read.

3. *Tables* A table is another way to present numerical data. If you wanted to present the average rate of employee turnover in departments of an organization, you could summarize that information in a table (see Exhibit 9.8).

Other visual aids In addition to the graphic aids we have discussed, there are many other types of visual aids. You should know something about some of these as well.

1. *Objects and props* In some presentations, you may want to display the actual object you are describing. For example, if you are explaining a new piece of equipment to a group of employees, it makes more sense to show them the equipment rather than try to describe it. This means that the object must be large enough for the group to see it and small enough for you to handle it.
2. *Models* A model may be a more appropriate choice than the actual object, and using a model is certainly more feasible in some cases. You

Exhibit 9.8 TABLE SHOWING AVERAGE RATES OF EMPLOYEE TURNOVER DURING A SIX-MONTH PERIOD

Average Rates of Employee Turnover Over a Six-Month Period	
Department	Number of Employees Replaced
Sales	35
Advertising	22
Marketing	8
Finance	4
Operations	11
Research and development	2
Personnel	5
Data processing	19

cannot display a huge piece of equipment during a presentation, but you might be able to display a model of the equipment. Architects use models on a daily basis, since it is so important to clients to see ahead of time what a building will look like. The model built to scale provides an excellent visual aid for the architect as she explains the structure to the client.

3. *Maps* Maps are commonly used visual aids. The people who report the weather on television rely on weather maps. Think how difficult it would be to visualize the location of an approaching storm without the map. If you wanted to present a group of executives with potential building sites, a map illustrating the location of those sites could be a very effective visual aid.
4. *Flip charts* A flip chart is a large tablet of paper. As the speaker discusses a point, he flips the page to display the next visual aid. Often the speaker puts main points on separate sheets. When he is ready to move to the next main point, he flips to the next sheet. In order to use a flip chart effectively, the speaker needs to have a stand to display the chart. A flip chart is too large and awkward to be used without a stand.
5. *Chalkboards* Sometimes the speaker finds that the old stand-by, the

Speakers often use flip charts when they have several visual aids to display.

chalkboard, is the only available visual aid. This is often the case when someone is called on to make an impromptu presentation during a meeting. You should avoid using the chalkboard if you have other alternatives; it is difficult to use the chalkboard well, and the presentation almost never appears professional. If the chalkboard is the only thing available to you, limit what you write on the board to just a few words, phrases, or drawings. Be sure to write large enough so the audience can see it, and avoid turning your back completely to the audience while you write. If you spend too much time writing on the board, you will lose the listeners' attention, particularly if you have your back to them. Be careful about where you stand as you explain what is on the board. Speakers often end up blocking the view of half of the people in the room.

6. *Electronic media* Speakers can also use videotapes, audiotapes, slide projectors, overhead projectors, and other electronic media as visual and audio aids. These should be used sparingly because otherwise they tend to dominate the presentation. Listeners focus more on the visual aid than on what you have to say. The key to effective use of electronic media is to know how to use the equipment and rehearse with it. There is nothing more distracting to a group of listeners than a speaker trying to figure out how to focus an overhead projector or how to display the slides right side up. Check your equipment before you use it, and be sure to check the room in which you'll be giving the presentation for outlets, lighting controls, and so forth. Electronic media can make a presentation appear to be very professionally done if they are used properly. But the speaker can look like a bumbling idiot if the equipment doesn't work or he doesn't know how to use it.

Guidelines for Effective Use of Visual Aids Regardless of the type of visual aid you decide to use, there are guidelines you need to follow to ensure that your visual aid is effective. Remember that the purpose of using a visual aid is to enhance understanding of your message and to maintain audience attention. Poorly handled visual aids will both confuse and distract your audience. Listeners will leave with the impression that you are either not competent or not well prepared. You are better off not using a visual aid than using one ineffectively. In this section we will examine seven guidelines for the effective use of visual and graphic aids.

1. Prepare visual aids as carefully as you prepare your oral presentation. If you are going to use visual aids, it is important that they look professional. Sloppy visuals will create a bad impression—that you did not prepare well or that you do not care about your presentation and your listeners. Professional-looking visual aids make a statement to your audience: they say that you are concerned about your message, yourself, and your listeners. So plan and prepare your

visual aids with care. Organizations usually have the necessary equipment and personnel to help you prepare professional visual aids. Once you become familiar with the facilities your organization has to offer, you will be able to produce first-class visual aids for your presentations.

2. Prepare visual aids so they can be seen by all members of the audience. We have all seen speakers display a chart with print that was too small for anyone to read, which detracts from the message. Keep in mind that all printing and drawing has to be large enough for people in the last row to see; all of the lines have to be dark enough and wide enough to be read or seen. The safest way to deal with this problem is to prepare your visual aid well in advance of your presentation, then take it to the location where you will give the presentation. Have some people sit in the back and tell you whether or not they can read the visual aid. If they cannot, then you know you need to rework the visual until it can be seen by everyone in your audience. If you decide to use an overhead projector, be careful of the size of the print you use; typewriter print will be too small for most groups of listeners.
3. Display visual aids only while you discuss them. Keep a visual or graphic aid out of sight until you are ready to discuss it. If you display it before the appropriate time, your listeners will pay attention to it rather than to whatever you are saying at the time. By the time you are ready to talk about the aid, they may be bored with it. So wait until you are ready to speak about whatever is on the visual aid. Then display it and talk about it, and then put it away.
4. Discuss the visual aid. You may have seen speakers with visual aids they never bothered to explain. This was probably because the visual was unnecessary to the presentation. If you decide that a visual aid is necessary, be sure to talk about it, and point to it as you discuss it. Otherwise, your listeners will be left wondering what the item was and why you displayed it.
5. Do not pass items around the audience. It is fairly common to see speakers who have a small visual aid pass it around the audience. In discussing a chip capacitor, for example, the speaker might be tempted to give it to the audience members to look at because it is too small to display. This is not an effective way to display a visual aid. As the listeners look at the object they are passing, they are not listening to what you are saying. There is a great deal of distraction in the audience when a speaker passes something around, and you'll quickly discover that almost no one is listening. The only time you should give an object intended as a visual to your audience is when you have one for each person. That way you can give them out, and when all the listeners have one, you can discuss the item.
6. Consider the visual aid from your listeners' point of view. Remember that your purpose in using visual aids is to make it easier for your listeners to understand the ideas you are conveying. Therefore, you

need to consider your visuals from the point of view of the audience. Is the aid too complicated for people to easily understand it? Is it placed where everyone in the audience can see it? Does it actually clarify ideas or help maintain listener attention? Is it in good taste, or might it be offensive to some members of the audience? Just as you considered your listeners when you prepared the content of your presentation, so you need to concern yourself with the audience as you prepare and use visual aids.

7. Rehearse with your visual aids. Sometimes a speaker who is very good about rehearsing oral presentations does not rehearse the use of visual aids. As a consequence, when giving the actual presentation, the speaker is awkward in the use of visuals. You need to do a complete rehearsal or two with your visual aids—if possible, in the location where you will do the presentation. You can perfect the timing and handling of your visual aids by rehearsing with them.

As you become experienced, you will discover that carefully prepared visual and graphic aids enhance your presentation if you use them effectively. For your classroom presentations, it is a good idea to practice with as many types of visuals as you can. If you are going to make any mistakes, you want to make them in the classroom, not when your job is at stake.

Stage 4: Rehearsing

The final stage in the process of preparing to deliver a presentation is rehearsal. We have already mentioned the importance of rehearsing, including rehearsing with visual aids. In this section we will offer some suggestions that will help you maximize the benefits of rehearsing. Before we discuss those suggestions, we need to mention the functions of practicing a presentation.

Functions of Rehearsal First, rehearsal will enable you to deliver your message more smoothly. It is always easier to do something that you've done before, and by rehearsing you will have that sense that you have given your presentation before.

Second, rehearsal increases your confidence. Because you have done this before, you can feel more self-assured. Reducing the sense of the unknown usually reduces apprehension. You know that you have given your presentation successfully and can do it again.

Third, rehearsal helps you commit your outline of ideas to memory, at least to some extent. You have a much clearer sense of where you are heading after you have practiced. As a result, you can concentrate on delivering the presentation in an enthusiastic manner; you don't have to worry so much about what comes next in the presentation. No director would ever think of letting the public see an unrehearsed play or a play that had not involved a dress rehearsal. You, too, need rehearsal, and in the next section we will offer some suggestions to help you rehearse.

Guidelines for Rehearsing There are five guidelines you should follow in rehearsing a presentation. Try using these guidelines for any classroom presentations you do. The guidelines should be helpful, although you may develop your own method of rehearsing after you have had experience in delivering presentations.

1. *Rehearse aloud.* Sometimes people think that staring at their notes or skimming through their notes is rehearsal. That is just not the case. You should practice your presentation aloud so you can hear how it sounds. If you are using an extemporaneous method of delivery, then you need to be sure that you can explain each point you want to make. Because your speech isn't written out, you will discover only by practicing *out loud* whether there are any ideas that might cause you trouble. If you are presenting a manuscript speech, you need to read it aloud to make sure that the markings you have made on your manuscript are useful in helping you convey the message in the way you intend to express it.
2. *Rehearse several times.* For most people, one rehearsal is not sufficient. You should probably rehearse your presentations about four or five times. Practice enough for you to know that you can explain all of your ideas. However, if you overpractice and commit the presentation to memory, particularly the extemporaneous presentation, you may sound like you are reciting your material rather than presenting fresh ideas.
3. *If possible, rehearse in the actual location of the presentation.* If it is possible to rehearse in the room where you will give the presentation, you should do so, particularly if you will be using visual aids. This will help you determine where to stand when you display the visuals, where the outlets are if you are using electronic media, and where you'll be in relationship to your listeners. Rehearsing in the actual location can increase your confidence by removing some of the ambiguity associated with the situation. It should be possible to rehearse in the classroom in which you'll deliver presentations. Take advantage of the times when the room is unoccupied.
4. *Time yourself as you rehearse.* People often say that they lose their sense of time when speaking before an audience. For most speaking situations, you will be limited to a specific amount of time. The most effective way to ensure that you will not exceed those limits is to time yourself as you rehearse. You should do this the last couple of times you rehearse. If you discover that the presentation is too long, then you need to cut out some material and practice again to assess the length of the new version of the presentation.

5. *Rehearse in front of people.* If possible, have a few friends, family members, or acquaintances listen to you as you rehearse. This will let you know what it feels like to be in front of an audience. It will also give you a chance to find out whether you are making your ideas clear to your listeners. Your presentation may have sounded clear to you as you rehearsed alone, but your audience may not be able to follow it. Rehearsing in front of someone will also give you an opportunity to try out your visual aids and determine their effectiveness. Perhaps your trial audience could sit in the last row to check that your visuals can be seen by those in the back.

If you follow these five guidelines, your rehearsal should really help you deliver your presentation smoothly and within the allotted time. Each person tends to develop idiosyncratic ways of rehearsing, and you will, too, but these guidelines provide the basis for practicing presentations.

As you can see, preparing to deliver a presentation is a fairly extensive process. It involves choosing a method of delivery, preparing notes, preparing visual aids, and rehearsing. Even if you carefully follow each of these stages, you may discover that you feel tense about having to speak before an audience. In the next section we will examine apprehension about speaking, and we will provide some suggestions for managing it.

UNDERSTANDING AND MANAGING SPEECH APPREHENSION

What Is Speech Apprehension?

There is no doubt that speaking before a group makes *most* people tense and uncomfortable. However, those of us who experience nervousness often think that everyone else is perfectly calm before giving a speech! That only serves to increase our apprehension because we assume there must be something wrong with us for feeling so nervous. You need to recognize that nearly everyone gets nervous when speaking before an audience. Often that nervousness does not show or shows very little, but that does not mean the speaker isn't experiencing it. So if you feel tension at the thought of making presentations, you can be certain that everyone in your class feels the same way—perhaps even your teacher.

Keeping in mind that nervousness is a natural response to speaking to a group, let's examine what that apprehension is all about and discuss some of the reasons why people experience it. Professionals in both communication and psychology have been interested in anxiety about speaking. People in both disciplines have coined terms, some of which denote apprehension about public speaking and some of which refer to apprehension about speaking in general. We are concerned here with apprehension about delivering presentations. Communication specialists have generally referred to this as *stage fright*[5] or *communication apprehension.*[6] Psychologists typically use the terms *speech anxiety* or *audience anxiety.*[7] The slight differences in meaning of these various terms is not important for our purposes. What is important is that you have an understanding of the apprehension you feel so that you can manage it effectively.

Several scholars have carefully examined the nature of apprehension about public speaking. They generally describe it as having four components: affective, cognitive, behavioral, and physiological.[8] Let's look briefly at these four components before we discuss how to manage speech apprehension.

1. ***Affective*** The affective dimension of apprehension refers to feelings and emotions. Apprehension about speaking usually involves an emotional reaction; people feel fearful of the situation. Often they feel embarrassment as well as fear, and they may feel a strong urge to avoid the presentation.
2. ***Cognitive*** The cognitive component of apprehension deals with people's thoughts about speaking. When people are apprehensive about making a presentation, they may worry and think negative thoughts ("I'll make a fool out of myself" or "My presentation is too boring"). These thoughts are, in part, the cause of the feelings of nervousness and fear.
3. ***Behavioral*** When we experience apprehension, we may avoid a situation, withdraw from the situation, or behave awkwardly in that situation. The behavioral component of apprehension is how it affects our behavior. Not showing up for a presentation, cutting a presentation short because of nervousness, or fumbling while delivering a presentation represent the behavioral aspect of apprehension.
4. ***Physiological*** In the past, when you have been apprehensive about speaking to a group, you may have noticed certain physical symptoms: perhaps trembling, increased heart rate, perspiration, blushing, or dry mouth. These kinds of reactions are common; they constitute the physiological component of apprehension.

There are a variety of reasons why you may feel apprehensive about public presentations. First, you may be very inexperienced, and you may lack the skills needed for effective speaking. (You may have been nervous when you got behind the wheel of a car the first time, too, because you didn't know what you were doing. The same can be true of speaking before an audience. If you are uncertain about how to approach a task, it can be very intimidating.)

Second, you may be interpreting a normal physiological response to public speaking in a way that makes you feel worse. If you accept the fact that you have increased adrenaline in your system and that is a natural response to public speaking, you may not feel quite so nervous. The problem occurs when people interpret the physiological response as a sure sign that disaster is about to occur. They claim that the reaction of their bodies will cause them to perform ineffectively, and as a result, they experience a great deal of fear about failing.

A third reason for your apprehension about speaking may be a past negative experience. Sometimes a person who does poorly in a particular speaking situation becomes afraid to try again. She assumes that failing once means she will fail again. It is like the person who gets in an auto accident and doesn't want to drive again.

A fourth reason people experience apprehension about speaking to a group is that they assume the audience expects more from them than they can deliver.[9] They believe their public speaking abilities will not measure up to audience expectations and that their deficiencies are in important areas. Thus, their apprehension is a response to their belief that because of their own inabilities, they cannot satisfy the listener's expectations.

There are certainly other reasons why people become tense and nervous about making presentations, but our intent is not to provide an exhaustive list. We have highlighted some of the most common reasons why individuals experience speech apprehension. More important than discovering reasons for speech apprehension is discovering ways to deal with it. Let's look at some ways that you can better cope with this nervousness.

Managing Apprehension

It is important for you to realize that you can probably never completely eliminate apprehension about speaking. Even if you could, we are not so sure that would be such a good idea. A certain amount of nervousness gives the speaker an energy boost that can translate into livelier, more effective delivery. Eliminating nervousness might result in a presentation that seems lifeless and dull, unless the speaker has the ability to inject enthusiasm into it in spite of the absence of apprehension.

Therefore, the first step in coping with speech apprehension is to recognize that it is a normal, natural response, experienced by nearly everyone, which can potentially enhance your presentation. You need to redefine your tension if you have been viewing it as certain to bring on failure. Continuing to view it in that light will only increase your nervousness.

A second major way to cope with speech anxiety is to do exactly what you are doing—enroll in a course and get some good training in how to prepare and deliver presentations. Training can increase your confidence by making you aware of what a presentation entails and how to approach it. Just as your nervousness about driving diminished once you learned how, tension about speaking can lessen through training.

The third way to alleviate apprehension is to practice, practice, practice. The more experience you get speaking to a variety of audiences in many situations, the more your fear will be diminished. This does not mean that all of your experiences will be total successes. You will be happy with some presentations and disappointed with others. That is normal. When you fail to perform at the level you had hoped, keep in mind that that has no bearing on your next presentation. Each speaking situation is unique, as we explained in Chapter 8. It is sometimes very difficult to predict how a presentation will be received. But if you carefully plan and practice, you can increase the likelihood that you will be successful. If a presentation does not go well because of some error on your part (for example, you may have used a visual aid that was too small, or you may have done insufficient research on the topic), you at least know what to work on for the next speaking situation.

If none of these suggestions helps you, you may need more specialized assistance. You might want to read a book designed for the person who is apprehensive about speaking. There are a variety of books available on the subject of apprehension and how to cope with it.[10] Some colleges offer special training programs for the apprehensive speaker. One such program, the Reticence Program, is offered at Pennsylvania State University. You may want to check out the programs being offered in your area.

Now that we have discussed the stages of preparing to deliver a presentation and have suggested ways to deal with apprehension about speaking, we need to move on to the actual delivery itself. In the next section we will focus on the process of delivering a presentation.

ASPECTS OF DELIVERY

Now that you are ready to deliver your message, you should think about some of the other aspects of delivery. We have not yet discussed your nonverbal communication during delivery, nor have we considered the effective use of your voice. In this section we will concern ourselves with those two major topics.

Your Physical Delivery

Because speakers generally stand before the listeners during a presentation, you need to be concerned about your physical delivery—your gestures and body movements, making eye contact, and your facial expressions. As you rehearse and actually deliver your presentation, you need to be conscious of these factors so that your physical delivery enhances your message rather than detracting from it.

Gestures The movements we make with our hands and arms are gestures. It is common for people to gesture during conversation, but they often think they shouldn't gesture during a presentation. Instructors frequently hear students say, "I shouldn't use my hands so much when I speak." Gesturing during a presentation is not only appropriate and natural—it can also enhance your message. For example, you may hold up two fingers for emphasis when you say, "There are two reasons for this situation." You can hold your hands apart at a particular distance to illustrate the size or length of an object. These gestures are effective because they enhance the speaker's message by reinforcing or clarifying it. Imagine a speaker who never moved her arms or hands; it would seem unnatural, and she would probably look silly. Our advice, then, is to let your arms and hands move naturally, as you would in a conversation. (If you try to plan gestures, they can look artificial. Only the most experienced speakers can look natural when they use planned gestures.)

The only thing you need to beware of is gestures that are too repetitious or unusual. For example, if you circled your hand at the wrist throughout your presentation, that motion would become very distracting to your audience. If your instructor videotapes you as you speak, you can observe your gesturing to determine whether it is too repetitive or odd. If you are not videotaped, you might ask your instructor about your gestures.

Body Movement Some speakers stay behind the lectern and never move during the course of a presentation. Others prefer to stay in front of it so they can move around. Either approach is acceptable, although some situations may dictate the use of one approach over the other. For example, if there is a fixed microphone, you may have to stand behind the lectern even if you prefer to move around. In other situations, there may be no lectern available, so you have nothing to stand behind.

If you are standing behind a lectern and either cannot or do not want to move away from it, the key is to avoid appearing rigid. Your body can still move even though you aren't going anywhere. We use our upper bodies to lean forward or backward. If you let yourself be natural, your body movements will reflect the emotion you are conveying or your attitude toward your topic or audience.

If you prefer to move about, you need to avoid pacing. Movement can help keep the listeners' attention, but if your movement is repetitive, it can become a distraction. You should try not to move constantly, because that could result in pacing. Again, watching yourself on videotape or getting criticism from your instructor can help you determine whether your movement is effective or distracting.

Eye Contact Some speakers are afraid to look their listeners in the eye. They think they can "fake it" by looking slightly over the heads of the audience. Although you may be able to get away with this in a large room, it looks silly to the audience, and the speaker loses the ability to adapt to the listeners. How can you adapt to your listeners if you can't see their faces? Direct eye contact with each and every member of your audience should be your goal. Obviously, you cannot do this if you have an audience of 500. Most of your speaking, however, will be in much smaller groups, where you not only can but should strive for eye contact. Maintaining eye contact performs several important functions.

First, as we have already suggested, through eye contact the speaker can observe the reactions of listeners and adjust the presentation as needed. Their eyes and facial expressions will let you know if your listeners are bored, confused, enjoying your talk, and so forth.

Second, eye contact with listeners helps keep their attention on you and your message. When you look at a person you are speaking to, he will snap back and attend to you if he had started to drift off. Remember, it is difficult for people to listen for a long period of time. Even when someone is motivated to listen, it is hard to listen to every word. Your eye contact can help to maintain the audience's concentration on your message.

Third, eye contact also communicates that you are involved with your listeners, that you are concerned with getting your message across to them. And it may even communicate that you have a positive attitude toward them. In our culture we are suspicious of people who cannot maintain eye contact. We tend to think that they are hiding something or that they lack self-confidence. Therefore, you can project a more positive image if you maintain good eye contact.

Facial Expressions Just as our whole bodies get involved when we speak, so too do our faces. The face is the main vehicle for conveying emotion. Again, our advice is to try not to control your facial expression, with the exception perhaps of smiling at your listeners when you start (even though you may not feel like smiling). Smiling is certainly not appropriate in every speaking situation, so be sure to determine what the occasion calls for before deciding to begin with a smile. A smile at the beginning of a presentation to inform employees that the plant is being shut down is obviously inappropriate.

One problem to beware of is facial expression incongruent with the idea being expressed. Speakers sometimes have a happy facial expression when talking about a serious, unhappy topic. This tends to call into question the speaker's sincerity, leaving the listeners wondering how anyone could smile while discussing that topic.

Overall then, our advice is to let your physical delivery be natural but to beware of repetitious or awkward movements or gestures. Even if eye contact does not come naturally to you, try to force yourself to maintain direct eye contact with listeners. That doesn't mean to stare at them; just look at each listener for a brief instant and then move on. Since you cannot see yourself, ask your instructor to help you assess your physical delivery.

Your Vocal Delivery

How you use your voice to deliver your message can also enhance or detract from your presentation. It seems to be somewhat easier to control our voices than our facial expressions, gestures, and body movements. You need to be conscious of how your voice sounds and how you are using it as you deliver your message. Consider each of the following aspects of the voice:

1. *Voice quality* This refers to how your voice sounds. Is it nasal, breathy, husky, or raspy? Vocal quality is the aspect of your voice that is most difficult to change, but it can be changed if you don't like the sound of your voice. There are courses available in voice and diction at many colleges and universities; you may want to consult a speech pathologist who can help you.
2. *Voice volume* How loud or soft you make your voice is one aspect you can control. It is frustrating to listeners if they cannot hear you speak; but on the other hand, a booming voice in a small room is difficult to listen to as well. Practice in speaking to audiences of different sizes will help you learn to adjust your voice volume. So will observing your listeners' responses to you. As you begin your speech, note whether the listeners lean forward as if straining to hear you. Note whether they are grimacing and leaning back as if to try to escape the loudness. Some listeners may not be very subtle at all—they will cup their hands to their ears if you are speaking too softly or cover their ears if your voice is too loud.
3. *Voice pitch* Pitch is how high or low your voice is. In general, women have higher-pitched voices than men, but pitch can be controlled. People tend to talk in a higher pitch when they are very excited, but a slightly lower pitch is easier to listen to. An extremely high-pitched voice can be hard on the ears. Voice pitch generally varies, but each of us has an optimum pitch that requires the least amount of effort.
4. *Speaking rate* We can also vary how quickly or how slowly we speak. Students often complain that they speak too quickly when they get nervous. For some people this is true, but just feeling like you talk too quickly does not mean that you do. You should seek your instructor's advice on this matter. It is a rare person who speaks too slowly, but when listening to a very slow speaker an audience can become quite restless. People can listen faster than others can speak, so a rate that is a little fast is preferable to a rate that is too slow.

What you should strive for in delivering a presentation is vocal variety. This involves varying these four aspects of your voice—quality, volume, pitch, and rate—so that your voice is interesting to listen to rather than monotonous. For some people, this may happen quite naturally. Others need to be conscious of these aspects and must work to add variety to their speech. If you listen to broadcasters, one thing you will notice is that they use their voices in an interesting way by varying these four aspects of their voices.

SUMMARY

In this chapter we have taken you through four stages of preparation to deliver a presentation. The first stage is to determine what method of delivery you will use: impromptu, extemporaneous, manuscript, or memorized. The second stage is to prepare the actual notes or manuscript from which you will speak. The third stage is to prepare any visual aids you need to use to enhance your listeners' understanding of your presentation. The fourth stage of preparation is to rehearse. The rehearsal should be a "dress rehearsal" if possible, in which you practice in the location where the presentation will take place. You also need to be sure to rehearse with your visual aids so that you can handle them smoothly.

Because delivering presentations makes most people nervous, we discussed the nature of speech apprehension and how to manage it. Apprehension has cognitive, affective, behavioral, and physiological components, and it is caused by a variety of factors. Apprehension can be dealt with in a number of ways: you can get training; you can practice giving speeches; you can accept apprehension as natural; and you can enroll in special programs and use self-help books.

In the last section of the chapter, we discussed the physical and vocal aspects of delivering a presentation. The speaker needs to be conscious of body movement, gestures, facial expressions, and eye contact in order to use them effectively. In addition, the speaker needs to strive for vocal effectiveness by varying vocal quality, pitch, volume, and rate. Good delivery can enhance a presentation, but poor delivery can detract from the speaker's message.

CHAPTER 9 ACTIVITIES

1. Attend a presentation and observe the speaker's delivery. Take notes on each of the following:
   a. Method of delivery (extemporaneous, manuscript, or memorized). How effective was it?
   b. Use of visual aids. What aids were used, and how effectively?

   c. Physical delivery. How well did the speaker maintain eye contact? Were gestures and facial expressions appropriate?
   d. Vocal delivery. Were the speaker's vocal quality, pitch, and loudness pleasing? Did the speaker use vocal variety?
2. Observe a videotape of yourself delivering a presentation. Take notes on the same items as in activity 1. What aspects of your delivery need improvement? How will you go about trying to improve?
3. For your first classroom presentation, use index cards for your notes, following the suggestions presented in this chapter for preparing them. After the presentation, evaluate your notes. Were they helpful? In what ways could your notes have been more helpful?
4. If your college computer center has graphics software for student use, experiment with that software to produce pie charts, bar graphs, and other kinds of graphic aids discussed in this chapter. If you are not familiar with using the computer, you should seek instruction from friends, take a computer course, or see what instruction services are available in your campus computer center.

CHAPTER 9 NOTES

1. See Cheryl Hamilton and Cordell Parker, *Communicating for Results: A Guide for Business and the Professions,* 2nd ed., Belmont, CA: Wadsworth, 1987, p. 330.
2. See Richard L. Weaver, II, *Understanding Business Communication,* Englewood Cliffs, NJ: Prentice-Hall, 1985, pp. 139–141.
3. See Patricia Hayes Bradley and John E. Baird, Jr., *Communication for Business and the Professions,* 2nd ed., Dubuque, IA: Brown, 1983, p. 368.
4. See Weaver, p. 141.
5. See, for example, Theodore Clevenger, Jr., "A Synthesis of Experimental Research in Stage Fright," *Quarterly Journal of Speech,* vol. 45, 1959, pp. 134–145.
6. See, for example, James C. McCroskey, "The Communication Apprehension Perspective." In *Avoiding Communication: Shyness, Reticence, and Communication Apprehension,* John Daly and James C. McCroskey (Eds.), Beverly Hills, CA: Sage, 1984, pp. 13–38.
7. See, for example, Mark R. Leary, "Social Anxiousness: The Construct and its Measurement," *Journal of Personality Assessment,* vol. 47, 1983, pp. 66–75.
8. See *Avoiding Communication: Shyness, Reticence, and Communication Apprehension,* John A. Daly and James C. McCroskey (Eds.), Beverly Hills, CA: Sage, 1984.
9. Joe Ayres, "Perceptions of Speaking Ability: An Explanation for Stage Fright," *Communication Education,* vol. 35, 1986, pp. 275–287.
10. See, for example, Lynne Kelly and Arden K. Watson, *Speaking with Confidence and Skill,* New York: Harper & Row, 1986; Gerald M. Phillips, *Help for Shy People and Anyone Else Who Ever Felt Ill at Ease on Entering a Room Full of Strangers,* Englewood Cliffs, NJ: Prentice-Hall, 1981; Philip G. Zimbardo, *Shyness: What It Is, What to Do About It,* Reading, MA: Addison-Wesley, 1977.

CHAPTER 10

Communication in the Socialization of Employees

In addition to developing skills for communication activities such as interviews, meetings, and presentations, you will need skill at "learning the ropes" of daily life in the organization. All employees experience the process of socialization when they enter organizations—a process that continues for the duration of their employment, although it tends to be most intense in the first several months. As an employee, you are not simply a passive recipient of whatever forces of socialization are directed at you. Instead, you are an active participant in that process, and the choices you make will influence whether or not you are successfully assimilated into the organization's culture. (This concept was developed further in Chapter 2.)

In this chapter we will examine the socialization of employees, with an emphasis on the role of communication. Our purpose is to provide you with both an understanding of the socialization process and guidelines for your communicative behavior throughout that process. We will begin with a definition of socialization and then outline its stages.

WHAT IS ORGANIZATIONAL SOCIALIZATION?

Organizational socialization, according to Van Maanen, is "the process by which a person learns the values, norms and required behaviors which permit him to participate as a member of the organization."[1] Employees at L&L Associates experience the process of socialization as they learn what is expected of them and what is valued within the organization. You have experienced this process in your college and in any other organizations in which you have been a member.

In Chapter 2 we discussed organizational culture; which we defined as a shared view of life in the organization, including its predominant values, norms for behavior, customs, and rituals. We emphasized that each organization develops its own unique culture, which is constantly, although usually subtly, changing. When you join an organization, you become assimilated into its culture. Jablin defines *organizational assimilation* as "the process by which organization members become a part of, or are absorbed into, the culture of an organization."[2] There are two components of the assimilation process:[3]

1. *Socialization*: the organization attempts to socialize members.
2. *Individualization*: the person tries to individualize her role in the organization, that is, to leave her unique mark on that role.

In the next section we will examine the phases of the socialization process, and later in this chapter we will discuss how employees attempt to individualize their roles.

PHASES OF ORGANIZATIONAL SOCIALIZATION

The socialization process does not happen overnight. At L&L Associates, for example, employees gradually learn the values, norms, and expected behaviors. When you became a member of your college community, it may have taken quite some time for you to learn the ropes, both in and out of the classroom. Scholars have typically outlined three stages or phases of organizational socialization: anticipatory socialization, an encounter phase, and metamorphosis.[4]

Anticipatory Socialization

Long before you accept employment with a specific company, you develop ideas about how to behave and communicate in various occupations and organizations.[5] Even as early as elementary school, you may have had ideas about what you wanted "to be when you grew up." Perhaps you wanted to be a doctor, a teacher, or an airline pilot. Even as a child you had some sense, as limited as it may have been, of what those occupations were like. *Anticipatory socialization* is the process of developing ideas about how to behave in particular occupations or work settings. According to Jablin, there are two stages in this process of anticipatory socialization: vocational choice socialization and organizational choice socialization.[6]

Vocational Choice Socialization In making decisions about what vocational direction to take, people acquire information about different occupations. Perhaps as a young teenager you thought about the possibility of becoming a teacher. Over the years prior to this choice and after making it, you developed ideas about what is expected of teachers and about how they behave. These ideas came from a variety of sources, including family members, schools, job experiences, peers, and the media.[7]

Thus, vocational socialization begins even before you have made a particular vocational choice. Through the information you acquire about vocations, you develop expectations about how people in those occupations behave.

Organizational Choice Socialization. In the job search process, people develop expectations about positions and organizations. Think about the expectations you developed about the various colleges to which you applied. You probably expected some schools to be more difficult or more competitive than others. You probably expected the social life to be exciting at some colleges and dull at others. You also developed expectations about your role as a student in those schools. You probably had ideas about how college students behave in class, when and how much they study, and what they do with their spare time.

Before joining organizations, then, people already have ideas about what those organizations are like and about what will be expected of organization members. People develop those ideas from reading material sent out by the organization (brochures, advertisements, and so on) and from interactions with others (recruiters, employees, or teachers).[8] The employment interview, which we discussed in Chapter 5, is a primary source of information about organizations. As Jablin notes, the interview is "an information-sharing, expectation-matching communication event and as such plays a key role in the assimilation of organizational newcomers."[9] Unfortunately, research has found that in general, applicants have unrealistic expectations about jobs and organizations.[10] They typically have higher expectations than the organization can fulfill. This may lead to lower job satisfaction, less commitment to the organization, and more job turnover.[11]

As you gather information about organizations from recruiters and company literature, remember that these sources generally try to paint the most positive picture they can. In Chapter 5 we talked about taking an active role in the employment interview. Ask questions about the specific position. You will want to know what your duties will be, what is expected in terms of the hours you'll work, and what potential problems you may encounter in performing your role. If you ask questions that dig beneath the glossy surface, you may be able to get information about the details of the job from the interviewer. Also, by seeking out other sources of information—perhaps by talking to employees—you may develop more realistic expectations about those organizations. The more realistic your expectations, the easier it will be to adapt to your new role and the greater your job satisfaction will be.

Encounter Phase

The *encounter phase* begins when you enter the organization as a newcomer. The expectations you developed in the anticipatory phase begin to be tested. Three situations are likely to occur when the newcomer confronts the reality of the job and the organization.

In some cases, the expectations the employee developed in the anticipatory stage are fairly realistic. The person with realistic expectations will adjust to the job and the organization relatively easily.[12] You may have had this experience as a student in a new school or when you began a new job. Careful gathering of information prior to entering an organization may help bring about this outcome.

At the other extreme, an employee's expectations may be so out of line that he experiences a traumatic period.[13] If this happens, the employee may be so disillusioned with the job and the organization that he withdraws from others or even leaves. In many cases, however, the newcomer goes through the difficult and exhausting process of changing those expectations and adjusting to the situation. The student who goes off to college expecting it to be just like high school may be in for a shock. Some of those students transfer to other schools, some of them quit college, and some of them make the necessary adjustments to do well.

In most instances, newcomers experience discrepancies between reality and expectations.[14] Louis referred to these as *surprises* employees encounter in this phase.[15] Conrad summarized four types of surprises that may be in store for newcomers.[16] Let's discuss these common types of problems.

1. ***Unmet expectations*** New employees are often surprised when what they expected does not match reality. If you are participating in the L&L Associates simulation, it is likely that some of your expectations have not been met. If your role in the simulation is a managerial position, you may have expected your subordinates to be easier or more difficult to manage than they are. If your role is in a project group, you may have assumed that the tasks would be relatively easy, and you may have been surprised that they were not. In Chapter 2 we discussed formal organizational rules and informal norms for behavior. Sometimes expectations are not met because there is a discrepancy between rules and norms. The policies and procedures manual may say one thing, but what is actually done may be another.
2. ***Self-surprise*** People often surprise themselves when they enter an organization. They may discover that they don't like tasks they ex-

pected to like or that they have worthwhile skills they never considered important. You probably experienced this kind of surprise as a newcomer at college. Perhaps you discovered your intended major was not for you or that you excelled at a subject you never took seriously before.

3. *Surprises resulting from taking things for granted* We all occasionally take things for granted. Employees may automatically assume that they will be rewarded for good work or that they will have the resources they need to perform their duties. Unfortunately, these assumptions may not be met. Perhaps when you went to college you assumed that you would do well in all of your courses, just as you did in high school. What an unpleasant surprise when you had trouble with a particular course!
4. *Surprise about the experience itself* Sometimes we understand something at the intellectual level but then encounter problems in the actual experience. You may say to yourself that you wouldn't mind a long commute to work, only to discover that you find the actual experience intolerable. All aspects of our jobs have this potential. Some people discover they aren't cut out for managerial positions because the experience of reprimanding or firing employees is too unpleasant, although they had understood that these duties are part of the job.

In the encounter phase, newcomers begin to adapt to the organization. Later in this chapter we will focus on the process of adaptation. We will also examine the companion process of individualization, which also occurs as employees are assimilated into an organization's culture.

Metamorphosis Phase

The final phase of the socialization process is *metamorphosis.* In this phase, the employee tries to make the adjustments necessary to become a participant in the organization. The employee must make adjustments in both attitudes and behaviors in order to meet the expectations of the organization.[17] Specifically, the employee needs to meet four requirements:[18]

1. *Develop a new self-image.* As Conrad explains, the employee must manage conflicts between a general self-concept and an organization-specific self-concept.[19] Each of us develops a general self-concept, which is how we see ourselves as individuals. When you enter an organization, the messages you receive from others may or may not be congruent with your general self-concept. For example, you may see yourself as a resourceful, independent person. Your role in the company, however, may not allow you to exercise these qualities. Superiors remind you not to make decisions without consulting them, and your ability to do your job hinges on the efforts of co-workers.

This situation presents a conflict between general self-concept and organization-specific self-concept, and you need to resolve it. Resolving it may require you to develop a new self-concept that is appropriate for your role. This does not mean you need to alter your general self-concept. It does, however, mean that you must develop an organization-specific self-concept that is congruent with the requirements of your role.

2. *Establish new interpersonal relationships.* In Chapter 2 we explained that the formal structure of an organization dictates relationships to some extent. For instance, you must have a relationship with your immediate supervisor and with the co-workers in your department. You will form other relationships voluntarily. Regardless of whether the relationships are voluntary or involuntary, they will need to be satisfactory and cooperative. Remember, the metamorphosis phase involves the attempt to become an accepted member of the organization. Part of that process is establishing relationships with others. Remaining isolated will not help you fit in.
3. *Acquire new values.* When we described the concept of organizational culture, we emphasized that an important part of culture is the set of values held by organization members. Some organizations value innovativeness and others value stability. Learning about an organization's culture involves identifying the values that are important. It takes some time to discover those values, but you can learn about them by reading company literature, such as newsletters and policy manuals. You can also learn about them by talking to employees who have been with the company for a long period of time. When employees are asked what values are rewarded by their organizations, most of them are able to identify such values.[20]

   You are expected to identify these values and to share them. If hard work is valued, you will be expected to work hard. If loyalty is held in high esteem, others will look for signs of loyalty from you. Employees who do not hold the organization's values as important may be viewed as uncommitted to the organization or as not fitting in. One study found that employees who did not identify with the organization (who did not feel a sense of belonging and did not share the organization's values) seemed to believe that the company's values placed excessive demands on them. They reported, for example, that the company wanted "blind loyalty," not just loyalty.[21] These employees were dissatisfied with communication in the organization, and perhaps with the organization itself.
4. *Learn a new set of behaviors.* The final requirement of the metamorphosis phase is to learn new behaviors that are appropriate for the job and the organization. These behaviors may be directly related to the job, such as learning how to use a particular piece of equipment, or

Exhibit 10.1 PHASES OF ORGANIZATIONAL SOCIALIZATION

1. Anticipatory socialization
   a. Vocational choice socialization
   b. Organizational choice socialization
2. Encounter phase
3. Metamorphosis

tangential, such as learning the norms for coffee breaks. The first type is essential to success on the job, and the second type is central to fitting in as an organization member.

The three phases of organizational socialization are listed in Exhibit 10.1. Newcomers become assimilated into an organization's culture through this process. In the next section we will discuss socialization as a communicative process, and we will focus on three sources of communication in this process.

ORGANIZATIONAL SOCIALIZATION AS A COMMUNICATIVE PROCESS

As Jablin notes, "Clearly, the process by which one learns about what the organization considers to be acceptable behaviors and attitudes is essentially communicative in nature."[22] Although the employee learns about the organization in part through observation, much of the learning that takes place occurs through communication. When you first went to college, you may have met other students who gave you advice about what courses to take or which professors gave the best lectures. Advisors gave you additional suggestions, as did college documents like the catalog and the student handbook.

That organizational socialization is a communicative process is illustrated by Cynthia Stohl's study of memorable messages.[23] Memorable messages are brief injunctions which people remember for a long period of time and which had a major influence on them. An example might be "Work smarter, not harder." Stohl found that employees had no trouble identifying memorable messages and that the content of these messages concerned norms, rules, values, requirements, and expectations of the organizational culture. Clearly, then, memorable messages—usually given by "older and wiser" employees to newer employees—functioned to socialize newcomers.

In this section we will look at three primary sources of information about the organization: upper management, co-workers, and the immediate supervisor.[24] These three sources of communication are important in the socialization process, particularly in the encounter and metamorphosis phases.

Upper Management

Top management provides employees with a great deal of information about expected behaviors and appropriate attitudes. Communication from management takes a variety of forms, both oral and written. The purpose of such communication differs, however, depending on the phase of the socialization process in which the messages are issued.[25]

Anticipatory Socialization As people gather information about organizations in order to make employment decisions, they collect brochures, annual reports, and other types of documents, as we have discussed. These materials are approved by top managers, although usually not prepared by them. The information in these documents provides potential employees with a sense of what is expected and an idea about what the organization is like. The purpose of these materials is to stimulate interest in the organization and attract qualified applicants.

Encounter Phase The major purpose of communication from upper management in the encounter phase is to orient newcomers.[26] Many companies, for example, offer an orientation program, just as your college does for first-year and transfer students. Newcomers usually receive some kind of employee handbook, similar to the student handbook you probably received when you entered college. These handbooks usually include information about the organization's history and its mission, policies, rules, procedures, and employee benefits.[27] Jablin concludes that most communication with upper management in the encounter phase is one-way (downward-directed) and that it functions to inform new employees about what is appropriate and preferred.[28] In a study in which he examined communication logs of nursing assistants, Jablin found that in the encounter phase newcomers primarily received information.[29]

How effective these communications from upper management are in orienting newcomers is not known. Studies have found that employee handbooks are not very readable[30] and that employees have little understanding of benefits such as life and health insurance even though management attempts to communicate this information.[31] Other studies have found that information about such matters as policies and benefits is better communicated in writing rather than orally.[32] We would suggest that as a new employee, you read over these materials carefully and make a list of questions. Although you don't have to get all of your questions answered right away, you should try to get them answered over the first month or so of employment. (If you have questions that pertain to your job, however, you should address them to your supervisor immediately.)

Metamorphosis Phase As your employment in an organization extends beyond the encounter phase, you will continue to receive communication from upper management. You may receive a *house organ,* such as a newsletter or magazine. Your college probably has a daily or weekly newspaper that reports about campus issues. Bulletin boards in the organization display announcements and changes, and you will receive letters and memos as well. The purpose of these communications from top management is, in part, to foster a sense of commitment to the organization.[33]

Co-workers

Co-workers are also involved in the socialization process. If you are participating in the L&L Associates simulation, other members of your project group have undoubtedly made suggestions about how you should behave. Students fulfilling managerial roles have probably discussed organizational policies and rules with others at their level in the organization. Let's examine how communications with co-workers change from the encounter phase to the metamorphosis phase of socialization. (You probably will have little or no contact with employees in the anticipatory socialization phase.)

Encounter Phase In any organization, each of us comes in contact with co-workers who help us "learn the ropes" in the organization. In fact, as newcomers we often initiate interactions with co-workers in order to obtain information from them. We learn shortcuts for getting tasks done; we learn about the informal communication networks and begin to become a part of those networks. In this phase we use our interactions with co-workers to gather information about what to do and not do.

Metamorphosis Phase In the metamorphosis phase, new employees continue to seek information from their co-workers, although less actively than in the encounter stage. During metamorphosis, new employees begin to share their views of events and of the organization.[34] We already pointed out that employees are not simply passive in the socialization process. During the metamorphosis phase, they usually begin to take a more active role in their own socialization. We will elaborate on this idea when we discuss the process of individualization of roles.

Because newcomers begin to offer their interpretations of events during the metamorphosis stage, conflict can occur between veterans and new employees.[35] The "old-timers" may think the newcomers are pushy or uncooperative. As a new employee, you need to recognize that this conflict is typical so that you will not overreact when it occurs. However, you also need to consider whether you are being too forceful in offering your views. Be sure to listen to

In informal situations such as lunch break in the company cafeteria, the process of socialization of employees continues.

Bonuses and other rewards encourage particular kinds of behavior from employees.

the views of others, and be ready to support your opinions. This is a good time to apply the characteristics of supportive communication we discussed in Chapter 5. Remember, too, that your work group is making adjustments to accommodate you and other newcomers. Thus, the process of socialization involves adjustments on everyone's part.

Immediate Supervisor

A key individual in the socialization of employees is the immediate supervisor. At L&L Associates, employees have a lot of contact with their supervisors, who provide them with information about what is expected of them. Again, let's examine the phases of socialization and the supervisor's role in those phases.

Anticipatory Socialization You may not interact with your supervisor prior to accepting employment with a company. There is a good chance, however, that you will meet her in the interview process. Often, a company recruiter conducts the first screening interview and then calls successful candidates in for a second, on-site interview. It is at this second interview that you are likely to meet and be interviewed by your immediate supervisor.

Use this opportunity to ask questions about your duties and responsibilities. Once again, you are trying to gather information about what is expected so that your expectations are not inflated. Your supervisor will be trying to collect information about you as well as to get a sense of whether he will be able to work with you. This is a chance for you to get an impression of how well you can work with him. Be honest with yourself. If you believe that working for this supervisor would be an intolerable situation, you probably should not take the job if it is offered, unless it is your only alternative. However, if the organization has a great deal to offer, you might decide to accept the job with the hope that you will be promoted quickly.

Encounter Phase As you might expect, the supervisor is an important source of information for a new employee, for several reasons. First, employees usually have a great deal of contact with their immediate supervisors. The more contact you have with someone, the greater the potential that person has to provide you with information. Second, your supervisor is typically the person who evaluates you—and who therefore has the power to dole out rewards and punishments.[36] Naturally, attending to your supervisor as a source of information is therefore important. And third, your supervisor serves as a mediator in the downward flow of communication. Information from upper management is often filtered through the supervisor, so not only does the supervisor provide her view of how tasks ought to be done, she interprets top management's directives.

Much of the communication from immediate supervisors in the encounter phase concerns job instructions rather than more general organizational issues. The study of communication logs of nursing assistants, mentioned earlier, revealed that 51.8 percent of messages received from superiors concerned job instructions; other job-related information was the subject of 23.2 percent of those messages.[37] Although you may think supervisors are too focused on the specific job, studies have shown that communication from first-level supervisors which emphasizes high standards for job performance has a positive effect on employees' performance.[38] By communicating information about your job performance, your immediate supervisor may be helping you succeed in the organization.

In the encounter phase, newcomers also seek information from their immediate supervisors. This is one way a new employee may play an active role in the socialization process. New employees need clarification of instructions and policies. They also need feedback about how they are performing, and they may choose to ask for such feedback. Unfortunately, however, many employees are reluctant to initiate interactions with their supervisors, and they may wait for information to be supplied.[39] They also may seek information from co-workers rather than ask their superiors.[40] We want to encourage you to initiate communication with your supervisor when you have questions that need to be answered. Decide what questions you want to ask; then approach your supervisor, explain that you have several questions, and ask them. If your supervisor does not have time to answer them at the moment, he will probably suggest an alternative time. If he doesn't, you might suggest one.

Metamorphosis Phase Communication with your immediate supervisor continues to be important in the metamorphosis phase of socialization. The purpose of that communication changes somewhat from the encounter phase to this phase. Newcomers no longer have as great a need for job-related information. Rather, new employees and their supervisors communicate to negotiate their relationship.[41] The quality of the communication relationship between employees and their immediate supervisors has a significant impact on employee satisfaction.[42] Therefore, reaching agreement on the nature of that relationship is an important activity.

In the metamorphosis phase, new employees seem to become less hesitant to initiate interactions.[43] Perhaps this is because they have negotiated a relationship in which initiating communication with their supervisors is appropriate. How does this occur? In part, it is a process of testing. You try certain behaviors and observe the response of the other person. The relationship also gets defined through open discussion. Your supervisor may tell you when you can talk with her and what topics are off limits. It is through both testing and direct communication that supervisor-employee relationships are defined.

Organizational socialization is a communicative process. Exhibit 10.2

Exhibit 10.2 COMMUNICATION SOURCES IN THE SOCIALIZATION PROCESS

1. Upper management
2. Co-workers
3. Immediate supervisor

summarizes the three key sources of communication involved in this process. It is primarily through interactions with others and through studying company documents that newcomers learn what life is like in the organization and what is expected of them. As we will discuss in the next section, new employees also bring their own unique mark to bear on their organizational roles in a process called individualization.

THE PROCESS OF INDIVIDUALIZATION

Earlier in this chapter we explained that organizational assimilation (the process by which newcomers become a part of an organization's culture) has two components: socialization and individualization. Socialization is the process by which the organization attempts to teach employees the values, rules, and expected behaviors important to that organization. Now that we have examined the socialization process, we can turn to the process of individualization. Unfortunately, individualization has not been studied nearly as extensively as socialization.

What Is Individualization?

Individualization is the companion process to socialization—it is the process by which employees attempt to adapt their roles to satisfy their own needs.[44] Two people do not fulfill the duties and responsibilities of the same position in the same way. Each newcomer leaves his mark on the position and the organization. That's because employees do not just follow rules and procedures precisely; they modify many of them to better suit their own ideas and needs. At L&L Associates, for example, several employees have the same position in the organization, as members of project teams. They have many of the same duties, but they will each perform their roles in different ways.

It is generally during the metamorphosis stage of socialization that a newcomer begins to individualize her role.[45] This is probably because the employee needs to fully understand her role and what that role requires before she can modify it. We have already cited some evidence that individualization begins to occur during metamorphosis. It is during this phase that the newcomer begins to initiate more interactions rather than simply receive information, and at this time she also begins to share her interpretations of events and situations. We already noted that this can increase conflict with co-workers and that the work group usually makes adjustments to accommodate the new employee.

As a student in this course, you will individualize your role, as will all the other students. You will develop your own unique ways of fulfilling duties and meeting responsibilities. Think about the differences in the ways students handle public presentations. Even though each of you is following the requirements of the assignment, there will be many variations in how the task is completed. It is in part because of the individualization process that an organization's culture is constantly, though subtly, changing.

The Supervisor's Role in Individualization

Although it is the employee who attempts to individualize his role, the immediate supervisor is important in this process.[46] Earlier we discussed the idea that the newcomer negotiates his relationship with his supervisor, particularly in the metamorphosis phase of socialization. In this negotiation process, the employee also defines his role and what is expected of him. How successfully an employee can individualize his role, then, depends on the negotiation of that role with the supervisor. If the employee tests behaviors (similar to the way a student may test an instructor by trying to turn in an assignment after the deadline has passed), the supervisor's response will either reinforce or reject those behaviors (as when the instructor won't accept the late assignment). Through this type of testing and direct discussion, the newcomer discovers what modifications of his role are acceptable to his supervisor. Thus, he negotiates his role with the supervisor. If the supervisor has little tolerance for deviation from specified procedures, the employee may have minimal success at individualization.

We have discussed the ways employees become assimilated into organizational cultures through the socialization and individualization processes. At one time or another—probably several times—each of you will enter an organization as a newcomer. In the final section of this chapter we will provide guidelines for managing these processes.

SUCCESSFUL ORGANIZATIONAL ASSIMILATION

We believe that you can and should take an active role in becoming assimilated into an organization. That is why we discussed the individualization process rather than focusing solely on socialization. In what ways can you take an active role? Although we have incorporated some suggestions throughout our discussion of these processes, in this section we will highlight three guidelines designed to help you in the assimilation process.

Become Involved in Communication Networks

As a newcomer, you should make the effort to become involved in communication networks. In Chapter 2 we discussed informal networks and their importance in the organization. Here we will elaborate that concept and provide suggestions for how to become involved.

Eisenberg, Monge, and Miller define involvement in communication networks as "the extent to which people establish and maintain direct and/or indirect communication contacts with others in their organizations."[47] Being involved in communication networks, then, means that you develop communicative relationships with others. We do not mean that these relationships have to be interpersonal in the sense that we used that term in Chapters 1 and 2. We simply mean that there must be *a relationship.* All of the employees with whom you interact regularly become part of a communication network.

By being highly involved in communication networks, you will be able to learn about the organization's culture much more quickly than if you remain fairly isolated. It is through interaction with other employees, particularly those who have been with the company for a long time, that you learn what is expected and what is valued in the organization. You discover the organization's culture in part through these interactions. In order to be successfully assimilated into the organization, you must understand what is expected and valued. You cannot effectively individualize your role if you are not aware of what is required of you. Thus, your involvement in communication networks will help you "learn the ropes."

Involvement in networks has other benefits. It becomes easier to get work done when you have contacts within the organization. When you need supplies, for example, it might ordinarily take several days or even longer to get a purchase order to buy them. However, if you have established a pleasant working relationship with someone in the purchasing department, you may be able to get your purchase order much more quickly. When you have a question about your employee benefits, you can use your contact in the personnel office to get an answer. If you are connected into communication networks, you can save a great deal of time and energy by using the shortcuts that will be made available to you.

High involvement in networks may also enhance your commitment to the organization. One study found that even employees who were uninvolved in their jobs were highly committed to the organization if their network involvement was extensive.[48] It is rewarding to be a part of a network; it provides a sense of belonging, acceptance, and involvement. This can translate into personal satisfaction and positive feelings about the organization.

Thus, when you begin the encounter phase of socialization, you should initiate interactions with other employees. Ask them questions about the organization, their positions, and events that occur. As long as you do not constantly barrage them with questions, the other employees will probably be flattered that you approached them. Just be sure to approach others at appropriate times, such as lunch and coffee breaks. They may be much less willing to talk to you when they are trying to get work done. The key to becoming involved is to *initiate.* If you wait for others to approach you, you may wait a long time. You don't have to become a pest; all you have to do is make the first move to show that you are interested in becoming an active, involved member of the organization.

Establish a Good Relationship with Your Supervisor

The second guideline we can offer to help you become assimilated into an organization is to try to develop a positive relationship with your immediate supervisor. In this chapter we have already suggested that the supervisor is an important source of communication in all three phases of the socialization process. We noted that how effectively you individualize your role depends in large measure on the supportiveness of your supervisor. This is a key relationship to which you should devote energy. Although there is no magic formula for establishing a good relationship with your supervisor, let's look at some important factors.

1. *Perform your job to the best of your ability.* Your supervisor is responsible for your performance. If the department is supposed to produce at a certain level, your supervisor is in charge of making sure that the standard is met. If you perform your job well, your supervisor will most likely have a positive attitude about you. We don't want to suggest that this is always the case, because people are not always rational. Sometimes a supervisor feels threatened by a competent employee, or he may dislike an employee for any of the reasons that people sometimes dislike each other. Doing a good job is no guarantee that your supervisor will respect and like you, but doing a poor job can ruin your relationship.
2. *Seek feedback and be willing to accept criticism.* To develop a positive relationship with your supervisor, seek feedback about your performance. By asking for feedback, you demonstrate an interest in doing a good job and in your supervisor's opinion. Just be willing to accept criticism or suggestions if any are forthcoming. It will damage the relationship if you ask for feedback and then make it clear that you are angry about the criticism. Before you ask for feedback, you might do a self-assessment of your performance. If your performance has been weak, it may not be a good time to seek feedback unless you need help to improve.
3. *Initiate communication.* New employees are hesitant to initiate interactions with others, particularly in the encounter phase of socialization. They are especially reluctant to approach their supervisors. Although we are not suggesting that you bombard your supervisor with questions, it is appropriate to ask some. Asking questions shows initiative and motivation. Our only caution is that you ask legitimate questions, that is, questions you actually need answered. Asking ques-

tions as an excuse to initiate interaction may backfire if your strategy is transparent to the supervisor. The supervisor may think you are just wasting time or trying to ingratiate yourself with her.

As a newcomer, you should not take your relationship with your supervisor for granted. It generally requires some effort and thought to develop a positive relationship. By doing your job well, seeking feedback, accepting criticism, and initiating interaction, you increase the chances that you will have a satisfying relationship with your supervisor. That relationship is an important one in your assimilation into the organization.

Be Willing to "Pitch In"

The final guideline for effective assimilation into an organization is to volunteer to "pitch in" to help your work group. Perhaps you have had a job in an organization where employees were happy to help one another when they had completed their own work. In some situations, they may have even sacrificed their own work to assist another employee. We believe that you should always be willing to cooperate. We are not suggesting that you do others' work for them. However, you should give other employees a hand when you aren't too busy and they are in need. By demonstrating a willingness to pitch in when it's necessary, you will send a message that you want to be part of the organization, part of the team. Employees who are unwilling to do this are often viewed as self-centered and uncooperative. If you want to be accepted by your work group, you need to show that you are willing to do your share for the good of the group.

SUMMARY

New employees must experience the process of socialization—the process by which they learn the norms, values, and behaviors required if they are to become active organization members. The socialization process consists of three phases. The first phase is anticipatory socialization. Before people choose occupations and enter organizations, they learn about what is expected in particular roles and types of organizations. Acquiring information about various occupations is called vocational choice socialization. Learning about what organizations and specific positions require is referred to as organizational choice socialization. Both of these processes occur before the individual enters the organization.

The second phase of socialization is the encounter phase. Once newcomers enter the organization, they begin to learn more about what is expected of them. They also have the opportunity to test the expectations they developed in the anticipatory phase. Newcomers may experience four types of surprises during the encounter phase: unmet expectations, self-surprise, surprises resulting from taking things for granted, and surprise about the experience itself. The more realistic their expectations were, the more easily newcomers adapt to the organization's culture.

The final phase of the socialization process is metamorphosis. At this point, the newcomer generally understands what is expected and is trying to make the necessary adjustments to become a participant in the organization. This involves developing a new self-image, establishing new interpersonal relationships, acquiring new values, and learning a new set of behaviors.

Socialization is a communicative process. It is primarily through communication that new employees learn what is expected. The three major sources of information about the organization are upper management, co-workers, and the immediate supervisor. The purposes of communication from these three sources vary, depending on the phase of socialization.

Socialization is one component of the organizational assimilation process. Assimilation is the process by which employees become part of an organizational culture. The other component process is individualization, which is the process by which employees attempt to adapt their roles to meet their own needs. It is through individualization that employees take an active role in their assimilation into an organization. The supervisor plays a key role in this process because the supervisor is the person with whom the newcomer negotiates his or her role.

There are three guidelines you should follow to help your assimilation into an organization occur smoothly and successfully. First, become involved in communication networks. Second, establish a good relationship with your immediate supervisor. And third, be willing to "pitch in" and help your coworkers when you can.

CHAPTER 10 ACTIVITIES

1. Reflect on your socialization experience at college or in a recent job. Describe each of the following aspects of that experience:
   a. Anticipatory socialization. What did you learn about the college or organization prior to entering it? What were your expectations?
   b. Encounter phase. What types of surprises did you experience? How realistic were your expectations?
   c. Metamorphosis phase. What adjustments did you have to make in your behavior in order to become an accepted member of the organization?

2. Look at some of the written documents given out by your college or company—handbooks, advertisements, catalogs, and so on. What expectations do these materials create for newcomers? What values do they suggest are important to the organization? What are the differences between what these materials suggest about the organization and what you know as a member of that organization?

3. Identify a memorable message that some other organization member directed to you. (A memorable message is a brief command about how you should behave in the organization.) Once you have identified such a message, answer the following questions:
   a. What was the source of the message? Who gave it to you?
   b. When did you receive the message?
   c. What was the situation in which you received the message?
   d. What does the message mean to you? What is your interpretation of its meaning?

CHAPTER 10 NOTES

1. J. Van Maanen, "Breaking In: Socialization to Work." In R. Dubin (Ed.), *Handbook of Work, Organization and Society,* Chicago: Rand McNally, 1975, p. 67.
2. Fredric M. Jablin, "Organizational Communication: An Assimilation Approach." In *Social Cognition and Communication,* M. E. Roloff and C. R. Berger (Eds.), Beverly Hills, CA: Sage, 1982, p. 256.
3. Fredric M. Jablin, "Assimilating New Members into Organizations." In *Communication Yearbook 8,* R. Bostrom (Ed.), Beverly Hills, CA: Sage, 1984, p. 595.
4. Ibid., pp. 595–596.
5. Fredric M. Jablin, "Organizational Entry, Assimilation, and Exit." In *Handbook of Organizational Communication: An Interdisciplinary Perspective,* F. M. Jablin, L. L. Putnam, K. H. Roberts, and L. W. Porter (Eds.), Newbury Park, CA: Sage, 1987, p. 680.
6. Ibid., pp. 680–693.
7. Ibid., p. 681.
8. Ibid., p. 685.
9. Ibid., p. 689.
10. Jablin, "Assimilating New Members," p. 621.
11. Jablin, "Organizational Entry," p. 687.
12. Charles Conrad, *Strategic Organizational Communication: Cultures, Situations, and Adaptation,* New York: Holt, Rinehart and Winston, 1985, p. 210.
13. Jablin, "Organizational Entry," p. 695.
14. Ibid.
15. Meryl Reis Louis, "Surprise and Sense-Making in Organizations," *Administrative Science Quarterly,* vol. 25, 1980, pp. 226–251.
16. Conrad, p. 211.
17. Fredric M. Jablin and Kathleen J. Krone, "Organizational Assimilation." In *Handbook of Communication Science,* C. R. Berger and S. H. Chaffee (Eds.), Newbury Park, CA: Sage, 1987, p. 713.
18. T. Caplow, *Principles of Organization,* New York: Harcourt Brace Jovanovich, 1964, cited in Jablin, "Assimilating New Members," p. 596.
19. Conrad, p. 209.
20. Patricia Geist, Monica Hardesty, and Lynne Kelly, "Consistency Inside and Out:

A Descriptive Study of Organizational Identification," paper presented to the Speech Communication Association, Boston, November 1987.
21. Ibid.
22. Jablin, "Organizational Entry," p. 696.
23. Cynthia Stohl, "The Role of Memorable Messages in the Process of Organizational Socialization," *Communication Quarterly,* vol. 34, 1986, pp. 231–249.
24. Jablin, "Organizational Entry," p. 696.
25. Jablin, "Organizational Entry," p. 706.
26. Ibid., p. 696.
27. P. Cowan, "Establishing a Communication Chain: The Development and Distribution of an Employee Handbook," *Personnel Journal,* vol. 54, 1975, p. 349.
28. Jablin, "Organizational Entry," p. 698.
29. Jablin, "Assimilating New Members," p. 622.
30. K. Davis, "Readability Changes in Employee Handbooks of Identical Companies During a Fifteen-Year Period," *Personnel Psychology,* vol. 21, 1968, pp. 413–420.
31. Jablin, "Organizational Entry," p. 697.
32. Ibid.
33. Ibid., p. 706.
34. Ibid., p. 711.
35. Ibid.
36. Jablin, "Organizational Communication," p. 269.
37. Jablin, "Organizational Entry," p. 700.
38. Ibid., p. 701.
39. Ibid., p. 699.
40. Ibid., p. 702.
41. Ibid., p. 708.
42. Fredric M. Jablin, "Superior-Subordinate Communication: The State of the Art," *Psychological Bulletin,* vol. 86, 1979, pp. 1201–1222.
43. Jablin, "Assimilating New Members," p. 623.
44. Ibid., p. 596.
45. Jablin and Krone, p. 714.
46. Ibid.
47. Eric M. Eisenberg, Peter R. Monge, and Katherine I. Miller, "Involvement in Communication Networks as a Predictor of Organizational Commitment," *Human Communication Research,* vol. 10, 1983, p. 180.
48. Ibid., pp. 191–192.

CHAPTER 11

Technology and the Performance of Everyday Tasks in the Organization

The communication activities we have been discussing in this text are primarily face-to-face oral interactions that take place as people go about their everyday work in the organization. There are, however, a number of other common modes of communication in the organization. These include making and receiving telephone calls, reading and writing memos, and sending and receiving business letters. In addition, in many business organizations within the last two decades, daily communication has begun to include using computers and other telecommunication technologies for even more rapid message exchange. In fact, face-to-face oral communication is not the primary way of doing business in most organizations.

In this chapter we will provide you with guidelines for enhancing your effectiveness in performing these everyday communication tasks. Let's look briefly at the evolution of the contemporary business organization so that we will have a frame of reference.

EVOLUTION OF THE BUSINESS ORGANIZATION

The industrial revolution took people away from their farms and out of their small family businesses and transplanted them into factories. The location and nature of the workplace changed: the workplace was no longer the home, and work was no longer rooted in the natural world. People who once worked at home on the farm were now going off to earn their livings at the factory. The office, as we have come to know it and as it has been discussed throughout this text, is a place in which workers congregate. It is an indirect outgrowth of the industrial revolution, with its emphasis on automation and centralization.[1] Communication in the workplace has changed, just as the workplace itself has changed. When families worked together to plow their fields, there was no need for many of the work-related communication activities described throughout this text.

Today another revolution is changing the nature of the workplace once again.[2] This "information revolution" is characterized by the fact that information, more than products or services, is becoming the basis of the economy. Factories for manufacturing products replaced the agricultural society during the industrial revolution; today we see information and information packages replacing other kinds of products and services as the major part of the gross national product.

Let's examine just what we mean when we say that we are in the midst of an information revolution. Basically, we mean that we are living in a time in which information, in various forms, surrounds us in dramatically increasing quantities. This is demonstrated in two ways. First, in the late 1960s it was predicted that the amount of technical information would double every ten years; however, by the mid-1970s, it was doubling every five and a half years. Second, each of us processes an enormous amount of information in everyday life. Studies of media use indicate that in one year, the typical American reads or completes 3000 notices and forms, reads 100 newspapers and 36 magazines, watches 2463 hours of television, listens to 730 hours of radio, reads 3 books, buys 20 records, talks on the telephone for almost 61 hours, and encounters 21,170 advertisements.[3]

Some information scientists point out that one of the consequences of the information revolution is the creation of a new class system in society: a differentiation between information "haves" and "have-nots." This is in part due to the cost of information when it is packaged, particularly in some of the electronic forms listed above. Think of going to the library to research a paper. Much more is being written and stored in libraries than ever before. Library users have more rapid access to that information than ever before, now that libraries are using automated information retrieval systems. If you know how to use the retrieval system to find the information stored in the library, you are potentially in the information "haves" class. Those who cannot get to a library, those who don't know how to use the retrieval system, those who are afraid of using computer technology as a means of access to information, and those whose libraries cannot afford to spend the money for up-to-date retrieval systems are the information "have-nots."

Communication has been said to be as necessary to an organization as the bloodstream is to a person.[4] Business communication has been dramatically affected in two ways by the advent of the information age. First, the explosion of information, particularly technical information, has affected businesses in much the same way as it has affected other organizations. There is simply more information available on most of the subjects relevant to any business, and therefore the people in that business need to know more in order to make decisions. Think, for example, of waiting in line at an airport ticket counter as the ticket agent searches a computer file to see whether you have a flight reservation. You tell him that you have bought tickets but lost them. He searches his computer files to check your story and verifies that your tickets were paid for and where and when they were issued. He has at his fingertips the ability to notify any other agent at any other linked computer terminal not to accept the lost ticket, and he issues you a replacement. The computer has saved your trip; it has also let the ticket agent do his job of checking you in at the airline.

The second way in which the information explosion has affected the business organization is by making available new media through which communication can take place. In addition to using telecommunication systems, office workers have to be able to use computers. Computer communication technologies provide many services useful to the organization—electronic mail, electronic bulletin boards, teleconferencing, electronic encyclopedias, and data bases, to name just a few. Through data bases, employees have access to all kinds of information about a variety of products, services, and goods, and can even find out details about the economic situation.

You may not need to use all of these technologies in fulfilling your responsibilities as an employee. But the effects of new information and communication technologies are still evident in carrying out your day-to-day tasks: making and receiving telephone calls, conducting correspondence, or working with computers.

In this chapter we look at these routine office communications and provide some guidelines to help you perform your job effectively. We will focus on everyday tasks, but we will also introduce you to the technological changes going on; this will help you understand how the nature of your everyday tasks may be changing even as you are working in your own organization. To provide a frame of reference, let's briefly describe the two classes of information and communication technologies that are beginning to affect communication activities in organizations.

Types of Information and Communication Technologies

New communication technologies associated with the collection, storage, and retrieval of information have led to big changes in the organization. Computer communication, retrieval systems for written documents, data bases, and other

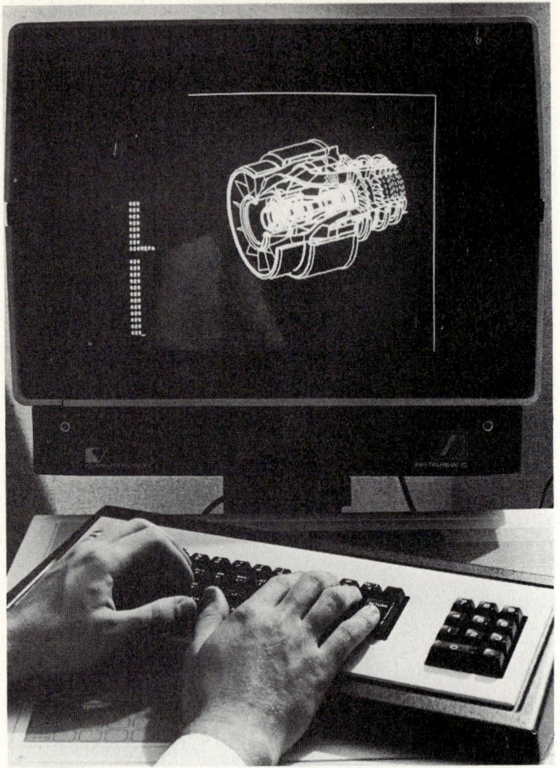

Computers have drastically changed the way information is collected, stored, and retrieved in organizations.

sorts of files represent the substance of information in the business organization. In fact, the contemporary business organization is so dependent upon information that a new class of workers has emerged in the last decade and a half: the information specialist. The term *information specialist* covers a wide group of employees whose common function is to deal with information in the organization. It would not be at all unusual for you to find yourself working for an organization that includes in its organization chart titles such as chief information officer, vice president of information systems, or information manager. These people are usually the ones responsible for compiling the information relevant to the organization's activities, so if you need information to help you do your job, the information specialist may be there to provide assistance. It's a good idea to review the organization chart when you start a new job, so you can find out whether such specialists exist and what is the acceptable way of using the services they provide.

Since the early 1970s, electronic information storage has become more prominent in organizations.[5] What, then, of oral communication in the organization? Oral communication is a way of working with information—and with the people who use information. In fact, one of the results of the explosion of technological advancement is that organization members need to be even more effective in communication. Nesbitt referred to this effect as "high tech, high touch."[6]

How is the workplace changing as a result of electronic communication technology, and how will these changes affect you as you perform your daily work? Basically, there are two kinds of technologies that are becoming commonplace in contemporary business organizations. These are interactive technologies and computer interface technologies. Let's talk briefly about each.

Interactive Technologies First, there are those technologies that are designed to facilitate or supplement face-to-face, written, or telephonic communication within the organization. These are referred to as *interactive technologies.* Interactive technologies bring about changes in the organization as computer-mediated communication replaces the face-to-face contact that was once necessary. Messages in written form may be transmitted in different ways, but they still retain an important place in communication in the organization.

Organization members who need to exchange written information do not have to travel to the same city or location. They can contact one another via telecommunication technologies without leaving their workplaces. Telephones have long been able to carry voice messages great distances. Today, people can transmit written messages over the telephone as well. You can write a memo on a personal computer at your desk in New York and send it via satellite to Tel Aviv, where the recipient can read it immediately. Progress in the development of technology—the "computer revolution"—is so rapid that by the time you read this chapter, the things we are talking about may all be commonplace.

Computer Interface Technologies The second new technology becoming common in the workplace involves humans interfacing with computers—the *computer interface technologies.* Such technologies change the way organizations work by replacing human–human exchanges with human–computer interfaces. For example, an executive who wants to update correspondence with a client does not have to ask a secretary to dig out files and review them. The executive can locate the correspondence in an electronic file in a personal computer right at her desk. And businesses do not need a secretary to answer routine correspondence. Form letters can be stored in computer files and used without secretarial assistance. In both instances, technology replaces the human being who would once have been responsible for getting the needed information. It was initially feared that this type of computer use would lead to the replacement of human beings by machines, but as it is working out, computers are replacing people in some areas while creating tasks for people in other areas.

Effects on the Performance of Everyday Tasks

Written and electronic forms of communication—via telephone or computers—are essential in organizations. Your day-to-day life in the organization is likely to be occupied with a variety of communication tasks—using the telephone, reading and writing memos and business letters, sending and receiving computer messages. We need to address these tasks from the perspective of professional and business communication.

These forms of communication—telephone use, business correspondence, and computer use—are important to the success of interviews, meetings, presentations, and other communication activities. You have become familiar with many of these activities while going through this text. Let's briefly examine the communication skills you will need when you perform these daily tasks. We'll begin with one of the mainstays of any business organization, the telephone.

TELEPHONE USE

In its primary business applications, the telephone is commonly used for its immediacy and its capacity to allow the people who use it to engage in a simultaneous exchange of information. Both of these factors—immediacy and simultaneousness—are what distinguish telephone use from other mediated

The telephone is widely used because it allows immediate simultaneous communication.

communication encounters. The telephone allows its users to experience the immediate and simultaneous contact that is usually associated with face-to-face conversation. We may use the telephone for human contact in our private lives. On the job, the telephone allows you to handle communication tasks efficiently without having to spend time in personal contact. Thus, in your private life, the telephone may extend your contact with others; in your business life, however, the emphasis is not on the personal contact. You use the telephone to communicate as needed with others; you can accomplish your tasks without having to spend time or energy in face-to-face contact. Think, for instance, of going into a meeting at L&L Associates. First, everyone has to leave their work areas to travel to the location of the meeting. People in the meeting begin by greeting one another and making small talk, and then they go on to the topic of the meeting. When the meeting ends, there is more small talk, and then everyone has to return to their own work areas. By using the telephone, you eliminate the travel and generally the small-talk time at the beginning and ending of a meeting. Business conversation via the telephone is far shorter than that which takes place in person.

Because time is money in the organization, the telephone is a way of saving time, and it is often cost-effective, regardless of the expenses associated with its use. For example, if the president of L&L wants to speak with one of the group project heads, the telephone saves the time it would take to travel to see her—even if that travel is within the same building. Sometimes people will call on the phone to talk to someone in an office that is only steps away, because it is faster to pick up the phone than to walk down the hall.

Business Uses of Telephone Communications

The telephone is an important communication tool that you will need to use effectively in various communication activities in your organizational life. Let's review some of the most important business uses of the telephone.

Asking Questions and Exchanging Information Probably the most frequent reason for you to call someone else is to ask a question (for example, "What is the current inventory of materials for the president's speech to the chair of the board?" or "Who is the new vice president of operations?"). The telephone allows you to have direct voice contact with the person you need to speak to about these matters. Exhibit 11.1 lists the most important elements of asking a question on the telephone.

If you are calling someone else within your organization, there is little financial cost in making an error such as calling the wrong person or the wrong number. The greatest expense is that your time and someone else's will be wasted if a call is pointless. Calling long distance can be expensive, however,

Exhibit 11.1 ASKING A QUESTION ON THE TELEPHONE

These are the important elements of asking a question over the telephone:

- Be sure you know what question you need to ask.
- Be sure the person you call is the one who should have the answer or can direct you to someone else who will have the answer.
- Be sure you know what a satisfactory answer will be.

so it is especially important that your call be prepared in advance and that you take advantage of your organization's long-distance facilities.

There are, of course, advantages to dialing direct. That is why there are so many directory index systems available. Dialing direct works best when you have good reason to believe your party will be available to take the call. Operator-assisted calls are very expensive and are sometimes inconvenient. If an operator handles your call at the receiving end, you may not be able to get all the information you need about when to call back, and you may not be able to get a message through to the other party within a short time.

Members of organizations often have secretaries who can handle their phone calls. If you have a secretary, he should be fully briefed in order to manage calls most conveniently for you. Remember that phone calls do not produce permanent records. (It is illegal to record calls, unless you notify the other party in advance.) Furthermore, even if you do record a phone conversation, the information is very hard to sort and retrieve. For these reasons, phone calls should not be used for complicated matters. Even for single-topic phone calls, it is important to keep a written record. If important information is exchanged over the phone, it is a good practice to follow up with a written memo to the other person, to summarize the sense of the call, so that both parties can have a permanent record of what was said.

The same features that make the telephone a convenience for business purposes also make it obtrusive. Some organization members are fortunate enough to have someone available to field and manage their phone calls. Most of us have to handle our own. If the phone rings while you are in the middle of a complicated task, you may be inclined to ignore it. Remember, though, that the telephone is an avenue through which information can reach you. That's why you have the phone there in the first place. Thus, you must deal with your calls in one way or another.

Corroboration Another reason to use the telephone in business is to corroborate your memory about some matter. For example, if your calendar indicates that you have an appointment with the vice president of operations at L&L Associates, you might make a quick telephone call to confirm your appointment on the morning of the meeting. You might also use the phone to get additional information about some matter. Keep a daybook or a card file and use it to record important information from phone calls. It is useful to have a log of phone calls. It serves as a reminder of what matters are discussed and what decisions are reached in the various conversations that take place during the calls you make and receive.

Personal Calls Organization members also use the telephone for friendly purposes, to keep in contact or touch base with their associates. Sometimes a friendly call is welcome during the working day. Sometimes a personal call is an annoyance that interferes with important work. You need to work out your own policy for handling personal calls. Most organizations have policies about personal calls. These range from forbidding personal telephone calls on company time to more lenient policies. But personal calls take you away from your work and are at the company's expense. It is smart to limit them to emergencies even if the company policy might allow you to be more casual about the matter.

Conference Calls We already mentioned that the telephone can be used for conference calls. Phone conferences can sometimes be a convenience when it is absolutely impossible for people to take the time or spend the money to get together. A few decades ago, futurists predicted that a great deal of business would be done via videophone. For the most part, however, conference calls in organizations do not include video. Instead, they are ordinary telephone calls in which more than two parties can listen and speak. The president of L&L Associates, for example, could have a conference call with three other executives if she thought that the call would be a better way to conduct a business meeting than an in-person conference.

Computer Interface The telephone is sometimes used in conjunction with other communication technologies (satellites and/or computers) in order to link people or data-base systems. As we have already mentioned, technology is changing so rapidly that our descriptions of the technology you are likely to use in the office will undoubtedly be outdated by the time you read this chapter. What will not change is that you will be expected to be familiar with whatever is available to you. You must be able to decide which of the technologies will best facilitate the communication for which you will be responsible. Computerized telecommunication systems are rapidly being incorporated into the day-to-day activities of many organizations, so you may well find that you need to understand and use these technologies in some aspects of your job.

Regardless of the state of technology as you enter the work force, however, you can be sure that you will use the telephone to aid and assist you in the performance of everyday tasks. You use the telephone when it is more efficient or effective than written or face-to-face communication and you do not need to have a written record or personal contact to accomplish your purposes. Let's discuss some of the factors that determine how to use the telephone well. One of them is your voice.

Telephone Voice

When you use the telephone, you and the other party rely on your voices and what they sound like in understanding what is being said. In face-to-face communication, you have lots of visual cues to go by—and so does the other person. But on the phone, this isn't true. So the words you use and what your voice sounds like as you say those words are probably even more important in telephone communication at work than they are in face-to-face contact. Exhibit 11.2 lists some important pointers for your telephone voice.

Your telephone voice is an asset when you use the telephone in business. You use the telephone to accomplish tasks when you don't want to take the time to write to someone or to travel to see them and talk to them. Effective use of the voice goes along with asking effective questions and providing effective answers on the telephone.

Telephone Courtesy

A final consideration when using the telephone is telephone courtesy. When placing a call, you should introduce yourself, give the name of the person to whom you would like to speak, give your company affiliation, and state the purpose of the call. If the person answering the call is well trained, he will ask you to answer these questions anyway, so it is best to begin by providing the information. You will save time this way, too.

Courtesy is also important when you answer the phone. The first consideration is what to say when you pick up the receiver. There is usually a company

Exhibit 11.2 POINTERS FOR YOUR TELEPHONE VOICE

- When you use the phone, be prepared to listen to yourself and the other person.
- Voices create images, so listen for your smiles and frowns and those of the other person.
- Use the sound of your voice to enhance the message you are trying to create; consider your speed, volume, pitch, articulation, and tone.
- Be pleasant and courteous; monitor your feelings and your voice.
- Give and take accurate messages.
- Pay attention to your choice of language.
- Remember the nature of your message and use your voice accordingly.

Exhibit 11.3 TELEPHONE COURTESY

Remember these points if you want to be effective and courteous in answering the business telephone call:

- Answer as promptly as possible—before the second ring, if you can.
- Answer your own phone when possible, unless you have a secretary.
- When you answer the telephone, identify yourself and provide whatever other information your company protocol calls for.
- Have your notepad handy for reminders. When writing notes on the pad, include date, time of call, and name of caller.
- If taking calls for others, get the necessary information about the caller.
- Don't keep callers on hold more than 30 seconds without warning them.
- Speak directly into the phone.
- Remember that your voice is you. Create the image you want to project.

protocol about these matters. It is a good idea to see whether your company has one. If not, then it is up to you or your immediate supervisor to determine what you say. It is not common practice in business to answer the phone by simply saying "Hello," as you might at home. Usually, the person answering uses some standard phrase, such as, "L&L Associates, Chris Jones speaking," "Good morning, L&L Associates," "Mr. Jones's office," or "Chris Jones speaking."

The first consideration in making a call is to identify both parties on the line. The next is to minimize the amount of time either party needs to be kept waiting if a third person needs to be brought to the phone. This can happen when a secretary or a co-worker answers the telephone. A few seconds seem very long when you are waiting for someone to come to the telephone. If you need to keep a caller waiting for more than 30 seconds, courtesy would dictate letting the caller know that. Exhibit 11.3 provides some suggestions for courtesy when you answer the telephone—and hopefully, for when others answer your calls.

BUSINESS CORRESPONDENCE: LETTERS AND MEMOS

Two common forms of written communication which are part of the everyday business of working in an organization are business letters and memos. *Business letters* are messages written to people outside the organization; *memos* are messages written to people within the organization. Letters and memos are related to the oral communication with which this text is concerned because they can be thought of as "written conversation." In this sense, written correspondence replaces the spoken message you might give to someone face to face. Instead, you address words to that person on a written page. This is not to say that there are not different conventions for written and spoken communication.

We simply wish to underscore that here we focus on the communication aspects rather than the grammar of written messages.

With the advent of computer technologies, some experts predicted that we were going to become a "paperless society." The meaning of this prediction was that we would be substituting electronic messages, sent via electronic media (telephones, satellites, computers), for paper messages (letters, memos, reports, and so on). Yet today, as for the past 50 years, organizations "run on paper," and members of most organizations spend enormous amounts of time and energy in writing and reading business correspondence in the forms of letters and memos. So let's talk about letters and memos.

Business Letters

Letters are used mainly to contact people outside the organization. The original reason for using letters—to permit communication between people who are physically separated—has become less important in the age of information and communication technologies. Use of the telephone and other telecommunication technologies is replacing written forms; these new communication forms are more immediate and relatively inexpensive compared to paper and pen. Yet business letters have not gone out of fashion in the contemporary organization, because they still serve some pretty important and perhaps irreplaceable communication functions.

Business letters provide a permanent, visible record for future reference. People who have relied on phone conversations, but later found out that they have no documentation of their transactions, have come to value the letter for its permanence and for its use to help them document their business transactions. There are several other valuable functions that business letters serve: (1) they can be written and read at the convenience of each party; (2) they allow for time to think and respond; (3) they serve as a formal "artifact," a visible message of organizational ritual; and finally, (4) they are often an expected form of communication.

Because a business letter is customarily written on the organization's letterhead, it is important to be sure that whatever you discuss in the letter adequately represents the company. It is considered unethical to use company letterhead for personal business.

Purposes of Business Letters Business letters are most frequently used for the variety of purposes summarized in Exhibit 11.4.

Exhibit 11.4 lists the purposes of letters; but another way to classify business letters is according to the anticipated reactions of their readers. We could classify letters according to the action or cessation of action desired of the reader.

Exhibit 11.4 PURPOSES OF BUSINESS LETTERS

- To request specific information from someone outside the company. You could, for example, request catalogs and price lists, a bid on a project, or information about a warranty.
- To provide information to someone who requests it.
- For ceremonial purposes. You can congratulate someone on a promotion, acknowledge the opening of a new branch, thank someone for a large order, commend a supplier for efficient service, and so on.
- To exchange ideas, handle arguments, present a point of view, or explain why an action is taken or why a requested action is rejected.
- To attempt to sell goods or services or to provide information about the company.

Business letters are usually about important matters, and they should adequately represent the organization. A good business letter gets to the point quickly. The first paragraph usually contains the main message, and everything else should relate to that main point. If you cannot state your message in two pages or less, add an appendix of materials. Sometimes it is necessary to accompany a letter with explanatory documents. These should not be included in the body of the letter.

Business letters, like business calls, are used for a specific purpose, and they are most effective when they get to the point. In fact, some people who specialize in written business communication say that the three basics of writing a business letter can be summed up as follows: keep it clear, courteous, and concise.

Memos: Internal Organizational Correspondence

We have said that business letters serve the primary purpose of contacting people outside the organization when a written form is preferred to a spoken contact. A memo (or memorandum) is a message written primarily for people inside the organization. Memos are *the* written form of communication within an organization. Memos can travel in all directions throughout an organization; they can convey messages upward, downward, or horizontally across departmental lines—and they often travel in all these directions at the same time, since a memo can be addressed to a number of people at once. See Exhibit 11.5 for a sample memo heading.

As you can see from Exhibit 11.5, memos can be sent to people at all levels of the organization. They are also written by people at all levels of the organization. At L&L Associates, for example, memos are likely to travel from the president, the vice president of operations, the manager of corporate communications, the project group heads, and the project group members.

Memos are short notes that serve the same purposes as written conversa-

Exhibit 11.5 SAMPLE MEMO HEADING

TO: S. A. Savitt, President; J. J. Jones, Chair of the Board; Jess Smith, Executive Vice President of Sales

FROM: M. Lopez, Vice President of Information Services

DATE: March 6, 1989

SUBJECT: New Rates for Presentations

tion. Memos can be used to exchange suggestions or ideas, to confirm agreements made over the phone, to make or confirm a date or appointment, to remind someone of something, to confirm the receipt of information, to issue instructions, or to announce an activity or action. They are written to transmit information—sometimes vital, at other times trivial. When memos are used wisely, they are an essential communication tool; used carelessly, they become a nuisance and annoyance. There are several advantages to using memos. Let's discuss these advantages.

Advantages of Memos Efficiently handled memos take considerably less time than phone calls, and they are considerably more convenient. You can write and mail a memo whenever you want; you do not have to wait to see if another person has time to talk on the phone. You can send a memo to several people at once. You can use the memo itself as a documentation that the message was sent. These are some of the more obvious advantages memos have over phone calls.

Memos are not suitable for extended discussions, negotiations, or arguments, nor can a memo substitute for the formal business letter. Ideally, a memo should make only one point. Each memo should contain several vital pieces of information: (1) the name of the sender, (2) the names of those to whom the memo is sent, (3) the date on which the memo is sent, (4) the subject of the memo, (5) the message, and (6) the method by which the message should be acknowledged.

It is good policy to reread and initial your memo before you send it. While you do this, check your spelling, grammar, and punctuation, and be sure the form of the memo is proper. Sloppy memos do not help your image. Make sure you have a copy for your own file. If you are using electronic mail, you can have your memo sent automatically to the people you want to contact. If you require a reply, make a note on your calendar so you can check back if the reply does not come.

COMPUTERS: EXTENDING VOICE AND MAIL MESSAGES

Although your job may or may not require you to have direct contact with computers, you can see from the technological developments we have described in this chapter that it is important to have a good working knowledge of what computers can do. If your job requires the use of a computer, you will need some specialized training and knowledge of how the computer is to be used in your job.

The computer is the hardware, the machinery that does the jobs it is programmed to do. In business, the most frequent application of the computer is for access to data bases. Data bases are collections of stored information which can be retrieved electronically. Many kinds of data bases, which store a vast array of information, are now at the fingertips of most organization employees. The information stored in the data base can be obtained rapidly through a set of simple commands. We can make complicated searches of records, provide instant information to customers or clients, or collect raw data for financial reports. Using other computer software, we can then process the data—for example, computing statistics or designing charts and graphs.

Sophistication in the use of computers is rapidly becoming a requirement for success in the workplace. And the variety of ways in which enhanced communication can take place grows daily. Computers assist in the creation of memos and letters—the lifeblood of every organization. They are a daily feature of work life on all levels. Let's briefly describe some of the most common forms of computer communication in business organizations.

Electronic Correspondence: Electronic Mail and Electronic Bulletin Boards

Electronic mail, electronic bulletin boards, and electronic banking are but a few of the computer services available today that can affect communication activities in organizations. More applications are becoming available all the time: electronic newspapers and encyclopedias, electronic directories, electronic shopping services, travel and entertainment services, and so on. You may find that you need to learn about some of these on the job in order to do your work better. Most training in the use of computer technology is done on the job because of the rapid changes in technology that we have been discussing. For our purposes it is sufficient that you are aware that you may need to use some of these tools. Let's examine some of the uses of computers in communication.

Other Computer Applications for Communication in Business

Currently, there are a great many ways in which people can communicate with other people using a computer. Through the use of a *modem* (modulator-demodulator), it is possible to connect two or more telephones in order to exchange messages through ordinary telephone lines. The messages are not oral—they consist of documents, which can be of virtually any length. Using a computer, you can keep an elaborate set of contacts, receive regular mail, and even communicate interactively. For example, a person either at home or in the office can use computer communication to access a data base, to direct questions to colleagues, or to compose and edit documents.

There are commercial networks that connect people to information sources and to each other—for example, CompuServe, The Source, and now even networks connected to cable television. These networks provide access to daily news, stock information, games, bulletin boards, interest groups, and shopping and bill-paying services. Some of them even allow computer users to send each other messages. In addition, through complicated switching facilities, messages can move from one network to another, so computer users are assured virtually instantaneous worldwide communication at relatively low cost.

The implications of computer communication are still not fully explored, but you can anticipate that computer use will be a daily aspect of whatever job you take. Consider, for example, organizations such as hotels, ticket agencies, airlines and railroads, and newspapers. These businesses rely on computers for the rapid exchange of information essential in today's world; the telephone is no longer their principal medium of communication.

Computers and Phones

By linking the computer with the telephone, you can receive calls, allow callers to leave messages when you are not available, and access data bases for rapid transmission of information.

A great many of the kinds of jobs that used to be handled over the telephone have now been taken over by computer-mediated communication. Inventories, financial balances, rosters of employees, and virtually any other kind of business information can now be accessed on-line. (Of course, in order to get accurate information via the computer, you must be able to phrase your request clearly and code it properly. Otherwise you get no response.)

Computer-mediated communication holds a great deal of promise for expediting contact between people, especially in large organizations. However, we can't give you specific information about how to handle computer-mediated communication, the way we did for telephone use. It is not possible to anticipate the changes in design and procedures for use that will take place in computer hardware and software. Yet it is important to understand computers as communication tools in organizations. You need to become familiar with their possibilities as they relate to your work in the organization.

There is one more important point to consider. Your workday will seem to be filled with communication activities—interviews, conferences, meetings, formal presentations, and so on. How can you develop a plan for being able to engage in all of these activities effectively? You need to know how to manage your time. Let's discuss time management briefly.

TIME MANAGEMENT

You can easily see that when you work in an organization, you will be faced with an unending stream of diverse messages in different forms, which will continually compete for your attention. In a workday filled with conferences, meetings, presentations, telephone calls, correspondence, conversations, and the various other kinds of communication activities we have been discussing, you will encounter a multitude of face-to-face verbal and nonverbal messages when dealing with fellow workers. You will also face an almost overwhelming world of paper and electronic messages. Yet you may be, or become, so accustomed to this "information society" that you automatically process communication of every kind in an almost unconscious way. Consider, for example, how quickly you might browse through a newspaper, sort your mail, and scan your electronic messages—all before going into your first meeting of the day, and perhaps before checking your materials (more information) for that meeting. One of the things that the information revolution takes away from workers in organizations is time: there is more information and more access to it, so the worker has to spend more time processing this information. One of your problems will be finding enough time and deciding how to dedicate your time. *Time management,* or planning how to use your time, is a necessary tool for the effective communicator in the organization. It will help you to prioritize your activities and to use your time well.

Planning the use of your time is a good way to spare yourself some of the stresses of daily life in a business organization. In order to manage your time well, you need to understand what is likely to happen during the course of a day. Then you can set up your schedule to accommodate both planned and unplanned parts of your workday.

On every job, there are some events that happen more often than others. You know that you will make and receive some phone calls; you will write and receive some memos and letters. You will also have to schedule appointments, meetings, trips, and other occasions when you must be out of your office. The idea is to set up your schedule so that you can deal with what has to be handled on a daily basis without impairing your ability to deal with matters that require large blocks of time.

Look at your job description and list the major tasks you must perform on a daily, weekly, monthly, quarterly, and annual basis. Estimate how much time each of these tasks should take. Apportion the weekly, monthly, quarterly, and annual tasks on a daily basis. Exhibit 11.6 presents a suggested format for your time log. If you come out with something less than an average of eight hours a day, you might have some hope of generating a working time plan.

Actually, you will probably find that in a typical day, you will need to put in no more than one-third of your allotted hours on activities that require uninterrupted blocks of time. In fact, a great many of your specified tasks may require you to be in contact with others. It is important that you have a sense of what these proportions are. This will make you more tolerant of what appear to be interruptions.

The fact is, when someone phones you or comes to see you on matters of ordinary business, that person has no idea what you might be doing at that moment. When you contact other people, you interrupt them, too. Interruptions actually represent the standard process of the conduct of business. If you accept this proposition, you can maintain an adaptable stance, since if you anticipate an interruption, you can hardly consider it an interruption.

Performing a time analysis will give you an overview of the way you spend your day within the organization. It will alert you to the routine and exceptional tasks you have to perform and will enable you to prepare more effectively to handle their communication requirements.

Exhibit 11.6 TIME LOG

Part 1: Daily Tasks

Instructions: Use this time log on several consecutive days to analyze your job. Do not fill out the form during special seasons (for example, just before a holiday or during inventory). You will get the best results if you start on a Tuesday or Wednesday. Keep track of your activities during a one-hour period, and fill out a copy of this form for each time slot. (For example, fill out a copy for the hour beginning at 8:00 A.M. on Tuesday; then do the same for the hours beginning at 9:00 A.M. on Wednesday, 11:00 A.M. on Thursday, 1:00 P.M. on Friday, 2:00 P.M. on Monday, 3:00 P.M. on Tuesday, and 4:00 P.M. on Wednesday. Then fill out a form for your work activities beginning at 5:00 P.M. on Thursday; skip Friday and Monday; and fill out forms for your lunch hours on Tuesday and Wednesday.)

Day____________ Date____________ Time____________

Step 1. List the name of a person you saw face-to-face.

a. How long did you spend with this person?
b. Where did you see this person?
c. What was the purpose of the contact?
   __ Give orders
   __ Take orders
   __ Give instruction
   __ Receive instruction
   __ Ask questions
   __ Answer questions
   __ Assigned task (for example, an interview)
   __ Casual chitchat
   __ Formal meeting
d. How important was your contact?
   Was it a scheduled appointment or meeting? How much notice did you have?
e. Were you interrupted? Why? How did you respond?
f. Have you ever seen this person for this purpose before?
   How often?

Repeat step 1 for each person you saw during the one-hour period.

Step 2. List the names of the people you called on the telephone.

a. Whom did you call?
b. For what reason?
c. How long did the call take?
d. How important was it?
e. Were you interrupted? Why? How did you respond?
f. Have you ever called this person for this purpose before?
   How often?

Repeat step 2 for each phone call you made.

Exhibit 11.6 (*Continued*)

Part 1: Daily Tasks

Step 3. List each telephone call you received.
a. Who called you?
b. For what reason?
c. How long did the call take?
d. How important was it?
e. Were you interrupted? Why? How did you respond?
f. Has this person ever called you for this purpose before? How often?

Repeat step 3 for each telephone call you received.

Step 4. List each memo you wrote.
a. To whom did you write it?
b. For what reason?
c. How long did it take?
d. How important was it?
e. Were you interrupted? Why? How did you respond?
f. How often do you write this kind of memo?

Repeat step 4 for each memo you wrote.

Step 5. List each memo you read.
a. Who was it from?
b. What was its message?
c. How important was it?
d. How long did it take?
e. Were you interrupted? Why? How did you respond?
f. How often do you receive this kind of memo?

Repeat step 5 for each memo you read.

Step 6. List each letter you wrote.
a. To whom did you write it?
b. For what reason?
c. How long did it take?
d. How important was it?
e. Were you interrupted? Why? How did you respond?
f. How often do you receive this kind of letter?

Repeat step 6 for each letter you wrote.

Step 7. List each piece of mail you opened, read, or disposed of.
a. What kind of mail was it?
b. What was its message?
c. How long did it take?
d. How important was it?
e. Were you interrupted? Why? How did you respond?
f. How often do you receive this kind of letter?

Exhibit 11.6 *(Continued)*

Part 1: Daily Tasks

Repeat step 7 for each letter you wrote.

Step 8. List time you spent reading and writing reports.
a. What did you do?
b. For how long?
c. For what reason?
d. Is this a regular duty?
e. Were you interrupted? Why? How did you respond?

Step 9. List time you spent filing and housekeeping.
a. What did you do?
b. Did you do it because you had to or because you had nothing else to do?

Step 10. List time you spent using equipment (for example, copy machines).

Step 11. List time you spent accessing data bases.

Step 12. List time you spent planning your work.

Step 13. List time you spent at meetings.

Step 14. List casual encounters with colleagues.

Step 15. List slack time.

Part 2: Job Responsibilities

Instructions: This part of your time log is a review of your job description. Use it to get an overview of the things you do on a regular basis.

1. List the tasks for which you are responsible hourly.
2. List the tasks for which you are responsible daily.
3. List the tasks for which you are responsible weekly.
4. List the tasks for which you are responsible monthly.
5. List the tasks for which you are responsible periodically. Stipulate the time period.
6. List the tasks for which you are responsible annually.
7. List the tasks for which you are responsible occasionally. How often and when are you responsible for them?
8. List the tasks which you have done on an emergency basis.
   a. What was the nature of the emergency?
   b. Why were you called on to do the tasks?
9. List the occasions you have covered for someone else. Explain why.
10. List the tasks you have done on a voluntary basis.

Exhibit 11.6 *(continued)*

Part 2: Job Responsibilities

11. Assess your social connections within your organization.
   a. On what matters is your decision final?
   b. To whom do you give instructions and orders? (Attach a list with job descriptions for each person.)
   c. Who gives you instructions and orders? To whom do you report?
   d. List the meetings and conventions you have attended in the last year. How much time did this take? How much did it cost?
   e. What are your meal arrangements? If you use meals for business reasons, what issues do you deal with?
   f. Do you take work home? What kind, and why?

SUMMARY

In this chapter we have looked at the organization as an environment that is in the process of being revolutionized by new communication technologies. These dramatic changes in the work environment have implications for the performance of everyday communication activities—using the telephone, reading and writing memos and business letters, and exchanging messages with co-workers and others.

Computer technology is producing an "information revolution," and organization members need to know how to gain access to the information stored in data banks. Employees need to use electronic retrieval systems, computer networks, and communication links in order to do their jobs effectively. Interactive technologies are electronic communication systems that facilitate communication. Telecommunication technologies allow extremely rapid exchange of messages. Computer interface technologies are replacing people for some tasks, such as answering routine correspondence.

Telephone conversations are still the best way to handle some types of business communications. The telephone's primary advantages are immediacy and simultaneity. Courtesy is always important in business communication. Some organizations have established telephone protocols that employees are expected to follow.

Business letters and memos are commonly used for exchanging messages. Letters are generally sent to people outside the organization, memos to people within the organization. Letters and memos are often used to document transactions made over the telephone or in person.

Employees are likely to use computers for many purposes—especially to access information stored in data bases and to compose and transmit electronic messages. Computer messages can be transmitted over ordinary telephone lines through the use of modems. Computer technology is advancing so rapidly that most employees are trained on the job in the specific procedures they need to use.

As an organization member, you will need to know how to manage your time effectively. By analyzing the time requirements of your various tasks, you will have an idea of how to apportion your time. You will be able to set aside the blocks of time you will need for jobs that require concentration; and by recognizing that interruptions are unavoidable in business, you will be able to minimize the stress you might otherwise feel when you are interrupted.

CHAPTER 11 ACTIVITIES

1. Use the time log to record your work responsibilities, either at L&L Associates, at your job, or as a student. What insights did you get by using the log?
2. Work with three others. Each person should make five phone calls to local companies, noting the protocol used to answer the phone. What are the images you get of the people answering? Compare notes.
3. Write a sample memo for L&L Associates. What would you suggest as a good form for company memos and business letters?
4. Write one letter to a friend, one request for information to a local company, and one other letter. Compare and contrast the styles you use.

CHAPTER 11 NOTES

1. Linda C. Lederman, "Communication in the Workplace: The Impact of the Information Age and High Technology on Interpersonal Communication in Organizations." In *Intermedia—Interpersonal Communication in a Media World,* Gary Gumpert and Robert Cathcart (Eds.), New York: Oxford University Press, 1986, p. 313.
2. Ibid., p. 314.
3. James Chesebro and Donald Bonsall, *Computer-Mediated Communication: Human Relationships in a Computerized World,* unpublished manuscript.
4. Keith Davis, *Human Behavior at Work,* New York: McGraw-Hill, 1972, p. 379.
5. James Chesebro and Donald Bonsall, "Computer-Mediated Communication," paper presented at the Eastern Communication Association Conference, Philadelphia, 1984.
6. John Naisbitt, *Megatrends: Ten New Directions Transforming Our Lives,* New York: Warner Books, 1982.

Index